Modernisation, National Identity and Legal Instrumentalism
(Vol. 2: Public Law)

Legal History Library

VOLUME 36

Series Editors

C.H. (Remco) van Rhee, *Maastricht University*
Dirk Heirbaut, *Ghent University*
Matthew C. Mirow, *Florida International University*

Editorial Board

Hamilton Bryson, *University of Richmond*
Thomas P. Gallanis, *University of Iowa*
James Gordley, *Tulane University*
Richard Helmholz, *University of Chicago*
Michael Hoeflich, *University of Kansas*
Neil Jones, *University of Cambridge*
Hector MacQueen, *University of Edinburgh*
Paul Oberhammer, *University of Vienna*
Marko Petrak, *University of Zagreb*
Jacques du Plessis, *University of Stellenbosch*
Mathias Reimann, *University of Michigan*
Jan M. Smits, *Maastricht University*
Alain Wijffels, *Université Catholique de Louvain, Leiden University, CNRS*
Reinhard Zimmermann, *Max-Planck-Institut für ausländisches und internationales Privatrecht, Hamburg*

The titles published in this series are listed at *brill.com/lhl*

Modernisation, National Identity, and Legal Instrumentalism

Studies in Comparative Legal History

VOLUME 2: PUBLIC LAW

Edited by

Michał Gałędek
Anna Klimaszewska

BRILL
NIJHOFF

LEIDEN | BOSTON

Cover illustration: Katarzyna Kapica, Doodlestudio.tv.

This publication was supported with funds of University of Gdańsk's Vice-Rector for Research and Foreign Cooperation, Professor Piotr Stepnowski, and with funds of the Dean of Faculty of Law and Administration, Professor Jakub Stelina.

Library of Congress Cataloging-in-Publication Data

Names: Gałędek, Michał, 1978- editor. | Klimaszewska, Anna, 1984- editor.
Title: Modernisation, national identity and legal instrumentalism : studies in comparative legal history / edited by Michał Gałędek, Anna Klimaszewska.
Description: Leiden ; Boston : Brill Nijhoff, 2020. | Series: Legal history library ; volumes 35-36 | Includes bibliographical references and index. |
Identifiers: LCCN 2019038551 | ISBN 9789004395282 (vol. I ; hardback) | ISBN 9789004417151 (vol. II ; hardback) | ISBN 9789004417274 (vol. I ; ebook) | ISBN 9789004417359 vol. II ; (ebook)
Subjects: LCSH: Law--History.
Classification: LCC K160 .M63 2019 | DDC 340.09--dc23
LC record available at http://lccn.loc.gov/2019038551

Typeface for the Latin, Greek, and Cyrillic scripts: "Brill". See and download: brill.com/brill-typeface.

ISSN 1874-1793
ISBN 978-90-04-41715-1 (hardback)
ISBN 978-90-04-41735-9 (e-book)

Copyright 2020 by Koninklijke Brill NV, Leiden, The Netherlands.
Koninklijke Brill NV incorporates the imprints Brill, Brill Hes & De Graaf, Brill Nijhoff, Brill Rodopi, Brill Sense, Hotei Publishing, mentis Verlag, Verlag Ferdinand Schöningh and Wilhelm Fink Verlag.
All rights reserved. No part of this publication may be reproduced, translated, stored in a retrieval system, or transmitted in any form or by any means, electronic, mechanical, photocopying, recording or otherwise, without prior written permission from the publisher.
Authorization to photocopy items for internal or personal use is granted by Koninklijke Brill NV provided that the appropriate fees are paid directly to The Copyright Clearance Center, 222 Rosewood Drive, Suite 910, Danvers, MA 01923, USA. Fees are subject to change.

This book is printed on acid-free paper and produced in a sustainable manner.

Contents

Abbreviations   VII
Notes on Contributors   VIII

1   Residential Right in the Course of Time: Changes in the Legal Institution of the Inkolat in the Bohemian Crown Lands   1
    Jiří Brňovják and Marek Starý

2   Legal Transfers and National Traditions: Patterns of Modernisation of the Administration in Polish Territories at the Turn of the 19th Century   33
    Michał Gałędek

3   National Modernisation through the Constitutional Revolution of 1848 in Hungary: Pretext and Context   51
    Imre Képessy

4   Restoring the Hungarian Historical Constitutional Order with a Coronation in 1867   69
    Judit Beke-Martos

5   The Privy Council Appeal and British Imperial Policy, 1833–1939   86
    Thomas Mohr

6   Direct Impact on Hungarian Migration Policy of the 1870 Agreement on Citizenship between the United States and Austria-Hungary (1880s–1914)   113
    Balázs Pálvölgyi

7   Political Systems in Transition and Cultural (In)dependence: The Limits of a Legal Transplant in the Example of the Brazilian's Court of Auditors Birth   131
    Marjorie Carvalho de Souza

8   Constitutional Systems of Free European States (1918–1939)   143
    Tadeusz Maciejewski and Maja Maciejewska-Szałas

| 9 | Local Citizenship in the Croatian-Slavonian Legal Area in the First Yugoslavia (1918–1941): Breakdown of a Concept?   171
Ivan Kosnica |

| 10 | Nazi Law as Pure Instrument: Natural Law, (Extra-)Legal Terror, and the Neglect of Ideology   192
Simon Lavis |

Index of Names   217
Index of Subjects   223
Index of Places   228

Abbreviations

AC	Appeal Cases
All ER	All England Law Reports
AT-OeStA HHStA MdÄ AR	Österreichisches Staatsarchiv, Haus-, Hof- und Staatsarchiv, Ministerium des Äußern, Administrative Registratur
BM	Decree of the Interior Minister
CLR	Commonwealth Law Reports
Cmd.	Command paper
DLR	Dominion Law Reports
EACA	Law Reports of the Court of Appeals for Eastern Africa
IR	Irish Reports
Képv. Ir.	Papers of the House of Representatives
KN	Journal of the House of Representatives
ME	Decree of the Prime Minister
MNL	Magyar Nemzeti Levéltár
OL	Országos Levéltár
TLR	Times Law Reports
TNA	National Archives of the United Kingdom

Notes on Contributors

Judit Beke-Martos
J.D., LL.M., Ph.D. is the managing director of the Center for International Affairs and a senior lecturer at the Legal Faculty of the Ruhr University Bochum (Germany). She holds a J.D. and a Ph.D. in law from the Eötvös Loránd University (Budapest, Hungary), and an LL.M. from Suffolk University Law School (Boston, MA, USA), where she spent a year in residence as a Visiting Scholar. She spent three months as a Foreign Legal Researcher at the Legal History Institute of Gent University (Belgium). She published a book and several scholarly articles in English, German and Hungarian.

Jiří Brňovják
(1978), Doc. Mgr., Ph.D. University of Ostrava, is Assistant Professor at the Department of History, Faculty of Arts, and a researcher at the Faculty's Centre for Economic and Social History. His specialist area of research is the aristocracy and the estates society in the Habsburg Monarchy during the early modern period. His research also includes regional history and archival and auxiliary historical sciences. He has published a monograph called *Šlechticem z moci úřední: Udělování šlechtických titulů v českých zemích 1705–1780* [Aristocrat from Official Power: Granting Aristocratic Titles in the Bohemian Lands 1705–1780] (Ostravská univerzita v Ostravě, 2015).

Marjorie Carvalho de Souza
holds a bachelor's degree in Law from the Federal University of Santa Catarina, Brazil (2018). Since 2019, she pursues a Master's degree in Global History from the same Institution and a graduated degree in Labour Law from the Pontifical Catholic University of Rio Grande do Sul, Brazil. During the 2015–2016 academic year, she experienced a research period at the University of Naples Federico II, within which this work was conceived.

Michał Gałędek
Ph.D. (2010), University of Gdańsk, is Professor in the Department of Legal History, Faculty of Law and Administration. In his research he focuses on the Polish administration, judiciary, constitutionalism, and political thought at the beginning of 19th century and in the interwar period.

Imre Képessy
(1986), Eötvös Loránd University, is assistant lecturer of Hungarian Legal History at that university as well as at the Széchenyi István University in Győr.

His area of research focuses on the tools of the constitutional protection in Hungary in the 19th century. He has published articles on the Hungarian constitutional development between 1848–1867, including *The 'Constitutional Court' (alkotmányőrszék) in Louis Kossuth's proposal for the Constitution of Hungary* (Dialóg-Campus, 2017).

Ivan Kosnica

(1982), Ph.D., works at the Faculty of Law at the University of Zagreb. He holds position of a Docent at the Chair of Croatian History of Law and State. His main research interest is history of citizenship and history of public law institutions in the second half of 19th and in the first half of 20th century. He is network chair of Politics, Citizenship and Nations Network at the European Social Science History Conference and editorial member of Journal on European History of Law.

Simon Lavis

Ph.D. (2015), Open University, is a Lecturer in law at that university. His research focuses on the nexus between law, history and theory in relation to the Third Reich, and the representation of Nazi law in academic discourse. His publications in this area include 'The Distorted Jurisprudential Discourse of Nazi Law: Uncovering the 'Rupture Thesis' in the Anglo-American Legal Academy' (2018) 31(4) International Journal for the Semiotics of Law 745–770.

Tadeusz Maciejewski

Ph.D. (1980), is head of the Department of Legal History at the University of Gdańsk. His research focuses on the municipal law, public law and the history of administration. He is also interested in the free cities of Europe in the 19th and early 20th centuries. In 1990, he was habilitated; in 1996, he was appointed professor of the University of Gdańsk; in 1999, he was made full professor. He has authored over 200 publications, including 20 monographs and textbooks. He has published a textbook entitled *History of the Polish Legal System*.

Maja Maciejewska-Szałas

Ph.D. (2012), is assistant professor at the Department of Civil Law (University of Gdańsk).

Thomas Mohr

is an associate professor at the School of Law, University College Dublin. He is vice president of the Irish Legal History Society and book review editor of the *Irish Jurist*, a law journal first published in 1848. His publications on Irish legal history range from medieval Gaelic law to the law of the independent Irish state in the twentieth century. His latest book is *Guardian of the Treaty – The Privy Council Appeal and Irish Sovereignty* (Four Courts Press, 2016). This concerns an important aspect of Ireland's relationship with the British Empire in the inter-war years. He has also recently published on the controversial topic of determining Ireland's 'independence day' in his article 'Law and the Foundation of the Irish State on 6 December 1922' (2018) 59 *Irish Jurist* 31–58.

Balázs Pálvölgyi
(1973), Ph.D. is associate professor at the University Széchenyi István in Győr (Hungary).

Marek Starý
(1974), Doc. JUDr., Ph.D. Charles University in Prague, is Assistant Professor at the Department of Legal History, Faculty of Law, and at the Department of Administrative Law and Public Administration at the University of Finance and Administration. The main areas of his research and publication activities are the early modern land law of the Bohemian Kingdom and the history of Wallenstein's Duchy of Frýdlant. He has written a number of studies and two monographs, e.g. *Cizozemci a spoluobyvatelé. Udělování českého obyvatelského práva (inkolátu) v době předbělohorské* [Foreigners and Co-inhabitants. Granting the Bohemian Inkolat in the Period before the Battle of White Mountain – 2018].

CHAPTER 1

Residential Right in the Course of Time: Changes in the Legal Institution of the Inkolat in the Bohemian Crown Lands

Jiří Brňovják and Marek Starý

1   Introduction

Two large legislative works emerged in quick succession in the territory of the Kingdom of Bohemia during the troubled period of the first half of the 17th century that became very important monuments of Bohemian legal history.[1] The first one was the Bohemian Confederation, adopted by the non-Catholic estates at the General Diet in 1619,[2] followed by the Renewed Land Constitution,

---

1   This study was completed within the resolution of the grant project of the Czech Science Foundation No. 14-12236S *Udělování českého inkolátu v době předbělohorské* [Granting the Bohemian Inkolat in the pre-White Mountain Period] and SGS11/FF/2017–2018 *Hospodářské a sociální dějiny vybraných lokalit Moravy a Slezska v 18.–20. století* [Economic and Social History of Selected Localities of Moravia and Silesia in the 18th–20th Centuries].

2   For edition accessibility of the text, cf. *Dějiny českého státu v dokumentech* [History of the Bohemian State in Documents], Zdeněk VESELÝ (ed.), Professional Publishing, Praha, 2012, 152–158. Cf. also Rudolf STANKA: *Die böhmische Conföderationsakte von 1619*, Ebering, Berlin, 1932; Winfried BECKER: *Ständestaat und Konfessionsbildung am Beispiel der böhmischen Konföderationsakte von 1619 = Politik und Konfession: Festschrift für Konrad Repgen zum 60. Geburtstag*, Dieter VON ALBRECHT et al. (eds.), Duncker & Humblot, Berlin, 1983, 77–99; Joachim BAHLCKE: *Modernization and state-building in an east-central European estates' system: The example of the Confoederatio Bohemica of 1619*, Parliaments, Estates & Representation 17(1997), 61–73; Karel MALÝ: *Die Böhmische Konföderationsakte und die Verneuerte Landesordnung: zwei böhmische Verfassungsgestaltungen zu Beginn des 17. Jahrhunderts*, Zeitschrift der Savigny-Stiftung für Rechtsgeschichte. Germanistische Abteilung 122(2005), 285–300; Jaroslav PÁNEK: *Od České konfederace k Obnovenému zřízení zemskému: (kontinuita a diskontinuita v proměnách českého státu a jeho ústavního zřízení na pomezí stavovství a absolutismu)* [From the Bohemian Confederation to the renewal of the land Constitution: (continuity and discontinuity in the transformation of the Bohemian state and its constitutional system on the edge of Estatism and Absolutism)] = *Vývoj české ústavnosti v letech 1618–1918* [Development of Bohemian Constitutionality in 1618–1918], Karel MALÝ, Ladislav SOUKUP (eds.), Karolinum, Praha, 2006, 13–29; Karolina ADAMOVÁ: *První česká federativní ústava z roku 1619* [First Bohemian Federative Constitution from 1619], Aleš Čeněk, Plzeň, 2009.

issued by Emperor Ferdinand II in 1627.[3] A similar Renewed Constitution was issued for the Margraviate of Moravia in the subsequent year.[4]

These documents reflect two alternative and, without exaggeration, conflicting ideas regarding the further functioning of the Bohemian state. As early as in the second half of the 15th century, the Bohemian state had become a state of the estates, where public power was divided between the monarch and the privileged social groups – corporatively associated in three estates.[5] Although set up slowly, the system was essentially instable because both the monarch and the estates were naturally inclined to efforts to extend their own powers and consequently increase their share of governing the state. In addition, the situation was complicated by religious tensions, as most estates and the population in general professed Protestantism, while both the Jagiellonian and the Habsburg dynasties were strictly Catholic. Moreover, stronger monarchs strove to make every effort to promote the position of Catholic Church in Bohemia (where it had lost its political and economic influence because of the Hussite Wars) – the most evident demonstrations of such efforts include the introduction of the Society of Jesus into Bohemia (1556) or re-filling the office of the Archbishop of Prague (1561), which had been vacant for a great many decades.

---

3 Edition accessibility of the text, cf. *Obnovené Právo a Zřízení zemské dědičného království Českého: Verneuerte Landes-Ordnung des Erb-Königreichs Böhmen: 1627*, Hermenegild JIREČEK (ed.), F. Tempský, Praha 1888. The digitized manuscript from 1627 is accessible at the website GDZ. Göttinger Digitalisierungszentrum (gdz.sub.uni-goettingen.de/dms/load/img/?PID=PPN626655234 (21. 2. 2017) or at the web Manuscriptorium. Digital library of Written Heritage, source: http://www.manuscriptorium.com/apps/index.php?direct=record&pid=rec1323815836_145#search, accessed: 21.02.2017). Among other literature, selectively: Hans-Wolfgang BERGERHAUSEN: *Die "Verneuerte Landesordnung" in Böhmen 1627: Ein Grunddokument des habsburgischen Absolutismus*, Historische Zeitschrift 272(2001), 327–351; Lutz RENTZOW: *Die Entstehungs- und Wirkungsgeschichte der Verneuerten Landesordnung für das Königreich Böhmen von 1627*, Peter Lang, Frankfurt a. M. et al., 1998; MALÝ: *Die Böhmische Konföderationsakte*, op. cit.; PÁNEK: *Od České konfederace...*, op. cit.

4 *Constitutiones Margraviatus Moraviae anno 1628 reformatae = Codex Juris Bohemici*, vol. 5, part 3, Hermenegild JIREČEK (ed.), F. Tempsy – J. Tempsky – G. Freytag, Pragae – Vindobonnae – Lipsiae, 1890.

5 The higher nobility was assembled in the estate of lords (Herren), the lower nobility in the estate of knights (Ritter), the third, the urban estate, comprised royal towns. In the other crown lands of the Bohemian Crown, there was also an estate of prelates, whose members were some of the leading representatives of the Catholic Church: On Central European Estatism in the 16th century, cf. e.g. *Crown, Church and Estates. Central European Politics in the Sixteenth and Seventeenth Centuries*, R.J.W. EVANS, T.V. THOMAS (eds.), St. Martin's Press, New York, 1991.

Growing tension between the monarch and the estates, as well as between Catholics – promoted by the monarch – and Protestants, escalated in the 1618 defenestration of imperial regents and the outbreak of the revolt by the estates, which precipitated a greater Europe-wide conflict known as the Thirty Years' War. The Bohemian Confederation and the Renewed Land Constitution, i.e. documents unilaterally dictated rather than resulting from a compromise, clearly define two visions of the further constitutional development of the state, which could develop either towards a republic of the estates, with an elected king having minimal and predominantly representative powers, or towards a state that would be more or less absolutist.[6] The fact that both the estates and the monarch incorporated their ideas into a legislative work is clear evidence of the importance already attached to law as an instrument to freeze social changes.

While the Bohemian Confederation was entirely about constitutional issues, the Renewed Land Constitution (as suggested by its title) built upon the older tradition of Land Law codifications, where constitutional issues stood side by side with statutes that, from today's perspective, fell within civil law (property law, family law, inheritance law, as well as law of obligations), criminal law, administrative law, and largely also procedural law.[7] However, the continuity reflected in the structure of the code, as well as in its external form, was accompanied by significant features of discontinuity in its content. Reinforcing the monarch's power and curtailing the powers and autonomy of the estates' institutions were the common denominator of major changes. The legal

---

6   The situation is the Netherlands is traditionally given here as inspiration, since it had broken free from the domination of the Habsburgs a few decades earlier.
7   In Bohemia, the Land Constitution was issued as branch-undefined codification of noble rights in 1500, 1530, 1549 and 1564. The earliest of them, called Vladislaus's, accessible as an edition *Vladislavské zřízení zemské a navazující prameny (Svatováclavská smlouva a Zřízení o ručnicích)* [Vladislaus's Land Constitution and Related Sources (St. Wenceslas's Contract and Constitution on Rifles)], Petr KREUZ, Ivan MARTINOVSKÝ, Jana VOJTÍŠKOVÁ (eds.), Scriptorium, Praha 2007. The texts of the remaining are brought to us today by the now obsolete edition *Zřízení zemská království českého XVI. věku* [Land Constitution of the Bohemian Kingdom of the 16th Century], Josef JIREČEK, Hermenegild JIREČEK (eds.), Všehrd, Praha, 1882. A number of stimulating studies on this Code are provided in the publication *Vladislavské zřízení zemské a počátky ústavního zřízení v českých zemích (1500–1619)* [Vladislaus's Land Constitution and the Beginnings of the Constitutional System in the Bohemian Lands (1500–1619)], Karel MALÝ, Jroslav PÁNEK (eds.), Historický ústav AV, Univerzita Karlova, Praha 2001. A similar development in Moravia with placement in the wider central European context was recently published by Jana JANIŠOVÁ, Dalibor JANIŠ: *Moravská zemská zřízení a kodifikace zemského práva ve střední Evropě v 16. a na začátku 17. století* [Moravian Land Constitution and Codification of the Land Law in Central Europe in the 16th and at the Beginning of the 19th Centuries], Scriptorium, Praha, 2016.

and philosophical background of this partial discontinuity was based on what is known as the theory of forfeited rights, under which the Bohemian estates had deprived themselves of their existing privileges by having revolted against the monarch and therefore it was unnecessary to take them into account during the recodification. After all, even the composition of the codification commission, which included only one representative of the Bohemian nobility, and at that, one who was gradually leaving the Bohemian environment (the imperial military leader Albrecht von Wallenstein who, when the code was issued, was already Prince of the Holy Roman Empire), was a clear signal that Ferdinand II would not allow his hands to be tied by the previous developments in any way.[8]

Of the important changes included in the opening section of the code, Article A 20 redefines the legal rules related to conferring the right of residence on foreigners (later, the term *Inkolat*, derived from Latin word *incolus* – inhabitant, became common for this legal arrangement).[9] Since the Middle Ages, foreigners in Bohemia had not been allowed to acquire real property holdings (free land property); they were also excluded from holding Land offices, from actively participating in Land Diets, as well as from many other options of participating in public affairs.

It should also be noted that, in fact, foreigners had always been coming to Bohemia to some extent, with the immigration clearly intensifying after the Lands of the Bohemian Crown became part (albeit independent in terms of their governance) of the emerging Danubian Monarchy in the wake of the Habsburgs' accession to the Bohemian throne. When the Imperial Court moved to Prague for almost thirty years in 1583, the capital of the Kingdom of Bohemia became a truly cosmopolitan city with a significant potential for integration. Hence, the aforementioned bans did not and actually could not aim to set up an impermeable border that foreigners could not cross. Conversely, the legal regulation was set up in such a way as to make immigration possible but, at the same time, to ensure that two fundamental requirements were met: i.e. to ensure that foreigners would settle in Bohemia under sufficient control of the Bohemian estates and that those who would be allowed to integrate themselves would truly integrate themselves into the Bohemian estates or bourgeoisie and would not be a centrifugal element affecting the homogeneity

---

8 On the preparation of the Renewed Land Constitution, see e.g. RENTZOW, *op. cit.*, 29–30.

9 *Obnovené právo...*, *op. cit.*, 28–30. O. Chalin uses the term "right of naturalisation", Olivier CHALIN: *Inside the Empire and for the House of Austria. The Buquoy Family from the Spanish Low Countries to Bohemia* = *The Holy Roman Empire, 1495–1806: A European Perspective*, Peter H. WILSON, R.J.W. EVANS (eds.), Brill, Leiden-Boston, 2012, 87.

of the Bohemian estates. The right of residence (*ius incolatus*) developed into a legal instrument of these requirements – as a specific set of subjective rights and obligations, which could only be held by noblemen or, if certain other conditions were met, also by burgesses of royal cities.

2 The Legal Base of the Right of Residence Before the Thirty Years' War

Although there is evidence of foreign noblemen buying property in Bohemia even in the pre-Hussite era, explicit legislation that governed conferring the right of residence on foreigners was not adopted before the late 15th century. This can be certainly placed in the context of the increasing role of written law generally – in Bohemia primarily reflected by publishing the first Land Code, what is known as the (King) Vladislaus Land Constitution, in 1500.[10] The two oldest preserved legislative acts, which had been adopted to address the Inkolat a few years earlier, were added to it in a slightly modified form. These acts included the Land Court ruling of 1486, which specifically addressed these issues (the wording of the relevant article in the Vladislaus Land Constitution was based on it), and the great resolution of 1497 by the Land Diet, which also marginally touched upon it.[11]

Formally, the relevant statutory article began with a ban – applicable to all domestic inhabitants – on alienating castles, cities or any other property to foreigners. The ban applied to all legal holding titles, i.e. allodial, fief, as well as mortgage and properties. Breaching the ban was penalized with loss of the seller's honor and lifetime banishment of the seller from the land, as well as with confiscation of the property concerned. Only such alienation was declared admissible that was carried out with the Bohemian King's permission and Land permission. The latter, apparently vague, term meant granting consent from the Land estates, which was supposed to be granted at the major estate institutions, i.e. the Land Diet and, where applicable, the Land Court (curiously, the 1486 ruling only mentioned advice, not permission). Furthermore, the Land Constitution required that the property should not be effectively assigned before the foreigner asserted that he would not recognize a lord

---

10 Cf. above.
11 These normative acts are accessible in the editorial series *Archiv český čili Staré písemné památky české i moravské* [Bohemian Archive or Early Written Monuments of Bohemia and Moravia], vol. 5, František PALACKÝ (ed.), Fridrich Tempský, Praha 1862, 427–428, No. 32, 465–477, No. 51.

other than the crowned King of Bohemia and that he would exercise the same duties as the other inhabitants of the Kingdom of Bohemia, that he would issue a document containing these promises and sell all of his property outside the territory of the Bohemian state. The ban on owning property outside the territory of the Bohemian Crown was incorporated into the Land Law by the 1497 resolution.

The legal situation laid down in the Vladislaus Land Constitution remained in force throughout the 16th century. Only another Land Code, issued in 1549, entailed minor progress; above all, the sentence that the foreigner to be admitted into the land must not own property in other countries was removed, probably to facilitate the integration of noblemen across Habsburg lands. In addition, it was explicitly specified how the foreigners to be admitted into the land should fulfil their promises: by depositing a sealed binding statement with the Office of Land Tables (*Landtafelamt*) and by an oral declaration (what is known as the Land confession) made before the same office and registered in the Land Tables (*Landtafel*).[12] However, this only involved exercising the older customary practices, which did not contradict the generally formulated legal sentences of 1486. Unfortunately, the knowledge of older practices is significantly limited by the fact that the devastating fire at Prague Castle in 1541 consumed the Land Tables, as well as other documents kept with them. This is also why we cannot state with certainty how far back these practices went and whether they may have developed in any way. In any event, the oldest preserved binding statement was issued in 1515[13] and some declarations in the Land Tables also come from the period prior to 1549.

Nonetheless, the Land Diet held the determining authority in conferring the Bohemian Inkolat until the outbreak of the estates' revolt. Yet we should note that the Inkolat could not be obtained without the monarch's consent either – each foreigner who presented his application before the Land Diet also had to provide evidence of the intercession of the monarch – produced as a letter, which the administrative terminology of the time referred to as Promotorial or Intercession. Only one exception to this rule can be found throughout the period prior to the Battle of White Mountain: Colonel Alexander Debner (1609). Nevertheless, this was just an administrative error, which allowed him to appear before the Diet prior to the Bohemian Court Chancellery making a fair

---

12   *Zřízení zemská...*, op. cit., 156–158, Article B 15.
13   Národní archiv (Praha) [National Archives (Prague)], Archiv českých stavů [Archives of the Bohemian Crown], No. 1905. Its publisher was Saxon aristocrat Johann von Saalhausen, who in that year purchased the North Bohemian estate Děčín.

copy of the letter of intercession. The key decision was up to members of the Diet, however.[14]

The importance that Bohemian estates attached to the Inkolat arrangement and to conferring the Inkolat is quite apparent in the fact that, during the 16th century and notably in the early 17th century, Diet resolutions included numerous statutory articles that continued to refine the legislation. Expanding and tightening the obligations imposed on the candidates to obtain the Bohemian right of residence were the common denominator of those articles. Thus, in particular the Diet sessions held in 1609 and 1610 provided that issuing the binding statement and making the personal Land confession before the Office of Land Tables had to take place within six weeks of the Diet granting admission, and if this deadline was not met, the admission had to be forfeited. Moreover, within the same period, the new inhabitants were required to buy property in the Kingdom of Bohemia, provide evidence of their membership in the estates before people elected by the Diet and have their children learn Bohemian.[15] In 1615, the Land Diet added that engagement in the estates (i.e. providing evidence of membership in the estates) had to precede *pro futuro* the Diet granting admission; the next article extended the obligation of having descendants learn Bohemian to include also those who had obtained their residential rights in the past, as well as those moving from foreign countries to cities, even if they did not wish to buy property registered in Land Tables and thus did not apply for the Inkolat.[16] Note that the obligation of buying property in Bohemia (for at least 10,000 kopa [or *sexagena*, a unit consisting of five dozen] of Meissen groschen) had been imposed on individual foreigners when they were admitted into the land by the Land Diet (without a normative basis!) as far back as 1607.[17]

With admissions to the land taking place at the Land Diet and on the basis of Land Constitutions (i.e. further normative acts of a regional nature), it is *a priori* evident that the practice of conferring the right of residence only

---

14   For more information, cf. Vladimír KLECANDA: *Přijímání cizozemců na sněmu do Čech za obyvatele* [Accepting foreigners at the diet into Bohemia as denizens] = *Sborník prací věnovaných prof. dru Gustavu Friedrichovi k šedesátým narozeninám* [Anthology of works dedicated to Prof. Dr. Gustav Friedrich on his 60th birthday], Historický spolek v Praze, Praha, 1931, 456–467 and especially Marek STARÝ: *Cizozemci a spoluobyvatelé. Udělování českého obyvatelského práva (inkolátu) v době předbělohorské* [Foreigners and Co-inhabitants. Granting the Bohemian Right of Residence (Inkolat) in the Period before the Battle of White Mountain], Auditorium, Praha, 2018.
15   Národní archiv (Praha), Desky zemské [Land Tables], Sg. DZSt 3, Fol. M 8r – M 9v.
16   *Ibid.*, Sg. DZSt 5, Fol. E 30v – F 2r.
17   KLECANDA: *op. cit.*, 466.

covered the Kingdom of Bohemia rather than the Bohemian state as a whole, consisting of Bohemia, Moravia, the Silesian principalities, Upper and Lower Lusitania and fragmented foreign (extraterritorial) fiefs. The Moravian Diet granted its Inkolat separately, yet very similarly.[18] While the legal arrangement of the Inkolat also existed in Silesia and Lusatia, it did not have such importance in their political or legal life and was not addressed by legislation in greater detail. With their Land-based admissions into the estates, Bohemia and Moravia used an arrangement similar to that of the Austrian Hereditary Lands, unlike, for instance, Poland and Hungary, where admissions took place at the National Diets, thus becoming legally applicable throughout the land.[19]

Although the individual Lands of the Bohemian Crown formally had their own rights of residence, there were effectively minimal barriers between them, with the inhabitants of one Land being allowed to settle in the others without any great obstacles. They could do so under unilateral legal acts, without having to obtain the monarch's intercession and undergo the admission process at the Land Diet. After all, all Land Constitutions of Bohemia stressed that

---

[18] On the Moravian situation, cf. Christian D′ELVERT: *Das Incolat, die Habilitirung zum Lande, die Erbhuldigung und der Intabulations-Zwang in Mähren und Oesterr.-Schlesien*, Notizenblatt der historisch-statistischen Section der Kais. königl. mährisch-schlesischen Gesellschaft zur Beförderung des Ackerbaues, der Natur- und Landeskunde 1882, 17–18, 29–32, 47–48, 51–55, more recently, cf. Jana JANIŠOVÁ, Dalibor JANIŠ: *Postavení cizinců a inkolát podle moravského zemského práva v 16. a na počátku 17. století* [Position of foreigners and inkolat according to Moravian Land Law in the 16th and at the beginning of the 17th centuries] = *"Morava jako zrcadlo Evropy". Etnické menšiny na Moravě do roku 1918* ["Moravia as a Mirror of Europe". Ethnic minorities in Moravia to 1918] = *"Mähren als Spiegel Europas". Etnische Minderheiten in Mähren bis zum Jahr 1918*, XXXIst Mikulov symposium, 13–14 October 2010, Miroslav SVOBODA (ed.), Moravský zemský archiv et al., Brno 2010, 191–201.

[19] Arnold LUSCHIN VON EBENGREUTH: *Inkolat, Indigenat, A: In den altösterreichischen Landen* = *Österreichisches Staatswörterbuch*, Ernst MISCHLER, Josef ULBRICH (eds.), vol. 2, Hölder, Wien, 1906, 886–897; Herbert HASSINGER: *Die Landstände der österreichischen Länder: Zusammensetzung, Organisation und Leistung im 16.–18. Jahrhundert* = *Festschrift zum hundertjährigen Bestand des Vereins für Landeskunde von Niederösterreich und Wien*, Karl LECHNER (ed.), Jahrbuch für Landeskunde von Niederösterreich, Neue Folge 36/1964, Verein für Landeskunde von Niederösterreich und Wien, Wien, 1964, 995–1015; Henryk SUCHOJAD: *Problem nobilitacji oraz indygenatów na sejmikach małopolskich i wielkopolskich w latach 1669–1696* [The problem of ennoblement and the Inkolat at the diets of Lesser and Greater Poland in 1669–1696], Śląski Kwartalnik Historyczny Sobótka 1–3(1996), 169–177; Jerzy MICHTA: *Nobilitacja i indygenat w szlacheckiej Rzeczypospolitej* [Ennoblement and the Inkolat in the noble Commonwealth], Annales Universitatis Mariae Curie-Skłodowska, Sectio F, Historia 45(1990), 355–363; Johann von JUNG: *Das Indigenat im Königreich Ungarn*, Zeitschrift für österreichische Rechtsgelehrsamkeit und politische Gesetzkunde, 2(1826), 134–158, especially 137.

Moravians, Silesians and Lusatians were not regarded as foreigners, with similar legal sentences also found in Moravian legal monuments.

3 Renewed Land Constitutions 1627/1628

While the Renewed Land Constitution of 1627, which ended several legal stopgap measures that occurred after the defeat of the Bohemian Revolt at the end of 1620, aimed at curbing the estates' rights in Bohemia, it was inevitable that curtailing the Land Diet's powers would become one of the main objectives of the recodification. Consequently, granting the residential right was one of the key powers. Hence it comes as no surprise that a quite significant change was also made to this specific item, with this effectively resulting in the obsolescence of the relatively detailed and sophisticated law-making activities by the Diet at the times before the outbreak of the revolt.

The Renewed Land Constitution firstly restructured the existing composition of the Estates' society. Article A 24 returned selected representatives of the Catholic Church in Bohemia headed by the Prague Archbishopric as members of the land estates. Only after them did the estate of lords follow (including the newly accepted titles of dukes, princes and counts – as had been known and used in the Holy Roman Empire and Austrian hereditary lands), than that of knights and finally the urban estate, which was traditionally limited only to royal towns (Art. A 25–35).[20] The Renewed Land Constitution created the legal basis to deprive estate corporations of their right to admit members into Land estates and fully transferred the right to the King. In addition, the relevant articles defined three basic conditions of the process of admission into the estates, with this process becoming completely formalized in the future. At first, Article A 20 legitimated the holding of free land property (*Landesgut, Landtafelgut*) confiscated from people who had compromised themselves by their involvement in or support for the revolt of the estates of 1618–1620. The monarch, specifically the royal chamber representing the monarch, assigned such confiscated property to meritorious foreigners or loyal inhabitants of the Bohemian state. However, the core of the cited article lies in the following provision, which states that foreigners who would intend to buy or otherwise acquire free land property in the Kingdom of Bohemia (e.g. by inheritance) could only do so with the monarch's permission (*Consens, Bewilligung*).[21] Issuing these writ-

---

20 *Obnovené Právo...*, op. cit., 34–50.
21 *Ibid*, op. cit., 28–29; Josef KALOUSEK: *České státní právo* [Bohemian state law], Bursík and Kohout, Praha, 1982, 148; Jan KAPRAS: *Právní dějiny zemí koruny České* [Legal history of the

ten permissions began as conventional (single-sheet) royal charters, where the monarch conferred the right on the person concerned and on all of his legitimate descendants to settle in the Lands of the Bohemian Crown, enjoy the rights and privileges of his estate, and freely buy and use free land property in a way in which only regular members of estate communities could do. Compared to the period prior to the Bohemian revolt, a substantial change results from the fact that the monarch admitted the foreigner, as the recipient of the charter, among the Inhabitants (*Landleuthe*) of literally all Lands of the Bohemian Crown, not just those of the Kingdom of Bohemia. Over the course of time, in the second half of the 17th century, the Latin legal term Inkolat (*ius incolatus*) started to appear in the texts of documents and other papers, and eventually prevailed.

As provided in the Renewed Land Constitution, the legitimate admission to the Bohemian estates required meeting the other two legal conditions. Under Article A 2 an applicant for membership in the estate community was obliged, before he accepted the property registered in the Land Tables, to swear an oath of loyalty to the monarch (*Erbhuldigung, Erbhuldigungseid, juramentum fidelitatis*). The oath had to be sworn before officials of the Bohemian Court Chancellery in Vienna, which just like at the time before the defeat of the uprising of the estates represented the Bohemian Lands at the Viennese Court and the person taking the oath, with the first two fingers of his right hand raised, pledged loyalty not only to the current monarch as the King of Bohemia but also to all of his hereditary successors.[22] In the end, under Article A 20, it was also necessary to deliver a written binding statement in relation to the Land (*Revers zum Lande*), provided with his own seal, to the land officials, whereby the person undertook to keep the existing and future regulations of the monarch, as well as the rights and constitutions of the Kingdom of Bohemia.[23]

The Inkolat after the Bohemian Revolt had been designed, from its inception, as a legal instrument with indubitable applicability in all Lands of the Bohemian Crown – "*im Unsers Erb-Königreichs Böheimb und dessen incorporirten Landen*" (i.e. Bohemia, Moravia, Silesia, Lusatia), being superordinate to

---

lands of the Bohemian Crown], vol. 3: *Dějiny státního zřízení* [History of the state system], part 2: *Doba pobělohorská*: [White Mountain Period], Česká grafická Unie, Praha, 1920, 26. On the confiscations of rebels' property, cf. Tomáš KNOZ: *Die Konfiskationen nach 1620 in (erb)länderübergreifender Perspektive: Thesen zu Wirkungen, Aspekten und Prinzipien des Konfiskationsprozesses* = *Die Habsburgermonarchie 1620 bis 1740: Leistungen und Grenzen des Absolutismus*, Petr MAŤA, Thomas WINKELBAUER (eds.), Franz Steiner Verlag, Stuttgart, 2006, 99–131.

22   *Obnovené Právo...*, op. cit., 10–13.
23   *Ibid.*, 30.

the existing admission practices of the Lands (Provinces) of the Bohemian state. Likewise, the legal applicability of the pledge of loyalty applied to the territory of the Bohemian state as a whole. In contrast, the applicability of the binding statement in relation to the Land was restricted to the Kingdom of Bohemia only.

Only after completing the entire above-described procedure of what is known as the habilation in the Land (*Habilitierung zum Lande*) the applicant for property registered in the Land Tables could apply to the Land Diet, where the estates had to assign him an appropriate position. The final provision of Article A 20 confirmed the equal status of all inhabitants of the Bohemian state, i.e. also Moravians, Silesians and Lusatians. However, even these were subject to the above-described procedure of admission to the Bohemian estates if they held property registered in the Land Tables in Bohemia. Naturally, they were not required to meet the condition of obtaining the monarch's consent, as this applied to foreigners only.

Obtaining the monarch's consent to buy free land property (*Landesgut, Landtafelgut*), swearing the oath of loyalty and submit Revers to the Land were the essential conditions of membership in the society of the land estates. The admitted person also acquired important estate rights: access to the land tables (*Landtafelfähigkeit*) registering besides the holding of free land property also the rights and privileges of the land estates, attending and voting at the Land Diet, and holding some of the Land Offices, which were traditionally filled by regular members of the Land's estate community.[24]

To clarify disputable provisions of the Renewed Land Constitution, what is known as the Declarations and Amendments (*Declaratoria und Novellen*) und were issued in 1640;[25] they also refined technical details of the habilitation process in the Land, such as swearing the oath of loyalty before Land authorities

---

24   The entry *Güterbesitz* in Peter Karl JAKSCH: *Gesetzlexikon im Geistlichen, Religions- und Toleranzsache, wie auch in Güter- Stiftungs- Studien- und Zensursachen für das Königreich Böhmen von 1601 bis Ende 1800*, vol. 2, Author and k.k. Gubernialregistratur, Prag, 1828, 213–221; the entry *Landtafelfähigkeit* edb., 4, 1828, 10–14; KALOUSEK: *op. cit.*, 147; Bohumil BAXA: *Inkolát (a indigenát) v zemích koruny české od r. 1749–1848* [Inkolat (and indigenat) in the Lands of the Bohemian Crown from 1749–1848], Sborník věd právních a státních, Praha, 1908, 11–12.

25   *Der Röm. Kays. auch zu Hungarn und Böheim..., königl. Majestät Ferdinandi des Dritten..., über der neuen Landes-Ordnung des Königreichs Böheim publizierte Declaratorien und Nouvellen*, Wien, 1753. Czech translation, cf. *Deklaratoria a Novely Obnoveného zřízení zemského* [Declarations and Amendments of the Renewed Land Constitution], Karel MALÝ, Jiří ŠOUŠA, Klára KUČEROVÁ (eds.) = *Vývoj české ústavnosti 1618–1918* [Development of Bohemian Constitutionality 1618–1918], Ladislav SOUKUP, Karel MALÝ, Karolinum, Praha, 2007, 793–873.

or even before regional governors. However, both forms of relief were conditioned upon obtaining the monarch's written permission (Dispensation). Article A.a.3 was of fundamental importance; pursuant to this article, not only persons habilitating themselves in the Land but as a new addition also all descendants of previously habilitated persons were obliged to swear the oath of loyalty to the monarch once they had reached the age of twenty. Failure to meet this obligation within a period of one-was to be penalized by temporary suspension of their estate rights in the Land. The Declarations and Amendments extended the obligation of swearing the oath of loyalty to include also those members of the clergy who were entitled to take part in Land Diets and Assemblies (archbishops, bishops, Grand Priors of the Order of Malta, abbots and other Land prelates). Swearing a *juramentum* also became a necessary precondition of acquiring royal cities burghers' rights.[26]

In Moravia, the same criteria of admitting people as inhabitants of the Bohemian state were effectively set up among the Moravian estates because of the Renewed Land Constitution, which was issued for this Land in nearly identical form in 1628.[27] The Declarations and Amendments (1650) were also adopted as applicable to this province (Land).[28] Thus, all of the previously mentioned conditions of habilitation in the Land, which were laid down in the Renewed Land Constitutions and in the Declarations and Amendments, issued for Bohemia and Moravia, formed a multistep process of admission into the Bohemian and Moravian society of the estates. This included traditional legal arrangements from the era prior to the Bohemian Revolt, which were appropriately modernized (Inkolat, Revers), as well as all-new elements (*juramentum*). Thus, the division between the monarch and the estates, as it had existed prior to the Bohemian revolt, was maintained but only at a purely formal level: as a new element, the monarch completely decided on behalf of both, having reduced the role of the estates to the factual execution of his will, i.e. taking care of the necessary formalities. Although the new legal conditions did not envisage that the scattered admissions by estates at Land Diets would be relevant, this traditional ceremony did not cease to exist. However, it completely turned into an initiative of the estates, the formal nature of which provided no option of reversing the admission of a new member into the estate community. The ceremony only symbolically confirmed the monarch's will, executed and supervised by monarchical offices.[29]

---

26   *Deklaratoria...*, op. cit., 823–824.
27   *Constitutiones...*, op. cit., 4–7, 32–33, 36–49, Articles II.2, XIV.23, XVI.26–XXI.38.
28   KALOUSEK: *op. cit.*, 460.
29   Jiří BRŇOVJÁK: *K úřednímu procesu přijetí do zemské stavovské obce v období od vydání Obnovených zřízení zemských do poloviny 19. století a jeho písemnostem* [On the official

4   The Administrative Reforms of the 18th Century

Despite the relatively clearly worded provisions of the Renewed Land Constitution and the Declarations and Amendments, apparently quite relaxed relations prevailed in the area of the legal holdings of land table properties in Bohemia and Moravia. At the beginning, the complicated period of the ongoing Thirty Years' War certainly was to blame in this situation. For the entire second half of the 17th century and first two decades of the 18th century, an increased effort by the sovereign to resolve the lingering unclear situation regarding the unhabilitated holders of land table estates continues to be characteristic. the large number of regulations issued, which very often repeated the wording of the preceding legal norms and set new dates for their fulfilment, proves that the Habsburgs were unable in the long term to ensure fully effective enforcement of the validity of the announced royal norms in Bohemia and Moravia.[30]

The expansion of the obligation to the holding of an Inkolat occurred in 1713, when Charles VI decreed that the members of the chapters, who in any of the Bohemian Lands owned land estates, would become only those, who before their election, nomination or presentation held an Inkolat. The Inkolat pragmatics did not take into account the fact whether the concerned clergyman was counted among the land prelates, who were already subject to the obligation to swear an oath of loyalty, or not. However, in practice, there was never complete fulfilment of this provision, despite the recurring effort of Maria Theresa, who in 1746 and 1747 almost verbatim repeated the provision of her father.[31]

Therefore, with identical texts of the Renewed Land Constitutions, the Declarations and Amendments, and numerous follow-up normative acts,

---

process of the acceptance into the land estate community from the issuance of the Renewed Land Constitutions to the middle of the 19th century and its documentation] = J. BRŇOVJÁK et al., *Nobilitace ve světle písemných pramenů* [Ennoblement in Light of the Written Sources], Nobilitas in historia moderna, vol. 2, Ostravská univerzita v Ostravě, Ostrava, 2009, 138–139; Jiří DAVID: *Kniha moravského rytířského stavu (1628–1690): Stavovský rozměr nobilitačního procesu* [Book of the Moravian Knightly Estate (1628–1690: Estates Dimension of the Ennoblement Process)] = *ibid.*, 148–159.

30   Jiří BRŇOVJÁK: *Šlechticem z moci úřední: Udělování šlechtických titulů v českých zemích 1705–1780* [Aristocrat from official power: Granting aristocratic titles in the Bohemian Lands 1705–1780], Nobilitas in historia moderna 7, Ostravská univerzita v Ostravě, Ostrava, 2015, 113–115.

31   Jiří BRŇOVJÁK: *In vim sanctionis pragmaticae: k interpretaci inkolátní pragmatiky z roku 1713 a nobilitací církevních hodnostářů v českých zemích v 18. století* [In vim sanctionis pragmaticae: on the interpretations of the Inkolat pragmatics from 1713 and ennoblement of ecclesiastical dignitaries in the Bohemian Lands in the 18th century]. Historica: Revue pro historii a příbuzné vědy 7(2016)/1, 1–22.

essentially the same rules for conferring the Inkolat and of the subsequent mechanism of admission into the society of the estates of both Lands had applied to both Bohemia and Moravia since the late 1620s. Lusatians were excluded from the individual right of residence in Bohemian Lands, as they were declared foreigners in 1651 because of a hereditary cession of Lower and Upper Lusatia to the electors of Saxony (1635).[32] The legal conditions of individual Silesian principalities and free state countries, which were stable parts of the Bohemian state, substantially differed from those in Bohemia and Moravia. Silesia was exempted on the strength of negotiating the Dresden (Saxon) Accord of 1621.[33] Given the specific settlement between Silesian estates and Ferdinand II, the original Land Constitutions remained in force in the individual Silesian principalities, but these constitutions did not regulate the process of admitting new members of local estate communities at all. The conditions of the process of estate admissions in the individual principalities/duchies and free estates domains (*freie Standesherrschaften*) could differ slightly. Paying homage to the holder of the principality was a generally widespread arrangement when allodial property covered by Land Law (*Landgüter, adelige Güter, Rittergüter*) was acquired. Some principalities/duchies and free estate domains required a written Revers from a new member of the estate community.[34]

During the second half of the 17th century and notably the first half of the 18th century, the necessity of the Inkolat for free land property was also slowly gaining ground in Silesian principalities. Silesian non-Catholics (only in Silesia did confessional freedom contintue to exist, in contrast to Bohemia and Moravia), whose official or economic activities were seen by the state as highly beneficial, were given the option of obtaining the Inkolat, which was explicitly restricted to the territory of Silesia – "*im Unseren Herzogthumb Nieder- und*

---

32   KALOUSEK: *op. cit.*, 148; KAPRAS: *op. cit.*, 26. On the resignation of Lusatia, cf. Jan ZDICHYNEC: *Předání Lužic Sasku v letech 1620–1635* [Transfer of Lusatia to Saxony in 1620–1635] = *Od konfesijní konfrontace ke konfesijnímu míru. Sborník z konference k 360. výročí uzavření vestfálského míru* [From confessional confrontation to confessional peace: Proceedings of the conference on the 360th anniversary of the conclusion of the Westphalian Peace], Jiří HRBEK, Petr POLEHLA, Jan ZDICHYNEC (eds.), Oftis, Ústí nad Orlicí, 2008, 70–86.

33   KALOUSEK: *op. cit.*, 162–163; *Geschichte Schlesiens*, vol. 2: *Die Habsburger Zeit 1526–1740*, Ludwig VON PETRY, J. Joachim MENZEL (eds.), Jan Thorbecke Verlag, Stuttgart, 1973, 54; Hermann PALM: *Der Dresdner Accord*, Zeitschrift des Vereins für Geschichte und Alterthum Schlesiens 13(1876)/1, 151–192.

34   BRŇOVJÁK: *Šlechticem..., op. cit.*, 116; Petr MAŤA: *Landstände und Landtage in den böhmischen und österreichischen Ländern (1620–1740): Von der Niedergangsgeschichte zur Interaktionsanalyse* = *Die Habsburgermonarchie..., op. cit.*, 363.

Ober-Schlesien", "im Unseren Erb-Herzogthumb Schlesien".[35] Silesia's complicated situation was substantially influenced by the events of the First Silesian War (1740–1742), which resulted in the final cession of an overwhelming majority of this Crown Land to victorious Prussia in 1742. In newly established Austrian Silesia, which occupied less than 14% of Silesia's original area, the Inkolat became a standard part of the procedure of admission among Austrian-Silesian estates.[36] Remarkably, the Prussian state left the Inkolat in force on its newly acquired Silesian territory.[37]

The merger of Bohemian and Austrian Hereditary Lands into a single administrative unit in 1749 had no significant impact on conferring the Inkolat and on the subsequent habilitation process in the Land (bear in mind that it fully existed on the strength of the Renewed Land Constitutions and subsequent regulations in Bohemia and Moravia only).[38] Thus, Bohemian Lands continued to differ from their Austrian counterparts – the original Austrian hereditary lands, where the arrangement of single Inkolat was unknown and where the powers of admission among Land estates, even after the defeat of the Bohemian Revolt there, were still held by the estates themselves.[39] In this regard, Bohemian Lands still maintained their unique nature of their former unity in the sense of single independent state within the western part of the Habsburg monarchy. Only one small modification was made: raising the level of coming of age from the original 20 to 24 years, which took place in 1754.[40]

The era of the 1770s onwards saw the state's pragmatically driven efforts for relaxing the rules of free land property in Bohemian Lands, but these efforts did not challenge at all the necessity of holding the Inkolat or undergoing the

---

35   BRŇOVJÁK: *Šlechticem...*, op. cit., 338–344.
36   Extensively, see Christian D'ELVERT: *Die Verfassung und Verwaltung von Oesterreichisch-Schlesien in ihrer historischer Ausbildung, dann die Rechtsverhältnisse zwischen Mähren, Troppau und Jägerndorf, so wie der mährischen Enklaven in Schlesien*, Schriften der historisch statistischen Sektion der k.k. mährisch-schlesichen Gesellschaft zur Beförderung des Ackerbaues, der Natur- und Landeskunde: Beiträge zur Geschichte von Statistik Mährens u. Oesterreichisch- Schlesiens 2/7, Nohrer's Erben, Brünn, 1854, 248–259.
37   [CUNOW]: *Beiträge für die Kunde des preussischen Staats*, Franzen und Grosse, Stendal, 1799, 47.
38   Friedrich WALTER: *Die österreichische Zentralverwaltung*, vol. 2: *Von der Vereinigung der österreichischen und böhmischen Hofkanzlei bis zur Einrichtung der Ministerialverfassung (1749–1848)*, part. 1.1 *Die Geschichte der österreichischen Zentralverwaltung in der Zeit Maria Theresias*, Böhlau, Wien et al., 1938, 92–193; in briefer form, cf. *Die Theresianische Staatsreform von 1749*, Verlag für Geschichte und Politik, München, 1958.
39   LUSCHIN VON EBENGREUTH: *op. cit.*; HASSINGER, *op. cit.*; MAŤA: *op. cit.* 353–365.
40   JAKSCH: *op. cit.*, vol. 2, 1828, 518–519; Václav ELZNIC: *Inkolát v českém státním právu* [Inkolat in the Bohemian state law], Listy Genealogické a heraldické společnosti v Praze 4(1976)/2, 58.

habilitation process in the particular Land (Bohemia, Moravia) in the end. Moreover, the estates themselves called for retaining these rules. This practice is aptly illustrated by the provision of the 1786 Civil Code that declared the legal equality of all inhabitants, i.e. people living in all Hereditary Lands under the single monarch's rule – even for property holdings registered in Land Tables – but also subjected this provision to the Land Constitutions of Bohemian Lands, which were still in force, and these still required holding the Inkolat and undergoing the habilitation process there (at that time, no longer with a *juramentum* – the only component of habilitation that was removed in the Land by Joseph II in 1781).[41] Hence the proclaimed equality of all inhabitants of Hereditary Lands in their access to free land property remained only theoretical. Nevertheless, reforms of Joseph II substantially relaxed confessional restrictions. After issuance of the Patent of Toleration in 1781, Vienna's office was obliged to grant the relevant dispensation to non-Catholics when they applied for the Inkolat.[42] Provisions of the Patent of Toleration and subsequent legal norms did not apply to the Jewish population and adherents of non-Christian religions (the period legal standards should refer specifically to the Muslims from the realm of the Ottoman Empire), and therefore they were still excluded from free land property and consequently from membership in the society of particular estates of Bohemian Lands.[43]

The period immediately following the death of Joseph II was characterized by efforts byt the estate communities at regaining their previous privileges, which had been threatened or even eliminated by Joseph II's reforms. In 1790, individual estate communities of former Bohemian Lands prepared their collections of demands (what is known as the Desideria), one of which was even the restitution of those historic freedoms already removed by Ferdinand II in the Renewed Land Constitution. Members of the estates demanded of Leopold

---

41 For the wording of the relevant paragraphs, cf. *Joseph des Zweyten Römischen Kaisers Gesetze und Verfassungen im Justitz-Fache.* [...]. *Jahrgang von 1785 bis 1786*, Kaiserlichkönigliche Hof- und Staats-Aerarial-Druckerei, Wien, 1817, 78–79; BAXA: *op. cit.*, 18–19. On the cancellation of the oath of loyalty to the sovereign, cf. BRŇOVJÁK: *K úřednímu procesu...*, *op. cit.*, 129.

42 Johann Thomas EDLER VON TRATTNER: *Sammlung der k.k. landesfürstlichen Verordnung in Publico-Ecclesiasticis*, Kaiserl. Königl. Hofbuchdruckern und Buchhändlern, Wien, 1782, 137–140, No. 133.

43 JAKSCH: *op. cit.*, vol. 2, 1828, *op. cit.*, 518–519; BRŇOVJÁK: *Šlechticem...*, *op. cit.*, 122–123; Jan ŽUPANIČ: *Židovská šlechta podunajské monarchie. Mezi Davidovou hvězdou a křížem* [Jewish Aristocracy of the Danube Monarchy: Between David's Star and the Cross], Nakladatelství Lidové noviny, Praha, 2012, 27–31.

11 that future Inkolats not be granted without consent and written opinion from representatives of the relevant Land estates. In 1791, the Bohemian estates were awarded the partial right to give their opinions on applications for the Inkolat (votum consultativum): the estate community could only comment on serious cases, the execution of which required a dispensation from statutory requirements.[44] As late as 1845, the Bohemian estate community was given the authority to evaluate all cases without exception. The necessity of the Inkolat and of the subsequent habilitation in the Land was not even challenged by the issuance of the General Civil Code of 1811, which put into place a common and equal Austrian citizenship. The Code did not at all comment on the existence of the Inkolat in all of the former Bohemian Lands; moreover, Section 355 suggested that each citizen was entitled to ownership, i.e. potentially also to the ownership of free land property. What is known as the Patent of Habilitation was issued immediately afterwards, requiring that non-habilitated candidates for free land property had to undergo the procedure of obtaining the Inkolat and of being admitted to the Land estates, or they had to apply to the Court Chancellery for a hereditary dispensation.[45]

The Bohemian estate system finally ceased to exist with the revolutions of 1848–1849. Estate constitutions were replaced with a constitutional monarchy, which no longer envisaged estate privileges and numerous traditional (judicial, military) freedoms enjoyed purely by the nobility.[46] The Inkolat, as the last

---

44 Ivo CERMAN: *Šlechtická kultura v 18. století: Filozofové, mystici, politici* [Aristocratic Culture in the 18th Century: Philosophers, mystics, politicians], Nakladatelství Lidové noviny, Praha, 2011, 507–581; cf. Anna M. DRABEK: *Die Desiderien der böhmischen Stände von 1791* = *Die böhmischen Länder zwischen Ost und West: Festschrift für Karl Bosl zum 75. Geburtstag*, Ferdinand VON SEIBT (ed.), Oldenbourg, München, 1983, 132–142; Christian D'ELVERT: *Die Desiderien der mähr. Stände vom Jahre 1790 und ihre Folgen*, Schriften der historisch-statistischen Section der k.k. mährisch-schlesischen Gesellschaft zur Beförderung des Ackerbaues, der Natur- und Landeskunde 14, Verlag der hist. Stat. Section, Brünn, 1865, 101–364.

45 Patent published in *Sr. k.k. Majestät Franz des Ersten politische Gesetze und Verodnungen für die Oesterreichischen, Böhmischen und Galizischen Erbländer 36*, Kurtzbeck, Wien, 1812, č. 48, 129–138. On the general civil code and habilitation patent, see BAXA: *op. cit.*, 61–62, cf. also the commentary on pp. 51–56.

46 Ernst BRUCKMÜLLER: *Sozialgeschichte Österreichs*, Böhlau, Köln et al., 2001, 265–282; Helmut RUMPLER: *Eine Chance für Mitteleuropa: Bürgerliche Emanzipation und Staatsverfall in der Habsburgermonarchie*, Österreichische Geschichte 1804–1914, Buchgemeinschaft Donauland et al., Wien, 2005, 279–286; cf. Helmuth FEIGL: *Die Stellung des Adels nach 1848 im Spiegel der Gesetzgebung* = *Adel im Wandel. Vorträge und Diskussionen des elften Symposions des Niederösterreichischen Instituts für Landeskunde Horn, 2.–5. Juli 1990*, Studien und Forschungen aus dem Niederösterreichischen Institut für Landeskunde

legal arrangement which continued to signify the integrity of the Lands of the Bohemian Crown after 1749 and also served as a precondition of free land property, was abolished in subsequent years (1849 1852, 1853).[47] Naturally, the elimination of the state of the estates also made the Revers unjustified. It can be noted that in the revolutionary years, the Hungarian Indignat was also cancelled, just like the Inkolat (Indigenat) used in the Kingdom of Galicia and Lodomeria, which became part of the Habsburg monarchy in 1772 during the First Partition of the Polish-Lithuanian Commonwealth (Rzeczpospolita).[48]

5 Comparison and Conclusion

The existence of the Inkolat in the Bohemian Lands is nothing extraordinary in the European legal and social history. It has already been implied above that the estate corporations had a similar institution in the individual Austrian Lands (*Landsmannschaft*), Hungary or Poland (*indigenat*). What would surely bring interesting analogies and incentives for comparison would be a more in-depth research of the actual procedure and registration of accepting new members into the estates of territorial units in the Holy Roman Empire and its successors or other western countries and their partial regions, e.g. in Spain, France or in the Netherlands, including its southern (Spanish/Austrian) part. A detailed analysis of the local situation far exceeds the possibilities of this paper – all the more so because this situation is reflected very little in the existing works.[49] We can, however, provide a preliminary hypothesis, which is that although it is possible to find certain analogies to the legal situation in the

---

15, Helmuth FEIGL, Willibald ROSNER (eds.), Selbstverl. d. NÖ Inst. für Landeskunde, Wien 1991, 117–135; Reinhard BINDER-KRIEGLSTEIN: *Österreichisches Adelsrecht 1868–1918/19: Von der Ausgestaltung des Adelsrechts der cisleithanischen Reichshälfte bis zum Adelsaufhebungsgesetz der Republik unter besonderer Berücksichtigung des adeligen Namensrechts*, Rechtshistorische Reihe 216, Peter Lang, Frankfurt a. M., 2000, 77–85.

47 Karolina ADAMOVÁ: *K českému inkolátu* [On the Bohemian Inkolat], Právněhistorické studie 41(2012), 193.

48 On the end of the Estate system in Hungary: Peter MOSNÝ, Ladislav HUBENÁK: *Dejiny štátu a práva na Slovensku* [History of State and Law in Slovakia], Právnická fakulta UPJŠ, Košice, 2005, 81–84. On the obligation of the so-called indigenat in Galicia, cf. *Alphabetisch geordnetes Repertorium aller für Galizien, Lodomerien und Bukowina erschienen Gesetze, Verordnungen, Patente, Gubernial- und Kreisschreiben im politischen, Justitz- und Kameralsache* […], E. Winiarz Verlags-Expedition, Lemberg, 1856, 153.

49 Cf. the literature above.

Lands of the Bohemian Crown, none of them had a completely identical layout.

In addition, in the actual Bohemian Lands the development of the Inkolat, which took several hundred years, from the late Middle Ages until the mid-19th century, by which time it, as an outdated relic of feudalism, ceased to be conferred, offers enough potential for comparison. Considering how fundamental a turning point the Battle of White Mountain and the immediately following defeat of the Bohemian Revolt against the Habsburgs was in the history of the Bohemian state, it is essential that we first ask to what extent the outlined turning point affected the changes in the legal institute, whose significance for the constitutional situation of the Bohemian state was, without exaggeration, crucial.

A more detailed analysis of the legal norms contained in sources of various types shows a range of discontinuous elements through which the content of the right of residence was considerably modified. The first essential shift was (like in many other regions) the strengthening of the role of the ruler, who, before 1620, stood more in the background of the entire process and his role was limited to issuing letters of intercession (Promotorials) for candidates who subsequently appeared before Land Diets, which had the ultimate authority. In contrast, in the post-White Mountain period conferring the Inkolat became one of the royal prerogatives, while the role of the Land Diets was marginalised. They now had only the right to assign the newly accepted inhabitant a place in their midst in the case this inhabitant decided to use the royal privilege to become a full member of the estate society, participating in the political running of the country. However, this process, which came to be called habilitation in the Land, represented only a kind of superstructure within the entire process. The charter, which later came to be known as the Inkolat, was issued based on the ruler's arbitrariness. Another novelty was the obligation of the newly accepted inhabitants to swear an oath of loyalty, which was, however, shared in Bohemia and Moravia with all members of the estate society based on the Declarations and Amendments.

Another significant change was the territorial scope of the Inkolat. In the pre-White Mountain period the right of residence had a distinctly provincial character, which corresponded with the competence of the individual Land Diets to make decisions about it. In contrast, after the Battle of White Mountain it became customary for the ruler to use one charter to confer the provincial citizenship for all Lands of the Bohemian Crown, i.e. Bohemia, Moravia and the Silesian principalities (an exception was the not very common specific Silesian Inkolat, whose existence was connected with a limited religious tolerance towards non-Catholics, which was, until the reforms of enlightened absolutism, unthinkable in Bohemia and Moravia). While the persisting Inkolat arrangement – even after Bohemian Lands administratively lost their independence in 1749, as well as its resistance to non-estate provisions of modern civil codes and the introduction of Austrian state citizenship in the General Civic Code of 1811 – looked rather out of date, it still helped to politically and culturally maintain the important concept of the exclusiveness of the union of historic Bohemian Lands and of the continuity of the historic Bohemian State. Numerous Bohemian politicians, lawyers and historians, who promoted the political ideology of Bohemian state governance in the Habsburg Monarchy, relied on this in the second half of the 19th and the early 20th centuries. Thus, the legal arrangement of the Inkolat contributed to maintaining the awareness of the identity of Bohemian Lands.

As indicated by the above overview, the Inkolat in Bohemian Lands is a fairly typical example of how law can be instrumental in changing social reality. This applies in particular to the period after 1620, when legislative modifications reflected the ideas of absolutist monarchs and quite significantly influenced the composition of estate corporations, which could partly serve as their political partners. Curiously, when the changes were made, they tended to weaken the national identity of the Bohemian state, but in the 19th century, when the Inkolat lost its actual gravity, it started to be retrospectively seen as an important state governance arrangement with a clearly integrative role, boosting the uniqueness of state governance in the Bohemian state.[50] This alone could be a topic for remarkable reflections on the "second life" of a legal statute after it expires, but such reflections exceed the scope of this paper. In any event, however, it would be highly desirable to develop comparative studies of medieval and early modern state or land nationalities across the European continent – after all, such a comparison would also be interesting for today's integration processes.

---

50 *Das böhmische Staatsrecht in den deutsch-tschechischen Auseinandersetzungen des 19. und 20. Jahrhunderts*, Ernst BIRKE (ed.), Lahn, Elwert, Marburg, 1960; Pavel MARŠÁLEK: *České státní právo v 19. století* [Bohemian state law in the 19th century] = *Vývoj...*, op. cit., 468–487; Luboš VELEK, *Böhmisches Staatsrecht auf "weichem Papier": Tatsache, Mythos und ihre symbolische Bedeutung in der tschechischen politischen Kultur*, Bohemia. Zeitschrift für Geschichte und Kultur der böhmischen Länder. A Journal of History and Civilisation in East Central Europe 47(2006/2007)/1, 103–118.

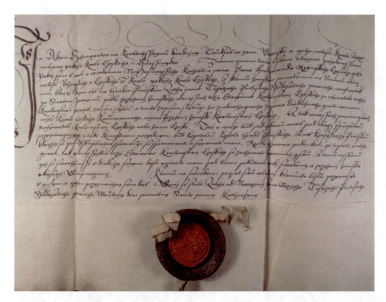

FIGURE 1.1 Binding statement (Revers) of Adam Hohenwartner of Gerlachstein (1561)
SOURCE: NÁRODNÍ ARCHIV (NATIONAL ARCHIVES), ARCHIV ČESKÝCH STAVŮ – REVERSY K ZEMI (LAND ESTATES ARCHIVES – REVERSES TO THE LAND), NR. 31

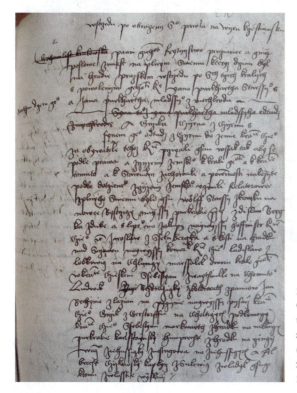

FIGURE 1.2
Conferring of Bohemian Inkolat to various persons (1545)
SOURCE: NÁRODNÍ ARCHIV (NATIONAL ARCHIVES), DESKY ZEMSKÉ (LAND TABLES), SG. DZST 42, FOL. F 10R

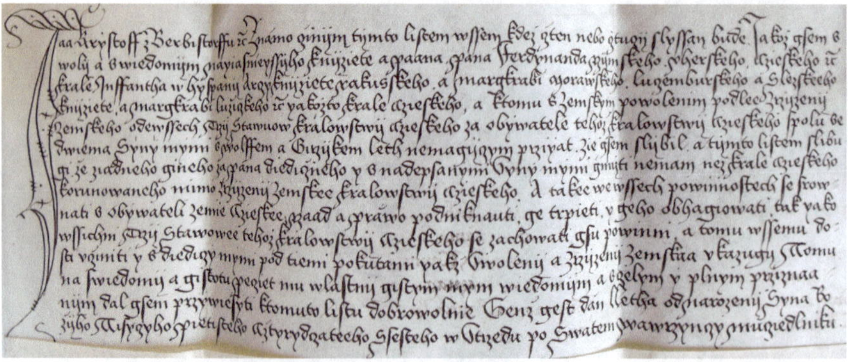

FIGURE 1.3 Binding statement of Christoph of Berbisdorf (1546)
SOURCE: NÁRODNÍ ARCHIV (NATIONAL ARCHIVES), ARCHIV ČESKÝCH STAVŮ – REVERSY K ZEMI (LAND ESTATES ARCHIVES – REVERSES TO THE LAND), NR. 5

FIGURE 1.4 Seal from binding statement of Julius Count of Hardegg (1558)
SOURCE: NÁRODNÍ ARCHIV (NATIONAL ARCHIVES), ARCHIV ČESKÝCH STAVŮ – REVERSY K ZEMI (LAND ESTATES ARCHIVES – REVERSES TO THE LAND), NR. 21

FIGURE 1.5 Title page of Moravian Renewed Land Constitution (1628)
SOURCE: MUZEUM TĚŠÍNSKA (MUSEUM OF THE LAND OF TĚŠÍN), KNIHOVNA SILESIA (SILESIA LIBRARY), NO. 1562

FIGURE 1.6 Patent of Inkolat for Blasius de Salasar (1656)
SOURCE: NÁRODNÍ ARCHIV (NATION ARCHIVES), ARCHIV ČESKÝCH STAVŮ – INKOLÁTY (LAND ESTATES ARCHIVES – INKOLATS), NO. 9

FIGURE 1.7 Binding statement (Revers zum Lande) of Maximilian Leopold von Cantelmo (1669)
SOURCE: MORAVSKÝ ZEMSKÝ ARCHIV (MORAVIAN LAND ARCHIVES), A 2 REVERSY K ZEMI (REVERSES TO THE LAND), SG. R 62

FIGURE 1.8 Moravian Book of royal deeds incl. documents of Habilitation in land (1773–1785)
SOURCE: MORAVSKÝ ZEMSKÝ ARCHIV (MORAVIAN LAND ARCHIVES), A 3 STAVOVSKÉ RUKOPISY (LAND ESTATES MANUSCRIPTS), LIT. K, NO. 68

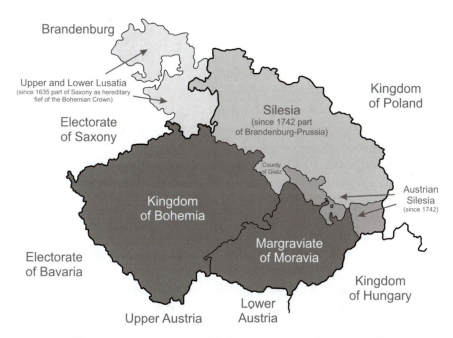

FIGURE 1.9 Changes of territorial extent of the Bohemian state during 17th and 18th centuries

Bibliography

Archival Sources

Národní archiv (Praha) [National Archives (Prague)], Archiv českých stavů [Archives of the Bohemian Crown], No. 1905.
Národní archiv (Praha), Desky zemské [Land Tables], Sg. DZSt 3, Fol. M 8r – M 9v.

E-sources

GDZ. Göttinger Digitalisierungszentrum (gdz.sub.uni-goettingen.de/dms/load/img/?PID=PPN626655234, accessed 21 Februar 2017).
Manuscriptorium. Digital library of Written Heritage (manuscriptorium.com/apps/index.php?direct=record&pid= rec1323815836_145#search, accessed 21 February 2017).

Literature

Karolina ADAMOVÁ: *První česká federativní ústava z roku 1619* [First Bohemian Federative Constitution from 1619], Aleš Čeněk, Plzeň, 2009.

Karolina ADAMOVÁ: *K českému inkolátu* [On the Bohemian Inkolat], Právněhistorické studie 41(2012), 179–198.

Alphabetisch geordnetes Repertorium aller für Galizien, Lodomerien und Bukowina erschienen Gesetze, Verordnungen, Patente, Gubernial- und Kreisschreiben im politischen, Justitz- und Kameralsache [...], E. Winiarz Verlags-Expedition, Lemberg, 1856.

Archiv český čili Staré písemné památky české i moravské [Bohemian Archive or Early Written Monuments of Bohemia and Moravia], 5, František PALACKÝ (ed.), Fridrich Tempský, Praha 1862.

Joachim BAHLCKE: *Modernization and state-building in an east-central European estates' system: The example of the Confoederatio Bohemica of 1619*, Parliaments, Estates & Representation 17(1997), 61–73.

Bohumil BAXA: *Inkolát (a indigenát) v zemích koruny české od r. 1749–1848* [Inkolat (and indigenat) in the Lands of the Bohemian Crown from 1749–1848], Sborník věd právních a státních, Praha, 1908, 11–12.

Winfried BECKER: *Ständestaat und Konfessionsbildung am Beispiel der böhmischen Konföderationsakte von 1619* = Politik und Konfession: Festschrift für Konrad Repgen zum 60. Geburtstag, Dieter ALBRECHT et al. (eds.), Duncker & Humblot, Berlin, 1983, 77–99.

Hans-Wolfgang BERGERHAUSEN: *Die "Verneuerte Landesordnung" in Böhmen 1627: Ein Grunddokument des habsburgischen Absolutismus*, Historische Zeitschrift 272(2001), 327–351.

Reinhard BINDER-KRIEGLSTEIN: *Österreichisches Adelsrecht 1868–1918/19: Von der Ausgestaltung des Adelsrechts der cisleithanischen Reichshälfte bis zum Adelsaufhebungsgesetz der Republik unter besonderer Berücksichtigung des adeligen Namensrechts*, Rechtshistorische Reihe 216, Peter Lang, Frankfurt a.M., 2000.

Das böhmische Staatsrecht in den deutsch-tschechischen Auseinandersetzungen des 19. und 20. Jahrhunderts, Ernst BIRKE (ed.), Lahn, Elwert, Marburg, 1960.

Jiří BRŇOVJÁK: *In vim sanctionis pragmaticae: k interpretaci inkolátní pragmatiky z roku 1713 a nobilitací církevních hodnostářů v českých zemích v 18. století* [In vim sanctionis pragmaticae: on the interpretations of the Inkolat pragmatics from 1713 and ennoblement of ecclesiastical dignitaries in the Bohemian Lands in the 18th century]. Historica: Revue pro historii a příbuzné vědy 7(2016)/1, 1–22.

Jiří BRŇOVJÁK: *K úřednímu procesu přijetí do zemské stavovské obce v období od vydání Obnovených zřízení zemských do poloviny 19. století a jeho písemnostem* [On the official process of the acceptance into the land estate community from the issuance of the Renewed Land Constitutions to the middle of the 19th century and its documentation] = Jiří BRŇOVJÁK et al., *Nobilitace ve světle písemných pramenů* [Ennoblement in Light of the Written Sources], Nobilitas in historia moderna 2, Ostravská univerzita v Ostravě, Ostrava, 2009, 138–139.

Jiří BRŇOVJÁK: *Šlechticem z moci úřední: Udělování šlechtických titulů v českých zemích 1705–1780* [Aristocrat from official power: Granting aristocratic titles in the Bohemian Lands 1705–1780,], Nobilitas in historia moderna 7, Ostravská univerzita v Ostravě, Ostrava, 2015.

Ernst BRUCKMÜLLER: *Sozialgeschichte Österreichs*, Böhlau, Köln et al., 2001.

Ivo CERMAN: *Šlechtická kultura v 18. století: Filozofové, mystici, politici* [Aristocratic Culture in the 18th Century: Philosophers, mystics, politicians], Nakladatelství Lidové noviny, Praha, 2011.

Constitutiones Margraviatus Moraviae anno 1628 reformatae = Codex Juris Bohemici, vol. 5, Part 3, Hermengild JIREČEK (ed.), F. Tempsy – J. Tempsky – G. Freytag, Pragae – Vindobonnae – Lipsiae, 1890.

Olivier CHALIN: *Inside the Empire and for the House of Austria. The Buquoy Family from the Spanish Low Countries to Bohemia* = *The Holy Roman Empire, 1495–1806: A European Perspective*, Peter H. WILSON, R.J.W. EVANS (eds.), Brill, Leiden-Boston 2012, 79–90.

Crown, Church and Estates. Central European Politics in the Sixteenth and Seventeenth Centuries, R.J.W. EVANS, T.V. THOMAS (eds.), St. Martin's Press, New York 1991.

[CUNOW]: *Beiträge für die Kunde des preussischen Staats*, Franzen und Grosse, Stendal 1799.

Jiří DAVID: *Kniha moravského rytířského stavu (1628–1690): Stavovský rozměr nobilitačního procesu* [Book of the Moravian Knightly Estate (1628–1690: Estates

Dimension of the Ennoblement Process)] = J. BRŇOVJÁK et al., *Nobilitace ve světle písemných pramenů* [Ennoblement in Light of the Written Sources], *Nobilitas in historia moderna*, vol. 2, Ostravská univerzita v Ostravě, Ostrava, 2009, 148–159.

Dějiny českého státu v dokumentech [History of the Bohemian State in Documents], Zdeněk VESELÝ (ed.), Professional Publishing, Praha 2012.

Christian D'ELVERT: *Das Incolat, die Habilitirung zum Lande, die Erbhuldigung und der Intabulations-Zwang in Mähren und Oesterr.-Schlesien*, Notizenblatt der historisch-statistischen Section der Kais. königl. mährisch-schlesischen Gesellschaft zur Beförderung des Ackerbaues, der Natur- und Landeskunde 1882, 17–18, 29–32, 47–48, 51–55.

Christian D'ELVERT: *Die Verfassung und Verwaltung von Oesterreichisch-Schlesien in ihrer historischen Ausbildung, dann die Rechtsverhältnisse zwischen Mähren, Troppau und Jägerndorf, so wie der mährischen Enklaven in Schlesien*, Schriften der historisch statistischen Sektion der k.k. mährisch-schlesichen Gesellschaft zur Beförderung des Ackerbaues, der Natur- und Landeskunde: Beiträge zur Geschichte von Statistik Mährens u. Oesterreichisch- Schlesiens 2/7, Nohrer's Erben, Brünn, 1854, 248–259.

Christian D'ELVERT: *Die Desiderien der mähr. Stände vom Jahre 1790 und ihre Folgen*, Schriften der historisch-statistischen Section der k.k. mährisch-schlesischen Gesellschaft zur Beförderung des Ackerbaues, der Natur- und Landeskunde 14, Verlag der hist. Stat. Section, Brünn, 1865, 101–364.

Deklaratoria a Novely Obnoveného zřízení zemského [Declarations and Amendments of the Renewed Land Constitution], Karel MALÝ, Jiří ŠOUŠA, Klára KUČEROVÁ (eds.) = *Vývoj české ústavnosti 1618–1918* [Development of Bohemian Constitutionality 1618–1918], Ladislav SOUKUP, Karel MALÝ, (eds.) Karolinum, Praha, 2007, 793–873.

Anna M. DRABEK: *Die Desiderien der böhmischen Stände von 1791* = *Die böhmischen Länder zwischen Ost und West: Festschrift für Karl Bosl zum 75. Geburtstag*, Ferdinand VON SEIBT (ed.), Oldenbourg, München, 1983, 132–142.

Johann Thomas EDLER VON TRATTNER: *Sammlung der k.k. landesfürstlichen Verordnung in Publico-Ecclesiasticis*, Kaiserl. Königl. Hofbuchdruckern und Buchhändlern, Wien, 1782.

Václav ELZNIC: *Inkolát v českém státním právu* [Inkolat in the Bohemian state law], Listy Genealogické a heraldické společnosti v Praze 4(1976)/2, 53–60.

Helmuth FEIGL: *Die Stellung des Adels nach 1848 im Spiegel der Gesetzgebung* = *Adel im Wandel. Vorträge und Diskussionen des elften Symposions des Niederösterreichischen Instituts für Landeskunde Horn, 2.–5. Juli 1990*, Studien und Forschungen aus dem Niederösterreichischen Institut für Landeskunde 15, Helmuth FEIGL, Willibald ROSNER (eds.), Selbstverl. d. NÖ Inst. für Landeskunde, Wien 1991, 117–135.

Geschichte Schlesiens, vol. 2: *Die Habsburger Zeit 1526–1740*, Ludwig VON PETRY, J., Joachim MENZEL (eds.), Jan Thorbecke Verlag, Stuttgart, 1973.

Herbert HASSINGER: *Die Landstände der österreichischen Länder: Zusammensetzung, Organisation und Leistung im 16.–18. Jahrhundert = Festschrift zum hundertjährigen Bestand des Vereins für Landeskunde von Niederösterreich und Wien*, Karl LECHNER (ed.), Jahrbuch für Landeskunde von Niederösterreich, Neue Folge 36/1964, Verein für Landeskunde von Niederösterreich und Wien, Wien, 1964, 995–1015.

Peter Karl JAKSCH: *Gesetzlexikon im Geistlichen, Religions- und Toleranzsache, wie auch in Güter- Stiftungs- Studien- und Zensursachen für das Königreich Böhmen von 1601 bis Ende 1800,* , vol. 2, Author and k.k. Gubernialregistratur, Prag, 1828.

Jana JANIŠOVÁ, Dalibor JANIŠ: *Moravská zemská zřízení a kodifikace zemského práva ve střední Evropě v 16. a na začátku 17. století* [Moravian Land Constitution and Codification of the Land Law in Central Europe in the 16th and at the Beginning of the 19th Centuries], Scriptorium, Praha 2016.

Jana JANIŠOVÁ, Dalibor JANIŠ: *Postavení cizinců a inkolát podle moravského zemského práva v 16. a na počátku 17. století* [Position of foreigners and inkolat according to Moravian Land Law in the 16th and at the beginning of the 17th centuries] = *"Morava jako zrcadlo Evropy". Etnické menšiny na Moravě do roku 1918* ["Moravia as a Mirror of Europe". Ethnic minorities in Moravia to 1918] = *"Mähren als Spiegel Europas". Etnische Minderheiten in Mähren bis zum Jahr 1918*, XXXIst Mikulov symposium, 13–14 October 2010, Miroslav SVOBODA (ed.), XXXIst Mikulov symposium, 13–14 October 2010, Moravský zemský archiv et al., Brno 2010, 191–201.

Joseph des Zweyten Römischen Kaisers Gesetze und Verfassungen im Justitz-Fache [...]. Jahrgang von 1785 bis 1786, Kaiserlich-königliche Hof- und Staats-Aerarial-Druckerei, Wien, 1817.

Johann VON JUNG: *Das Indigenat im Königreich Ungarn*, Zeitschrift für österreichische Rechtsgelehrsamkeit und politische Gesetzkunde, 2(1826), 134–158.

Josef KALOUSEK: *České státní právo* [Bohemian state law], Bursík and Kohout, Praha, 1982.

Jan KAPRAS: *Právní dějiny zemí koruny České* [Legal history of the lands of the Bohemian Crown], vol. 3: *Dějiny státního zřízení* [History of the state system], part 2: *Doba pobělohorská*: [White Mountain Period], Česká grafická Unie, Praha, 1920.

Vladimír KLECANDA: *Přijímání cizozemců na sněmu do Čech za obyvatele* [Accepting foreigners at the diet into Bohemia as denizens] = *Sborník prací věnovaných prof. dru Gustavu Friedrichovi k šedesátým narozeninám* [Anthology of works dedicated to Prof. Dr. Gustav Friedrich on his 60th birthday], Historický spolek v Praze, Praha, 1931, 456–467.

Tomáš KNOZ: *Die Konfiskationen nach 1620 in (erb)länderübergreifender Perspektive: Thesen zu Wirkungen, Aspekten und Prinzipien des Konfiskationsprozesses = Die Habsburgermonarchie 1620 bis 1740: Leistungen und Grenzen des Absolutismus*, Petr MAŤA, Thomas WINKELBAUER (eds.), Franz Steiner Verlag, Stuttgart, 2006, 99–131.

Arnold LUSCHIN VON EBENGREUTH: *Inkolat, Indigenat, A: In den altösterreichischen Landen = Österreichisches Staatswörterbuch*, Ernst MISCHLER, Josef ULBRICH (eds.), vol. 2, Hölder, Wien, 1906, 886–897.

Sr. k k. Majestät Franz des Ersten politische Gesetze und Verodnungen für die Oesterreichischen, Böhmischen und Galizischen Erbländer 36, Kurtzbeck, Wien, 1812.

Karel MALÝ: *Die Böhmische Konföderationsakte und die Verneuerte Landesordnung: zwei böhmische Verfassungsgestaltungen zu Beginn des 17. Jahrhunderts*, Zeitschrift der Savigny-Stiftung für Rechtsgeschichte. Germanistische Abteilung 122(2005), 285–300.

Pavel MARŠÁLEK: *České státní právo v 19. století* [Bohemian state law in the 19th century] = *Vývoj české ústavnosti 1618–1918* [Development of Bohemian Constitutionality 1618–1918], Ladislav SOUKUP, Karel MALÝ (eds.), Karolinum, Praha, 2007, 468–487.

Petr MAŤA: *Landstände und Landtage in den böhmischen und österreichischen Ländern (1620–1740): Von der Niedergangsgeschichte zur Interaktionsanalyse = Die Habsburgermonarchie 1620 bis 1740: Leistungen und Grenzen des Absolutismus*, Petr MAŤA, Thomas WINKELBAUER (eds.), Franz Steiner Verlag, Stuttgart, 2006, 345–400.

Jerzy MICHTA: *Nobilitacja i indygenat w szlacheckiej Rzeczypospolitej* [Ennoblement and the Inkolat in the noble Commonwealth], Annales Universitatis Mariae Curie-Skłodowska, Sectio F, Historia 45(1990), 355–363.

Peter MOSNÝ, Ladislav HUBENÁK: *Dejiny štátu a práva na Slovensku* [History of State and Law in Slovakia], Právnická fakulta UPJŠ, Košice, 2005.

Obnovené Právo a Zřízení zemské dědičného království Českého: Verneuerte Landes-Ordnung des Erb-Königreichs Böhmen: 1627, Hermenegild JIREČEK (ed.), F. Tempský, Praha 1888.

Hermann PALM: *Der Dresdner Accord*, Zeitschrift des Vereins für Geschichte und Alterthum Schlesiens 13(1876)/1, 151–192.

Jaroslav PÁNEK: *Od České konfederace k Obnovenému zřízení zemskému: (kontinuita a diskontinuita v proměnách českého státu a jeho ústavního zřízení na pomezí stavovství a absolutismu)* [From the Bohemian Confederation to the renewal of the land Constitution: (continuity and discontinuity in the transformation of the Bohemian state and its constitutional system on the edge of Estatism and Absolutism)] = *Vývoj české ústavnosti v letech 1618–1918* [Development of Bohemian Constitutionality in 1618–1918], Ladislav SOUKUP, Karel MALÝ (eds.), Karolinum, Praha, 2006, 13–29.

Lutz RENTZOW: *Die Entstehungs- und Wirkungsgeschichte der Verneuerten Landesordnung für das Königreich Böhmen von 1627*, Peter Lang, Frankfurt a.M. et al., 1998.

Der Röm. Kays. auch zu Hungarn und Böheim etc., königl. Majestät Ferdinandi des Dritten etc., über der neuen Landes-Ordnung des Königreichs Böheim publizierte Declaratorien und Nouvellen, Wien, 1753.

Helmut RUMPLER: *Eine Chance für Mitteleuropa: Bürgerliche Emanzipation und Staatsverfall in der Habsburgermonarchie*, Österreichische Geschichte 1804–1914, Buchgemeinschaft Donauland et al., Wien, 2005.

Henryk SUCHOJAD: *Problem nobilitacji oraz indygenatów na sejmikach małopolskich i wielkopolskich w latach 1669–1696* [The problem of ennoblement and the Inkolat at the diets of Lesser and Greater Poland in 1669–1696], Śląski Kwartalnik Historyczny Sobótka 1–3(1996), 169–177.

Rudolf STANKA: *Die böhmische Conföderationsakte von 1619*, Ebering, Berlin, 1932.

Marek STARÝ: *Cizozemci a spoluobyvatelé. Udělování českého obyvatelského práva (inkolátu) v době předbělohorské* [Foreigners and Co-inhabitants. Granting the Bohemian Right of Residence (Inkolat) in the Period before the Battle of White Mountain], Praha, Auditorium, 2018.

Luboš VELEK, *Böhmisches Staatsrecht auf "weichem Papier": Tatsache, Mythos und ihre symbolische Bedeutung in der tschechischen politischen Kultur*, Bohemia. Zeitschrift für Geschichte und Kultur der böhmischen Länder. A Journal of History and Civilisation in East Central Europe 47(2006/2007)/1, 103–118.

Vladislavské zřízení zemské a navazující prameny (Svatováclavská smlouva a Zřízení o ručnicích) [Vladislaus's Land Constitution and Related Sources (St. Wenceslas's Contract and Constitution on Rifles)], Petr KREUZ, Ivan MARTINOVSKÝ (eds.), Scriptorium, Praha 2007.

Vladislavské zřízení zemské a počátky ústavního zřízení v českých zemích (1500–1619) [Vladislaus's Land Constitution and the Beginnings of the Constitutional System in the Bohemian Lands (1500–1619)], Karel MALÝ, Jaroslav PÁNEK (eds.), Historický ústav AV, Univerzita Karlova, Praha 2001.

Friedrich WALTER: *Die österreichische Zentralverwaltung*, vol. 2: *Von der Vereinigung der österreichischen und böhmischen Hofkanzlei bis zur Einrichtung der Ministerialverfassung (1749–1848)*, part. 1.1 *Die Geschichte der österreichischen Zentralverwaltung in der Zeit Maria Theresias*, Böhlau, Wien et al., 1938, 92–193.

Friedrich WALTER: *Die Theresianische Staatsreform von 1749*, Verlag für Geschichte und Politik, München 1958.

Jan ZDICHYNEC: *Předání Lužic Sasku v letech 1620–1635* [Transfer of Lusatia to Saxony in 1620–1635] = *Od konfesijní konfrontace ke konfesijnímu míru. Sborník z konference k 360. výročí uzavření vestfálského míru* [From confessional confrontation to confessional peace: Proceedings of the conference on the 360th anniversary of the conclusion of the Westphalian Peace], Jiří HRBEK, Petr POLEHLA, Jan ZDICHYNEC (eds.), Oftis, Ústí nad Orlicí 2008, 70–86.

Zřízení zemská království českého xvi. věku [Land Constitution of the Bohemian Kingdom of the 16th Century], Josef JIREČEK, Hermenegild JIREČEK (eds.), Všehrd, Praha 1882.

Jan ŽUPANIČ: *Židovská šlechta podunajské monarchie. Mezi Davidovou hvězdou a křížem* [Jewish Aristocracy of the Danube Monarchy: Between David's Star and the Cross], Nakladatelství Lidové noviny, Praha, 2012.

CHAPTER 2

Legal Transfers and National Traditions: Patterns of Modernisation of the Administration in Polish Territories at the Turn of the 19th Century

Michał Gałędek

The purpose of this chapter[1] is to demonstrate the sources of inspiration drawn on by the authors of the Polish administrative system and its legal framework from the late 18th century onwards. I make an attempt to prove that, under certain political circumstances, where the political elites are under great pressure toward modernisation brought on by both intellectual influences and a threat to the existence of the state, they become prone to quickly change their convictions and to conduct thorough structural reforms, at the same time focusing on the effectiveness of their solutions without abandoning the elements of their own republican tradition of statehood. Nevertheless, these are just a few elements, often referring to the past in a merely symbolic dimension. From this perspective, Polish legal history and administrative history may be viewed as a reliable reflection of the legal and political history of the semi-peripheral countries and their elites, both in Central Eastern Europe and in other regions of the world that had been under the constant influence of Western European legal culture, especially since the Enlightenment.

It should be emphasized that during a relatively short period in the Polish territories at the turn of 19th century, a number of events took place that created the need for legal transfers which would permit the building of an efficient state on the basis of a mix of different models. The reforms occurred within a climate of incessant confrontations between traditionalists, who emphasized an attachment to national solutions, and "progressive enlightened occidentalists", who opted for radical modernisation reforms based on foreign experiences.

---

1 The present chapter was prepared under the project "Administrative Thought in the Kingdom of Poland 1814–1831" financed by the National Science Centre (Narodowe Centrum Nauki) on the basis of decision no. DEC-2013/11/D/HS5/01901.

1 Administrative Reforms During the Reign of Stanisław August Poniatowski

The first period of political changes and of transformations in administration began in 1764, with the ascension to the throne of Stanisław August Poniatowski, an enlightened ruler and reformer. He was the last in the line of kings in what had once been a European power, namely the Polish-Lithuanian Commonwealth, a state with a number of particular administrative and legal institutions that made for a fairly specific and original republican tradition of this country. Alongside the reformist camp that was consolidating at the time, Stanisław August strove to pull the country out of the stagnation and political collapse in which it had been moored for over 100 years. A great part of the erstwhile political elites had grown convinced of the backwardness of the Polish territories in relation to Western Europe as their main point of reference, as well as of its weak statehood resulting from numerous systemic defects and mistaken assumptions upon which the hithertofore existing concept of the Polish-Lithuanian Commonwealth had existed. An attempt at conducting complex reforms, however, ended in failure and in the collapse of the state in 1795, by way of the series of partitions carried out by the neighbouring powers. On the eve of the collapse, a number of comprehensive reforms in governance were successfully implemented, especially as regarded the functioning of the Four-Year Sejm (1788–1792). The greatest success of this period was the adoption of the republican – and thus liberal – Constitution (the Government Act) of 3 May 1791, which consisted in adapting Polish traditions to the requirements of a modern state.

We may point out a few characteristic features of the Polish administrative system that existed until the end of the 1780s, and which were subsequently only slightly modified in the 3 May Constitution and its accompanying legal acts.

The specificity of the administrative system of Poland under the reign of Stanisław August Poniatowski stemmed primarily from the maintenance of relatively weak monarchical power, in line with Polish tradition. Unlike in many other Enlightened countries, and not only not absolutist ones, the Polish transformations in the system of central administration were moving in the direction of severe limitation of the king's role as the head of executive power. The success of this trend was ultimately secured with the principles on which the system of power was organised following the establishment of the Permanent Council in 1775. Members of the Council were selected by the Senate and members of the "knight estate", while the king was deprived of this right,[2] with the reservation that it was he who appointed ministers and senators, chosen from three candidates presented by the Permanent Council. Moreover, Stanisław August Poniatowski had lost to the Council his right to issue individual orders to the organs of administration, as well as his prerogatives of appointment. In all that he did, he was obliged to respect the collegial decisions of the Council, over which he could only preside with a regular voting right. Within such arrangement, his status was therefore closer to that of a prime minister than to the head of state who stood at its helm. Such a system of organisation of state power in which the monarch had been deprived of legal instruments ensuring his dominant position in the executive sphere was, at the time, an exception in all of Europe. The prerogatives of the Permanent Council, on the other hand, went beyond executive competences.[3] It was designated as second highest national magistracy, after the Sejm, and all the state organs and general population were obliged to respect its decrees, called "reminders".[4]

This model, that reduced the position of the monarch in the government to the extreme, was modified by the reformers, who supplanted it with a new system based on the Government Act of 3 May 1791, enacted by the Four-Year Sejm. The role of the Permanent Council was taken over by the Guardianship of Laws, whose functioning was fashioned by the Polish reformers based on English solutions.[5] From then on, the binding principle was that "a royal decision shall prevail after all opinions [of the Guardianship] have been heard, that there be a single will in the execution of law. Therefore, every resolution from the Guardianship shall be issued under the King's name and with the signature by his hand, but it shall also be signed by one of the ministers seated in the Guardianship, and thus signed, it shall oblige obedience, and shall be carried out by the commissions of any executive magistracies".[6] The validity of the

---

2   Aleksander CZAJA: *Między tronem, buławą a dworem petersburskim. Z dziejów Rady Nieustającej 1786–1789*, Państwowe Wydawnictwo Naukowe, Warsaw, 1988, 54; Marek KRZYM-KOWSKI: *Wybory członków Rady Nieustającej (aspekty organizacyjno-prawne)*, Studia z Dziejów Państwa i Prawa Polskiego 16(2013), 119–120.
3   Witold FILIPCZAK: *Sejm 1778 roku*, Semper, Warsaw, 2000, 158–159.
4   Wojciech ORGANIŚCIAK: *Wincenty Skrzetuski o Radzie Nieustającej*, Dzieje Prawa 4(2011), 74, 76–79; Władysław KONOPCZYŃSKI: *Geneza i ustanowienie Rady Nieustającej*, Akademia Umiejętności, Krakow, 1917, 212–214, 336–361.
5   Józef WOJAKOWSKI: *Straż Praw*, Wydawnictwo Uniwersytetu Warszawskiego, Warsaw, 1982, 54.
6   *Ustawa Rządowa*, Volumina Legum 9(1889), 223.

monarch's decision, who thus wielded the power of a one-man head of administration, depended on the counter-signatures of a minister, but this minister could be any member of the Guardianship of the Laws. Only in a situation in which all ministers refused to give their signature, would the king have to "abandon his decision".[7] The English model is reflected in the principle that the king could not be held responsible for his decisions, unlike the counter-signing ministers, who could face penal liability (named constitutional liability). The conjoint chambers of the Sejm could also recall a minister by a two-third majority of votes, which established a legal mechanism for making them politically accountable to the Parliament.[8]

Despite the emphasis of the monarch's leading role in the executive power, the solutions put forward in the 3 May Constitution still failed to ensure his supremacy in this sphere; on the one hand owing to the prerogatives of the Sejm, and on the other hand by shifting the burden of running the country onto the ministers.

What also stood apart was the specificity of the relationship between the Permanent Council and ministerial bodies in the form of treasury commissions, which resulted from the fact that ministers that headed commissions were not members of the Council. Within the Permanent Council, on the other hand, the offices of treasury ministers were held by councilmen who were members of the Treasury Department, but not of treasury commissions. This solution must have proven itself successful in Polish circumstances, since also the authors of the 3 May Constitution supported the division between ministers of the Guardianship of the Laws as a successor to the Permanent Council and ministers in great commissions, which supplanted the previous ministerial bodies. In light of the definition of administration, pursuant to which management, handled by administrative structures, must be perceived separately from governance, handled by government structures, it must be noted that it was in this very model that this principle found institutional expression, while in the system that did not become more widespread until the 19th century and in which ministers combined their functions as heads of departments with membership in a collegial council of ministers, this functional division started to blur.

---

7 *Ibid.*
8 Bogusław LEŚNODORSKI, *Dzieło Sejmu Czteroletniego (1788–1792): Studium historyczno-prawne*, Wydawnictwo Zakładu Narodowego im. Ossolińskich, Wrocław, 1951, 59–64, 67–70, 188–189, 318–319; Wojciech WITKOWSKI, *Historia administracji w Polsce 1764–1989*, Wydawnictwo Naukowe PWN, Warsaw, 2007, 68–69.

The Permanent Council was divided into departments, which the literature concerned with the history of law quite universally regards as an early form of ministries.[9] In the Polish-Lithuanian Commonwealth, this was the first attempt to implement a systematic division of the administrative structure. The result was the emergence of the Department of Foreign Interests, Department of Treasury, Military Department, Police Department (i.e. Department of Good Order) and Department of Justice. The educational sector, subordinate to the Commission of National Education, maintained its fully autonomous character. A separate department was not created for this sphere of public administration.[10]

The division into departments as established for the Permanent Council caught on and gained a lasting foothold, and it was not significantly modified in the 3 May Constitution. The legislators behind this legal act decided that the Guardianship of the Laws would include the ministers of foreign affairs, treasury, war, police and a minister of the seal. As regards the division of the Permanent Council into departments, a basic modification stemmed from the fact that also the primate was now a member of the Guardianship of the law as head of the Commission of National Education and the sole person in the government who combined chairmanship in a great commission with membership in the Guardianship of the Laws. Respectively to this division of ministerial positions, four great commissions shared by the Crown and Lithuania were created: national education, treasury, a military commission and a police commission.[11] No great commissions were established for the departments of foreign interests (foreign affairs) and for the department of the seal, which were peculiar and organised in a different way.

Under the rule of Stanisław August Poniatowski, the reformers of administrative structures strove to create a ministry that would integrate all the fundamental functions of managing the country's internal affairs. This function was to be fulfilled by the police branch. The first police magistracy in the

---

9   Andrzej ZAHORSKI, *Centralne instytucje policyjne w Polsce w dobie rozbiorów*, Państwowe Wydawnictwo Naukowe, Warsaw, 1959, 31–33; Marek KRZYMKOWSKI, *O składzie Rady Nieustającej* = *W kręgu nowożytnej i najnowszej historii ustroju Polski: Księga dedykowana Profesorowi Marianowi Kallasowi*, Sławomir GODEK, Dariusz MAKIŁŁA, Magdalena WILCZEK-KARCZEWSKA (eds.), InterLeones Halina Dyczkowska, Warsaw, 2010, 119–134; Katarzyna BUCHOLC-SROGOSZ, *Departament Wojskowy Rady Nieustającej w latach 1775–1789 i 1793–1794*, Wydawnictwo Poznańskie, Poznań, 2007, 18–19, 23–27.
10 Ambroise JOBERT, *Komisja Edukacji Narodowej w Polsce (1773–1794): jej dzieło wychowania obywatelskiego*, Wydawnictwo Zakładu Narodowego im. Ossolińskich, Wrocław, 1979, 70.
11 ZAHORSKI: *op. cit.*, 252–273.

Commonwealth was the Police Department of the Permanent Council. The scope of its activities was initially quite narrow, but it was somewhat expanded as early as in 1776. Nevertheless, it still concentrated mainly on urban affairs.[12] The situation did not change considerably until the period of the Four-Year Sejm reforms. In the 1791 act, the Police Commission received a much broader range of tasks. The legislators decided it would become responsible for all broadly understood matters of public safety and order, including, among others, supervision over physicians, pharmacists and the sanitary conditions in the country, correction facilities, weights and measures, population and economic censuses. The competences of the Police Commission also included comprehensive oversight over cities, as well as duties concerning the so-called general comfort, entailing social care, infrastructure matters or the postal service.[13] Thus, the reformers gave the Police Commission the role of a meta-department, so to speak.

A system of collegial administrative bodies was fashioned after the 18th century solutions then functioning in Europe. At the central level, such bodies were the ministerial commissions. The first ones created were the treasury and military commissions (separate for the Crown and for Lithuania), and the next one was the Commission of National Education, established as a single body for the entire Commonwealth. On other levels, the reformers first set up commissions of good order, which it then replaced with other collegial organs called civil and military order commissions. The principle of collegiality in administration, widespread in Enlightenment Europe, took root in Poland in the organisation of both central and local offices. The forefathers of Polish administrative reforms of the latter half of the 18th century resolved, at the same time, that these bodies should be relatively numerous. As concerned great commissions, they deemed six members to be sufficient, but order commissions could have even in excess of twenty members. The principle of collegiality was accompanied by that of terms of office. Commission members were appointed for a fairly short period of time, usually two years. The third complementary principle, that of unpaid (honorary) offices, was introduced only on the local level. Such a system did not provide proper conditions for the professionalisation of staff. If anything, it ran contrary to them, especially since the designers of the new administration had no intention to require any professional qualifications from candidate officials. Nevertheless, the Republican conviction that bureaucracy was obsolete had enough time to sink in with

---

[12] Cf. *ibid.*, 30–32.
[13] *Ibid.*, 91–92.

some of the representatives of Polish political elites and it sprang back to life a few decades later. As a consequence, on the eve of the establishment of the Kingdom of Poland (until 1815), this model of collegial, elected, tenured unpaid offices (not only administrative, but also judicial) was still widely supported. Its advocates argued for the supremacy of solutions from the times of Stanisław August Poniatowski over the bureaucratic, career-based structure, which – in their eyes – had been discredited in the times of the Duchy of Warsaw (1807–1813).

On the other hand, what clearly emerges in the balance of reforms under Poniatowski's reign, and especially in a comparison between the accomplishments of the Four-Year Sejm and earlier initiatives, is a bureaucratic vector of the transformations. Professionalisation of staff was taking place especially in the treasury and education sectors. Moreover, the gradual process of bureaucratisation was attested to by the strivings to expand, order and render uniform the entire administrative structure, as well as to separate more discernibly the administrative apparatus from other authorities, and to organise it more consistently in line with the rules of a bureaucratic system. There was also a more visible striving to base the entire system of public management on the principle of hierarchical subordination of ministerial bodies (commissions) to the government (first the Permanent Council and later the Guardianship of the Laws), as well as the organs of local administration (initially the commissions of good order and then the civil and military order commissions) to central authorities. Moreover, the rationalisation of the entire administrative structure was furthered by the development of legislation that laid down the methods and the scope of operations of the administration and the division of tasks between individual offices.

According to Jerzy Gordziejew, "While the authors of the concept behind the political reforms of the late Saxon period and the early days of the reign of Stanisław August exhibited interest in the issue of reorganisation of the administrative apparatus, the problem of territorial management did not receive sufficient attention in their works".[14] Thus, the unambiguous breakthrough that took place in the organisation of administrative structures on the local level did not come until the introduction of civil and military order commissions in 1789, while their predecessors – the good order commissions of 1768 – had, owing to their limited scope of tasks and competences, an incomparably

---

14   Jerzy GORDZIEJEW: *Komisje porządkowe cywilno-wojskowe w Wielkim Księstwie Litewskim w okresie Sejmu Czteroletniego (1789–1792)*, Wydawnictwo Uniwersytetu Jagiellońskiego, Krakow, 2010, 18.

weaker power to influence the socioeconomic life of the province. Nevertheless, their very establishment was tantamount to the implementation of a general territorial management in the country, which had been virtually non-existent in Poland, as the country was in disarray. When creating new offices, the reformers did not reject the key elements of the Polish local government system.[15] For this reason, they determined that local officials had to be elected, and that the nobility would retain its privileges in such elections. Moreover, the order commissions were subordinated not only to the central administrative authorities but were also dependent on the local social representation in the form of dietines and communal assemblies. On the other hand, "the crystallisation of the concepts of rebuilding the administration and of appointment of order commissions may have been influenced by the political experiences of enlightened absolutist countries, including the directions of the development of local public administration".[16]

The administrative system created by the camp of Polish reformers under the reign of King Stanisław August Poniatowski represented an original, native solution. Its originality stemmed from the attempt to transform state structures in a spirit that did not reject certain elements of the old republican tradition, albeit in a modified, improved or modernized form. The fundamental sources of inspiration for these modifications may be traced back to both Western European Enlightenment thought (republican and liberal), and especially to Montesquieu's concept of the separation of powers, as well as to the English system. Both these models were compatible with the Polish systemic tradition. It rested on the maintenance of the leading role of the Sejm as the legislative power, which also had some instruments to wield influence over the executive. At the local level, the Polish tradition was in turn expressed by the self-governing nature of local administration. Reforms introduced under the rule of Stanisław August Poniatowski also laid the first foundations for the bureaucratic structure of administration, in principle inspired by the organisational models typical of states that embraced Enlightened absolutism, with the reservation, however, of avoiding excessive centralism and instruments of state interference whenever it jeopardized the sphere of freedoms and rights of citizens, mainly noblemen. The excessive strengthening of executive power ran against the Polish republican tradition and was out of the question.

---

15 Cf: Józef GIEROWSKI: *Na szlakach Rzeczypospolitej w nowożytnej Europie*, Księgarnia Akademicka, Krakow, 2008, 127–135.
16 GORDZIEJEW: *op. cit.*, 23.

2 New Administration in the Duchy of Warsaw

The situation changed after the fall of the Polish state. The central Polish territories, along with the capital city of Warsaw, fell under the control of Prussia and under the management of its highly bureaucratized and centralized administration, in keeping with the Enlightened absolutism model. The direct contact with the orderly and modernized state left a rather lasting impression on the subsequent attitude of Polish elites to the typically Prussian mechanisms of the functioning of the state. Prussian models became an important point of reference. Especially those mechanisms on which the organisation of Prussian administration was built were generally deemed as progressive and worth keeping.

This political configuration was overturned by the Napoleonic Wars. The year 1807 marked the establishment of the Duchy of Warsaw, which, albeit under the French protectorate, was ruled with a degree of sovereignty by the Polish political elites, who considered Napoleon's initiative of 22 July 1807 an attempt at restoration of Polish statehood. Napoleon's constitution, however, accounted for the pre-partition Polish political and legal traditions only to a very limited extent. This was not met with enthusiasm by the majority of Polish political elites, similarly to the introduction on Polish soil of numerous legal and political institutions transplanted from Napoleon's France. This legal transfer was particularly visible in the manner of administrative organisation.

In determining the administrative system of the Duchy of Warsaw in the constitution of 22 July 1807, the French emperor decided to fashion it after the way that administration was organised in France. This was the first time in the history of Polish administration when it was organised according to bureaucratic principles and strictly centralized, and the authority was passed into the hands of officials (ministers, prefects, subprefects, municipal and commune mayors). Napoleon decided to separate the offices of the minister of internal affairs, of police, justice, treasury and war. This model of departmental division was widespread in Europe, with just a few exceptions,[17] which was an expression of a broader tendency, characteristic of the first half of the 19th century, to make the administrative organisation throughout the continent more uniform. The tenets of Napoleon's model were the fundamental point of reference.[18] This departmental division imported from France did not, on the

---

17 Hubert IZDEBSKI: *Historia administracji*, Liber, Warsaw, 1997, 119.
18 Hubert IZDEBSKI: *Rada Administracyjna Królestwa Polskiego w latach 1815–1830*, Wydawnictwo Uniwersytetu Warszawskiego, Warsaw, 1978, 8.

other hand, have any direct links to the Polish traditions from the times of Stanisław August Poniatowski. The most glaring changes were the disappearance of the separate department of education, the establishment of the Ministry of Internal Affairs which replaced the former Police Commission and the creation of the Ministry of Police with different features and operations. The Council of State was another new institution, as well as the Council of Ministers, characteristic to the Duchy of Warsaw. The organisational model of local administration was also antipodal to the pre-partition solutions. It was now based on the French office of prefects in departments and their strictly subordinate sub-prefects in poviats, which in principle were to hold all administrative power out in the field. French modelled administrative courts, exercised by prefectural councils and the Council of State, was also a new institutional form in the Polish territories.

However, in octroying the constitution to the Duchy of Warsaw, Napoleon only specified the basic institutional model, and he introduced a number of modifications to it. In France, for example, there was no Council of Ministers. He also set up the lowest level of local administration differently, as he did not introduce uniform communes nor the office of the *maire*. Instead, the constitution provided for the establishment of the office of rural commune mayors (*wójt*) and of the office of municipal mayors (*burmistrz*), which were subsequently organised to account for Polish peculiarity. Above all, however, the authorities, in executing the constitutional provisions, decided against fuller adoption of the French administrative system. There were some specific cases of searching for organisational models in the French legislation, but this was not a widespread, coordinated endeavour.[19] Nevertheless, situations in which concrete French institutions and solutions were taken as one of the points of reference, whether in the course of debates preceding the introduction of the constitutional system in the Duchy of Warsaw (until 1809), or later, in the preparation of the reform of the feeble administrative apparatus (1809–1812) were still rather rare. A few such occurrences did take place, however. It was French inspirations that led, among others, to the division of the Council of State into

---

19   Władysław ROSTOCKI: *Z badań porównawczych nad ustrojem administracyjnym Księstwa Warszawskiego i Francji*, Czasopismo Prawno-Historyczne 13(1961)/1, 112–125; Jerzy MALEC: *Administracja terytorialna na ziemiach polskich w pierwszej połowie XIX wieku. Wpływy obce a rodzima tradycja = Polskie tradycje samorządowe a heraldyka: Materiały sesji naukowej zorganizowanej w dniach 4 i 5 czerwca 1991 r. w Lublinie*, Piotr DYMMEL (ed.), Wydawnictwo Uniwersytetu Marii Curie Skłowskiej, Lublin, 1992, 123–125.

sections,[20] and they were also one of the reasons behind a tighter integration of local administration under prefects.[21]

In the remaining scope, however, the authorities of the Duchy of Warsaw decided to introduce a number of divergences from the French original model. They resulted both from the acts that executed the constitution differently than in France, as exemplified by the manner in which the Polish government organised the office of the prefect, as well as from the distinct evolution of individual institutions in practice, as was the case of the Council of State. Some of these divergences had weak legal justifications, and were the effect of improper execution of the constitution, a crowning example of which was the limitation of the prefect's authority over other domains of local administration. Moreover, the Duchy's authorities tolerated the unconstitutional existence of certain institutions that preceded the introduction of the constitutional system (in the first half of 1807) and drew on the local political traditions to a much greater extent than they were expected to. Such was the case of the Chamber of Education, which the Polish government (the so-called Governing Committee that functioned prior to the octroyment) established based on the model that had underpinned the pre-partition Commission of National Education. The departmental councils also differed from their French counterparts, as they effectively laid claim to greater influence over the course of events out in the provinces.

It was however impossible to draw on the Polish pre-partition traditions to a broader extent owing to the fundamental differences between the bureaucratic French model and the 18th century inkling of bureaucratic structures that the Polish authorities had only started to build in the time of Stanisław August Poniatowski. Just as it was impossible, owing to the Constitution of 1807, to return to the concepts underpinning the organisation of the Guardianship of the Laws, of the great commissions or of the civil and military order commissions, the authorities of the Duchy of Warsaw decided not to use native solutions from the times of King Poniatowski in the internal organisation of offices (for example in the division of official tasks or in organising the filing system), even though this was not banned by Napoleon's constitution. The pre-partition Polish authorities had not managed to

---

20   Cf: Marek KRZYMKOWSKI: *Rada Stanu Księstwa Warszawskiego*, Ars boi et aequi, Poznań, 2011, 53; Marek KRZYMKOWSKI: *Status prawny urzędników Księstwa Warszawskiego*, Wydawnictwo Uniwersytetu im. Adama Mickiewicza w Poznaniu, Poznań, 2004, 32–35.
21   Cf: Tomasz KNOPP: *Prefekci Księstwa Warszawskiego, Przyczynek do portretu zbiorowego*, Studia Historyczne 4(2012)/3–4, 360.

come up with their own management solutions that would be efficient enough to return to in the times of the Duchy of Warsaw. In organising the work in offices, they preferred to lean on Prussian and Austrian experiences, which they had been exposed to over throughout the several years under their rule (1793/5–1806/9) that fell between the era of King Poniatowski and the Napoleonic Duchy of Warsaw. The fact that many tested foreign officials at the lower level, especially Prussian ones, were still employed in the administration, worked in favour of maintaining these management and internal organisation solutions.[22]

This entire situation was a reminder of the fact that the introduction of numerous solutions foreign to the Polish tradition had divided the political elites of the Duchy. Part of them supported the implementation of Napoleonic ways. Even before the octroyment, the circle of so-called Jacobins endorsed the fullest possible adoption of the French model.[23] Some even appealed to Napoleon to introduce the French constitution *en bloc*.[24] The Polish occidentalists accepted *a priori* the superiority of Napoleonic institutions, departing from the assumption that an emperor who propagates revolutionary postulates is a repository of civilisational progress, and thus that the legal and political solutions proposed by him are worthy of reception as universally valuable, "eternal, unyielding, general, same for all times, places and countries".[25]

Yet the majority of the political elite approached foreign political institutions with caution or reluctance. Many still remembered the times of King Poniatowski well; they had participated in the reforms of those times and expected the reinstatement of the pre-partition system, and most notably of the 3 May Constitution. For example, all three presidents of the Council of

---

[22] Marian KALLAS: *Organy administracji terytorialnej w Księstwie Warszawskim*, Wydawnictwo Uniwersytetu Mikołaja Kopernika, Toruń, 1975, 53; KRZYMKOWSKI: *Status prawny urzędników...*, op. cit., 32–35.

[23] Marceli HANDELSMAN: *Z dziejów Księstwa Warszawskiego. Geneza Księstwa i jego statutu* = Marceli HANDELSMAN: *Studia Historyczne*, vol. 1, E. Wende i Spółka, Warsaw, 1911, 127–128; Bogusław LEŚNODORSKI: *Polscy Jakobini: karta z dziejów insurekcji 1794 roku*, Książka i Wiedza, Warsaw, 1960, 303–311.

[24] Marian KALLAS: *Konstytucja Księstwa Warszawskiego, jej powstanie, systematyka i główne instytucje w związku z praktyką i ustawodawstwem szczegółowym*, Państwowe Wydawnictwo Naukowe, Toruń, 1970, 28.

[25] *The Founding Act* of the Republican Society of 1798. Quoted after Marceli HANDELSMAN: *Rozwój narodowości nowoczesnej*, Państwowy Instytut Wydawniczy, Warsaw, 1973, 169, 174. Similarly, the leading representative of the Polish intellectual elites, Hugo Kołłątaj, professed that a time was approaching when "the inhabitant of any part of the Earth, whichever way he goes [...] will find in each country [...] the same constitution, the same laws". Hugo KOŁŁĄTAJ, *Uwagi nad teraźniejszym położeniem tej części ziemi polskiej, którą od pokoju tylżyckiego zaczęto zwać Księstwem Warszawskim*, Leipzig, 1808, 127.

Ministers and of the Council of State – Stanisław Małachowski, Ludwik Gutakowski and Stanisław Potocki, had been active deputies of the Four-Year Sejm, and the first of them, as speaker of that Sejm, had participated in the drafting of the 3 May Constitution. Criticism of the system introduced in the Duchy of Warsaw mounted as the shortcomings of the organisation of central and local administration became more visible. Soon, parts of the ruling elites, as well as representatives of departmental councils and Sejms convened in the years 1809, 1811 and 1812, began to call for reform of the administrative system that was still in the making, but those who voiced such demands usually steered clear of the issue of possible constitutional amendments. More far-reaching postulates could only be articulated surreptitiously, as, owing to the stance of the French side and of the monarch (Duke of Warsaw was the Saxon king, Frederic Augustus), changing the constitution was out of the question. Thus, since the constitution was immutable, the reformist circles seldom debated on issues that could not be modified without constitutional amendments, such as introducing the constitutional liability of ministers before the Sejm, introduction of self-governmental administration, changing the departmental division or appointment of collegial offices. The constitutional act, however, only outlined the administrative system, making it perfectly feasible to go through with a complex political reform without having to interfere with its contents. Therefore, the first proposals and drafts for administrative reform soon emerged. In fact, the issue of fixing the political and administrative relations occupied an important position in the Duchy of Warsaw throughout the entire period of its existence.[26]

3 At a Crossroads. Administration of the Kingdom of Poland

Napoleon's fall was tantamount to the twilight of the Duchy of Warsaw, which brought about another significant systemic reform associated with the establishment of a new state form, namely the Kingdom of Poland (1815), this time under the rule of Alexander I, a liberal Emperor of Russia. The Polish elites at that time wielded significant influence on the development of the Kingdom's administrative system and were in a position to build on experience from different governance models, which had previously been in place in the Polish territories, as well as new models, previously unknown (e.g. the French one).

---

26 Paweł CICHOŃ: *Rozwój myśli administracyjnej w Księstwie Warszawskim 1807–1815*, Księgarnia Akademicka, Krakow, 2006, 69.

In moulding the new state, Polish political elites in reality maintained the core of the bureaucratized administrative model assumed in the times of the Duchy of Warsaw, de facto maintaining a host of existing institutional solutions, such as the Council of State, the strictly hierarchical construction of the administrative apparatus or the professionalisation of administrative work. The Polish political elites did so despite having officially broken with the systemic heritage of the Duchy of Warsaw. In public discourse, this was presented as defective, foreign, and maladjusted to Polish customs and the character of the country.

Irrespective of this discourse, however, we will not find much evidence of a return to the native solutions from the previous century in the manner of organisation of the administrative apparatus of the Kingdom of Poland. What had been reinstated was the Polish nomenclature; Napoleon's departments were replaced by Polish voivodeships (palatinates), the prefects with palatinate commissions, etc. What is truly symptomatic, however, is the fate of reforms that went further than superficial modifications. For example, what may be interpreted as a sign of a true return to Polish traditions is the restitution of collective administrative organs in the form of the mentioned palatinate commissions that replaced prefects, or government commissions that succeeded Napoleonic ministers. In reality, these other reforms were introduced so as to ensure that administration kept on functioning according to principles similar to those in place in the period of the Duchy of Warsaw. This was a two-dimensional problem. In the systemic dimension, the issue boiled down to the fact that a detailed regulation of a given institution caused it to function differently from what was to follow from its general characteristics. Such was the case of the above-mentioned collective organs, both in the central and local administration. This is due to the fact that they were constructed in such a way that their presidents could easily dominate the other members of these bodies, and in practice they were the ones who directed the course of administrative matters and had a decisive influence on the decisions taken. The political dimension overlapped this situation. For example, the authors of the administrative system of the Kingdom of Poland attempted to design it so as to return, at least partially, to the self-governing nature of local administration, for instance by providing conditions conducive of the elective nature of offices. Yet the government of the Kingdom of Poland quelled these efforts under Russian pressure. As a result, the local administration was controlled by the local community which was *de facto* deprived of influence over the appointment of official posts by way of legal acts of lower force and by way of practice that bent – if not violated – the binding principles.

4 Conclusion

The analysis of source materials from work conducted regarding the reformation of the administrative system first in the Duchy of Warsaw and then in the Kingdom of Poland has brought me to the following conclusions. Firstly, the rulers of the Duchy of Warsaw and then of the Kingdom of Poland (largely the same people) were capable of adopting the organisational principles of modern bureaucratic administration, even if it was based on foreign solutions. Indeed, practical concerns prevailed. All those who were considering the choice of an optimal administration system were rather prone to adapt Western-European ideas. The need for a fully developed bureaucratic system was not questioned, despite the lack of native traditions and long-lasting concerns for strengthening the executive power in the state. In the new reality of the beginning of the 19th century, the centralized Napoleonic model was criticized, but the criticism was largely for show. However, certain influences of the previous period were also present there. As a result, the Polish administration in its most mature form in the Kingdom of Poland was, in its general principles, mainly based on the Napoleonic model, which, however, was partly altered. As far as details were concerned, it borrowed from different solutions, not only French but also Prussian, and embraced some local Polish traditions – legal survivals of the pre-partition period. Secondly, as far as the place of administration in the political system was concerned, the Polish elites were typically prone to bind administrative operations with provisions of law as strict and detailed as possible. At the time of the establishment of the Kingdom of Poland, the Polish elites even believed that it would soon be possible to draft a complex administrative code, as well as to introduce a system of internal oversight over the operations of the executive power both at the local and central levels. In keeping with pre-partition traditions, Polish political elites supported giving the Sejm competences to exert real control over central administration and giving the self-government authorities competences to exert real control over the local administration. All these elements suggest that the Polish legal tradition, which had been developing since at least the 16th-century blossoming of the Polish-Lithuanian state, had been imbued with some well-rooted core elements that served as the foundation for the 19th-century idea of a state of law and of the rule of law. The evolution of the perspective on this issue, drawing on the old republican traditions, under the influence of new liberal trends, was clearly moving in this direction and it represented a natural path of development, compliant with both the existing tradition and with what was deemed modern, that is wholly Western European.

This was reflected in the opposition to and increasing criticism of other forms of governance originating from absolutist monarchies and adopted in the Duchy of Warsaw and in the Kingdom of Poland. The strength of that opposition derived from two sources – on the one hand, from the conservative attachment to national solutions and, on the other hand, it gained support from the ever-strengthening liberal circles. Both trends, the conservative-traditional and the liberal, invoked the traditions of their respective versions of constitutionalism symbolized by the Constitution of 3 May. However, the postulate of the restoration of the Constitution of 3 May, still quite lively at the time of the establishment of the Duchy of Warsaw in 1807, was losing momentum, and started to fulfill a more symbolic role of return to the main ideas, and not to the full restoration of institutions and mechanisms that by then were deemed archaic.

The impact of pre-partition Poland's legacy, mainly the Constitution of 3 May 1791, on the awareness of Poland's political elites at the turn of 19th century was quite noticeable. It was against this backdrop – combined with Western European ideas – that the Polish version of constitutionalism took shape, which also determined the particular place of administration within government authorities. Polish concepts of political systems were based on solutions developed during reforms undertaken by the Four-Year Sejm, which culminated in the drafting of said Constitution. Polish reformist elites had already incorporated a number of Western European ideas of the Age of Enlightenment into the political system which came into being back then. They transplanted it into the Polish political system and then transformed it by combining it with intrinsically Polish elements.

When considering the influence of native and foreign administrative and legal traditions on Polish elites, the following issues have to be taken into account. The local political elites were of the opinion that Western Europe was much ahead of Poland in terms of development of the state and of civilisation, and that it had much greater experiences in designing an administrative system that responded to the needs of the new times. The West provided ready models that could be followed. The sense of backwardness which solidified in the political and intellectual elites made the vision of accelerated modernisation along a path that had already been cleared all the more attractive – and, as it may have seemed, it provided a guarantee of success. The strong conviction of the need to catch up was at the same time a catalyst for advancing increasingly bold reformist postulates. The list of necessary reforms was headed by the programme of a complex transformation of the state apparatus, as it was precisely the modern state that would drive the process of subsequent civilisational conversion, and then watch over their correct course.

Acknowledgements

The Author would like to thank dr habil. Rafał Mańko for reading and commenting on an earlier version of this chapter.

Bibliography

Katarzyna BUCHOLC-SROGOSZ: *Departament Wojskowy Rady Nieustającej w latach 1775–1789 i 1793–1794*, Wydawnictwo Poznańskie, Poznań, 2007.

Paweł CICHOŃ: *Rozwój myśli administracyjnej w Księstwie Warszawskim 1807–1815*, Księgarnia Akademicka, Krakow, 2006.

Aleksander CZAJA: *Między tronem, buławą a dworem petersburskim. Z dziejów Rady Nieustającej 1786–1789*, Państwowe Wydawnictwo Naukowe, Warsaw, 1988.

Witold FILIPCZAK: *Sejm 1778 roku*, Semper, Warsaw, 2000.

Józef GIEROWSKI: *Na szlakach Rzeczypospolitej w nowożytnej Europie*, Księgarnia Akademicka, Krakow, 2008.

Jerzy GORDZIEJEW: *Komisje porządkowe cywilno-wojskowe w Wielkim Księstwie Litewskim w okresie Sejmu Czteroletniego (1789–1792)*, Wydawnictwo Uniwersytetu Jagiellońskiego, Krakow, 2010.

Marceli HANDELSMAN: *Rozwój narodowości nowoczesnej*, Państwowy Instytut Wydawniczy, Warsaw, 1973.

Marceli HANDELSMAN: *Z dziejów Księstwa Warszawskiego. Geneza Księstwa i jego statutu* = Marceli HANDELSMAN: *Studia Historyczne*, vol. 1, E. Wende i Spółka, Warsaw, 1911, 107–240.

Hubert IZDEBSKI: *Historia administracji*, Liber, Warsaw, 1997.

Hubert IZDEBSKI: *Rada Administracyjna Królestwa Polskiego w latach 1815–1830*, Warsaw, Wydawnictwo Uniwersytetu Warszawskiego, 1978.

Ambroise JOBERT: *Komisja Edukacji Narodowej w Polsce (1773–1794): jej dzieło wychowania obywatelskiego*, Wydawnictwo Zakładu Narodowego im. Ossolińskich, Wrocław, 1979.

Marian KALLAS: *Konstytucja Księstwa Warszawskiego, jej powstanie, systematyka i główne instytucje w związku z normami szczegółowymi i praktyką*, Państwowe Wydawnictwo Naukowe, Toruń, 1970.

Marian KALLAS: *Organy administracji terytorialnej w Księstwie Warszawskim*, Wydawnictwo Uniwersytetu Mikołaja Kopernika, Toruń, 1975.

Tomasz KNOPP: *Prefekci Księstwa Warszawskiego, Przyczynek do portretu zbiorowego*, Studia Historyczne 4(2012)/3–4, 357–370.

Hugo KOŁŁĄTAJ: *Uwagi nad teraźniejszym położeniem tej części ziemi polskiej, którą od pokoju tylżyckiego zaczęto zwać Księstwem Warszawskim*, Leipzig, 1808.

Władysław KONOPCZYŃSKI: *Geneza i ustanowienie Rady Nieustającej*, Akademia Umiejętności, Krakow, 1917.

Marek KRZYMKOWSKI: *O składzie Rady Nieustającej = W kręgu nowożytnej i najnowszej historii ustroju Polski: Księga dedykowana Profesorowi Marianowi Kallasowi*, Sławomir GODEK, Dariusz MAKIŁŁA, Magdalena WILCZEK-KARCZEWSKA (eds.), InterLeones Halina Dyczkowska, Warsaw, 2010, 119–134.

Marek KRZYMKOWSKI: *Rada Stanu Księstwa Warszawskiego*, Ars boi et aequi, Poznań, 2011.

Marek KRZYMKOWSKI: *Status prawny urzędników Księstwa Warszawskiego*, Wydawnictwo Uniwersytetu im. Adama Mickiewicza w Poznaniu, Poznań, 2004.

Marek KRZYMKOWSKI: *Wybory członków Rady Nieustającej (aspekty organizacyjno-prawne)*, Studia z Dziejów Państwa i Prawa Polskiego 16(2013), 119–129.

Bogusław LEŚNODORSKI: *Dzieło Sejmu Czteroletniego (1788–1792): Studium historyczno-prawne*, Wydawnictwo Zakładu Narodowego im. Ossolińskich, Wrocław, 1951.

Bogusław LEŚNODORSKI: *Polscy Jakobini: karta z dziejów insurekcji 1794 roku*, Książka i Wiedza, Warsaw, 1960.

Jerzy MALEC: *Administracja terytorialna na ziemiach polskich w pierwszej połowie XIX wieku. Wpływy obce a rodzima tradycja*, in: *Polskie tradycje samorządowe a heraldyka: Materiały sesji naukowej zorganizowanej w dniach 4 i 5 czerwca 1991 r. w Lublinie*, ed. Piotr DYMMEL, Wydawnictwo Uniwersytetu Marii Curie Skłodowskiej, Lublin, 1992, 51–65.

Wojciech ORGANIŚCIAK: *Wincenty Skrzetuski o Radzie Nieustającej*, Z Dziejów Prawa 4(2011), 25–46.

Władysław ROSTOCKI: *Z badań porównawczych nad ustrojem administracyjnym Księstwa Warszawskiego i Francji*, Czasopismo Prawno-Historyczne 13(1961)/1, 112–125.

Ustawa Rządowa, Volumina Legum 9(1889), 220–226.

Wojciech WITKOWSKI: *Historia administracji w Polsce 1764–1989*, Wydawnictwo Naukowe PWN, Warsaw, 2007.

Józef WOJAKOWSKI: *Straż Praw*, Wydawnictwo Uniwersytetu Warszawskiego, Warsaw, 1982.

Andrzej ZAHORSKI: *Centralne instytucje policyjne w Polsce w dobie rozbiorów*, Państwowe Wydawnictwo Naukowe, Warsaw, 1959.

CHAPTER 3

National Modernisation through the Constitutional Revolution of 1848 in Hungary: Pretext and Context

Imre Képessy

1   Introduction

In this chapter I wish to prove that since the revolutionary waves of the Spring of Nations made it possible to introduce fundamental changes to the Hungarian political, economic and social system, the 31 Acts enacted by the Hungarian Parliament in 1848 (the so-called April Laws) served as an attempt to modernize the country's constitutional order with legal instruments. Said laws aimed to strengthen the national identity by laying down the foundation of an independent Hungarian Government within the Habsburg Empire.[1] To prove that, we need to analyse the constitutional development prior to 1848 from two aspects. First, we need to look at the relation between Hungary and its rulers. Since the House of Habsburg ruled many territories, the Hungarian noblemen came into conflict with them from time to time. Second, we need to identify the characteristics of the contemporary Hungarian society which affected the chances of modernisation. (Parts 1 & 2).

Subsequently, we have to look at the events that occurred during the Spring of 1848 in order to determine whether the April Laws were of constitutional nature or not (Part 3). To do so, we have to analyse the circumstances in which these laws were enacted. In my research, I focus on three acts that aimed to change the Hungarian constitutional order fundamentally (Part 4). The insufficiencies of the April Laws have to follow (Part 5). The importance of this aspect cannot be overstated since the events of 1848 led to a war with the House of Habsburg, which Hungary lost.[2] Consequently, the country was ruled through absolutist methods for a decade,[3] until the situation was resolved

---

1   Cf. Barna MEZEY: *Magyar alkotmánytörténet* [Hungarian Constitutional History], Osiris, Budapest, 2003, 246.
2   *Ibid.*, 253.
3   As Franz Joseph I put it, the Hungarians forfeited their right to their own constitution with the rebellion. Cf. Ferenc ECKHART: *Magyar alkotmány- és jogtörténet* [Hungarian Constitutional and Legal History], Osiris, Budapest, 2000, 354.

through the Austro-Hungarian Compromise in 1867.[4] Ultimately, we have to determine whether these laws played a role in strengthening the national identity or not (Part 6).

2 A Brief Look at the Various Interpretations Regarding the Events of 1848 in the Hungarian Historiography

Until the early 20th century, most Hungarian historians focused on the war of independence (and the national struggles it involved), that broke out in September of 1848 and lasted until the following summer.[5] According to them, the strongest determinant factor in the country's history was the armed conflict and not the social and political changes introduced by the contemporary legislation. In the public eye, 15 March 1848 became the most iconic moment, when the revolution broke out in the city of Pest. Even according to the Fundamental Law of Hungary of 2011, this day shall be celebrated in the memory of the *"1848–49 Revolution and War of Independence"*.[6] However, as we will see, in the Spring of 1848, the Hungarian political leadership did everything to deny the revolutionary nature of the events.[7] This is proven by the documents written by Sándor Petőfi,[8] one of the leading figures of the Revolution in Pest. According to his notes, Pál Nyáry (one of the leading members of the Opposition Party, who was elected as chair of the Commitee for Public Order in Pest) "vehemently, almost furiously protested against every revolutionary word, denied, that this would be a revolution" – just a day after the events, on 16 March.[9]

The first major change occurred in the late 1940s, when József Révai (an influential communist politician)[10] argued that the leaders of the revolution set out to achieve two interrelated goals: they wanted to strengthen national

---

4   *Ibid.*, 357–358.
5   András GERGELY: *Magyarország története a 19. században* [Hungarian History in the 19th Century], Osiris, Budapest, 2005. 236.
6   The Fundamental Law of Hungary, Article J.
7   György SPIRA: *A negyvennyolcas nemzedék nyomában (Following the generation of 1848)*, Magvető Kiadó, Budapest, 1973, 231–232.
8   Petőfi is considered to be Hungary's national poet, also one of the key figures of the Hungarian Revolution. Cf. John BOWRING: *Translations from Alexander Petőfi*. Trübner & Co., London, 1866, 1–5.
9   SPIRA: *op. cit.*, 231–232.
10 Cf. *Révai József pályaképe: egy veszedelmes elme (The Path of József Révai: A Dangerous Mind)*, Magyar Narancs Online. (http://magyarnarancs.hu/belpol/revai_jozsef_palyakepe_-_egy_veszedelmes_elme-71583, accessed 15. 3. 2017).

independence, but this was attainable only together with the abolition of serfdom.[11] He also argued that this "bourgeois revolution" helped the transformation of the economic system into a capitalist one, and therefore, made the development of civil society possible.

The most important change in the interpretation of the events of 1848 occurred in 1979, when István Deák published his book called "The Lawful Revolution". The author analysed the circumstances of the development of the civil state from a new perspective.[12] He argued that the "revolutionary" transition was made possible first and foremost thanks to the negotiations between the Viennese Court and the contemporary members of the last feudal Diet (the legislative body). He concurred with the view arguing that the leaders of the Revolution of 15 March in Pest did not have any real political power.[13] He quoted Louis Kossuth,[14] who said in the Summer of 1848, (just before the war broke out), that the era of consolidation began with the enactment of the so-called April Laws (see later).[15] The following spring, when he read out loud the Declaration of Independence about the dethronement of the House of Habsburg, he mentioned once more that the establishment of the constitutional monarchy was not the consequence of any revolution. With this statement, all contemporary politicians would have agreed.[16]

3 Part 1: Hungary's Constitutional Status in the Habsburg Empire between 1526–1790

Hungary maintained a special position in the Habsburg Empire, even after it came under the dynasty's rule in 1526. In 1547, the estates of the country pledged their loyalty not only to the reigning King (Ferdinand I), but also to his

---

11 SPIRA: *op. cit.*, 10–12.
12 GERGELY: *op. cit.*, 241.
13 István DEÁK: *A törvényes forradalom: Kossuth Lajos és a magyarok 1848–1849-ben* [The Lawful Revolution: Louis Kossuth and the Hungarians (1848–1849)], Gondolat Kiadó, Budapest, 1994, 100.
14 The leading figure of this era, member of the Diet, member of first Hungarian Cabinet, later president of the Committee of National Defense, and after the proclamation of the dethronement of the House of Habsburg, Regent President of Hungary. Cf. Tarján TAMÁS: *1802. szeptember 19.: Kossuth Lajos születése* (*19th September 1802, The Birth of Louis Kossuth*), Rubicon Online (rubicon.hu/magyar/oldalak/1802_szeptember_19_kossuth_lajos _szuletese, accessed 15. 2. 2017). Cf. also DEÁK: *op. cit.*, 28.
15 DEÁK: *op. cit.*, 121.
16 Barna MEZEY: *Szuverenitáskérdések* [The issue of sovereignty], Jogtörténeti Szemle 3(2015)/3, 56.

heirs.[17] In 1687, at the end of the Ottoman occupation, the Diet (i.e. the medieval General Assembly, which existed until 1848) enacted the Act of Settlement, which permanently abolished the nobility's right to elect the king.[18] The line of succession was fixed from that point,[19] and the Hungarian throne passed automatically to the firstborn male heir of the previous king. This was extended to the female heirs in 1723 through the *Pragmatica Sanctio*.[20] The Habsburg rulers vowed in return that they would exercise their powers in accordance with Hungarian Laws.[21]

The Habsburgs tried to concentrate executive power in their own hands.[22] Their efforts relied mostly on the traditionally extensive royal prerogatives of the Hungarian kings and on their constitutional status (which meant that the person of the king was sacred, inviolable and not directly responsible). After successfully establishing absolute monarchy in the Habsburg Hereditary Lands, they sought to introduce this form of government numerous times also in Hungary between the 17–19th centuries.[23] Furthermore, in accordance with their efforts towards centralisation, the dynasty sought to rule the country as part of their empire. This required the establishment of a central government which was based in Vienna. Among its authorities there was the State Council, later the State Conference, and therefore many important decisions regarding Hungary were made abroad.[24] These efforts generated tension between the Viennese Court and the Hungarian nobility. The noblemen tried to defend their political privileges, and according to them by doing so, they also protected the Hungarian constitution.

Every conflict between the King and the nobility ended with a compromise. Leopold I's attempt to introduce an absolutist regime in Hungary was followed by a war of independence at the beginning of the 18th century. This lasted for almost a decade, but the peace agreement guaranteed peaceful

---

17 Cf. Act Nr. v of 1547 § 5.
18 Act Nr. II of 1687, § 1.
19 Between 1547 and 1687, the family laws of the House of Habsburg settled the order of succession, then the chosen successor had to be formally elected by the Assembly. Cf. MEZEY: *Magyar alkotmánytörténet...*, *op. cit.*, 63.
20 Act Nr. II of 1723, §§ 5–10.
21 Act Nr. III of 1723.
22 DEÁK: *op. cit.*, 21.
23 SPIRA: *op. cit.*, 24.
24 In the 1840s, the members of this commission were Grand Duke Ludwig, Grand Duke Franz Karl (father of the future King Franz Joseph), State Chancellor Metternich and other ministers. After 1835, they essentially governed the Empire instead of the mentally ill king, Ferdinand v. See: DEÁK: *op. cit.*, 91.

cooperation for many years thereafter. At the end of the century, Joseph II sought to modernize his Empire and in doing so, to centralize and Germanize the administration in the whole country (including Hungary).[25] This interfered with the interests of noblemen in the whole realm. After his death, Leopold II had to give his royal assent to the Act, which explicitly stated that Hungary was a free, independent country with its own constitution. It had to be governed by respecting its laws and customs, and it could not be ruled like other territories of the Habsburg Empire.[26]

4 Part 2: The Reform Era (1825–1848) and the Origins of the "Revolution"

The political situation grew tense again at the end of Franz I's rule. The Emperor, as one of the leaders of the Holy Alliance, needed to impose new taxes upon Hungarian serfs and obtain new recruits at the end of the Napoleonic Wars. To achieve these goals, he needed the consent of the Diet, which he received. In return, however, the king refused to assemble the legislative body between 1811 and 1825 and ruled the country by absolutist means instead.

In addition, the state of the economy worsened. In the first half of the 19th century, Hungary was lagging not only behind the countries of Western Europe, but also some territories of the Habsburg Empire. The fundamentals of the economy were based mostly on agriculture even at the beginning of the industrial revolution, primarily because of the country's geopolitical situation. We cannot state that this situation solely depended on the actions and decisions of the Viennese Court, because the country's economic development had already taken a turn for the worse before 1526.[27] The endless wars with the Ottoman Empire left their mark on the country in the 16–17th century, and in the 18th century, the Habsburg army was a reliable market for the noblemen to sell their agricultural products. Under these circumstances, the nobility did not feel the need for economic reforms, and therefore any social reforms. Moreover, without their support, no changes were possible. Only a nobleman had the right to possess any real estate in the whole country (apart from urban society, but they were restricted in this regard to the royal free cities). Furthermore, noblemen were the only ones allowed to hold office due to their strong

---

25 Peter F. SUGAR, Péter HANÁK, Tibor FRANK: *A History of Hungary.* Indiana University Press, Bloomington-Indianapolis, 1994, 175.
26 Act Nr. X of 1790.
27 SPIRA: *op. cit.*, 15.

political privileges.[28] They had most of the seats in both chambers of the feudal Diet and apart from the church only they could act as judges etc.

To really understand their importance, we shall look at Hungarian society of the period, which divided itself into four estates: the prelacy, the barons, the (lesser) nobility and the representatives of the cities. In addition, there were the serfs and the intellectuals. The (Catholic) prelacy was one of the strongest allies of the crown, because without the consent of the Hungarian King no one could be appointed to a position in the church.[29] Most of the barons were also close allies of the Habsburgs, since many of them had won their titles and wealth from the dynasty. In the 16th and 17th centuries, many of those who opposed the House were tried and executed.[30] The political and economic influence of civil society was not considerable. In the lower chamber of the Diet, they had only one (!) vote vs. the nobility's 100 votes. At the beginning of the 19th century, trade guilds still existed in the royal free cities, which hindered their development. Furthermore, most of their citizens were of German descent, so the (lesser) nobility did not treat them as allies. The intellectuals consisted mostly of writers and poets without any real power and the serfs had no political rights whatsoever. They were also the ethnically most diverse group in society, and in the wake of nationalism, this even led to armed conflict during the war of 1848–1849. However, with civil society so weak, which estate could represent ideas like the emancipation of serfs, or equality under the law? We can state that only the nobility had the power – and from the 1820s, the incentive – to form an opposition even against the crown.

At the end of the Napoleonic Wars, the currency was greatly devalued in the Habsburg Empire. This development adversely affected the noblemen, along with the shrinking Austrian market. Therefore, the idea of much needed economic and political reforms slowly but steadily spread, starting in the early 1820s. This period (1825–1848) is designated as the "Reform era" in Hungarian history, when the principles of liberalism started to influence politicians. Alexis Tocqueville's book "Democracy in America" was well-known, as was the 1831 Constitution of Belgium, which served as an example of parliamentary monarchy for the whole continent. The influence of these new ideas cannot be overstated: in these decades, the liberals tried to abolish the death penalty and incorporate the jury system into the judiciary. Part of the nobility grew willing

---

28   MEZEY: *Magyar alkotmánytörténet...*, op. cit., 241–242.
29   Levente VÖLGYESI: *Városi kegyúri jogok az újkori Magyarországon* [The right of representation in the royal free cities in Hungary in the modern times], Iustum Aequum Salutare, 6(2010)/1, 125–129. 125.
30   Mária HOMOKI-NAGY: *Hűtlenségi perek a reformkorban* [The Crime of Infidelity in the Reform Age], Rubicon, 27(2015)/10, 75.

to accept the idea of universal taxation. Between 1825 and 1848, the Diet convened several times and certain steps were taken in the direction of the much-needed reforms. Many noblemen, including some aristocrats, believed that economic and social changes were first needed to achieve the political reforms. Therefore, the Diet enacted an Act about the voluntary liberation from serfdom.[31] This gave emancipated serfs the right to possess real estate, regulated the status of merchants and trading corporations,[32] and so on. These changes only laid down the legal foundation, because only the wealthiest one percent of serfs could liberate themselves. Also, by establishing a few joint stock companies, Hungary's economy would not transform into a capitalist one if the Act of Entailment was still in effect[33] (this Act meant that "the noble estate was the common property 'in perpetuity' of the ancestor i.e. the original owner and his male descendants".)[34] István Széchenyi's[35] works played a great role in the awakening of the nobility,[36] showing that the supposedly "cheap" labour of the serfs was in fact expensive owing to its inefficiency.[37] These changes led to political tensions with Vienna, because the imperial government opposed any changes under Metternich's rule. They felt the need for changes too – but they did not find any answers regarding how should they transform their empire.[38]

I must add that both the members of the aristocracy and the lesser nobility were not equally interested in these reforms. Among the members of the aristocracy we can find the country's first prime minister (Lajos Batthyány, who became one of the strongest allies of Kossuth); István Széchenyi, who strongly supported the economic reforms but opposed the political ones, which he deemed too radical. There was also a group which opposed any changes (such as the ultraconservative György Apponyi). The lesser nobility supported the reform ideas, but in some ways, they were divided too. The most important

---

31 Act Nr. IV of 1836.
32 Act Nr. XVI of 1840.
33 Barna MEZEY: *Magyar jogtörténet* [Hungarian Legal History], Osiris, Budapest, 2007, 156.
34 SUGAR, HANÁK, FRANK: *op. cit.*, 44.
35 Gróf István Széchenyi: aristocrat, Kossuth called him "The Greatest Hungarian". He played a great role in establishing the Hungarian Academy of Sciences, funded the building of the "Chain Bridge", and incorporated the first firm in Hungary. For more information see: *A Pallas Nagy Lexikona*, vol. 17, Pallas Irodalmi és Nyomdai Rt., Budapest, 1897 (mek.oszk.hu/00000/00060/html/095/pc009589.html, accessed 15.3.2017).
36 For more information cf. István SZÉCHENYI: *Hitel*, Neumann Kht., Budapest, 2002 (mek.oszk.hu/06100/06132/html). Also István SZÉCHENYI: *Világ*. Neumann Kht., Budapest, 2002–2003 (mek.oszk.hu/11800/11842/11842.htm).
37 DEÁK: *op. cit.*, 44.
38 *Ibid.*, 18.

issue was the future of the *noble counties*, which for example had the authority to deny the execution of any order on the grounds of unconstitutionality. Kossuth and Deák (the so-called "municipalists") stood for their preservation, whereas Eötvös on the other hand, as a so-called centralist, strongly believed in a strong central government responsible only to Parliament and wanted to redefine their role in the civil state.[39] For a "municipalist" like Kossuth, this idea was incomprehensible until 1848 because he saw the counties as the guardians of the Hungarian constitution.[40] On the other hand, his ideas were way more radical than Deák's or Eötvös' – for him even the abolition of monarchy was not out of the question.

As we have seen, civil society was too weak to influence the course of events – just as in the entire Central-Eastern-European region. On the other hand, the serfs played a role nonetheless, as the Viennese Court feared that in absence of any political and social reforms (like their emancipation) they would rebel against Habsburg rule, and this increased their (temporary) willingness to accept the proposed constitutional changes.[41]

It is also worth mentioning, that the Hungarian political sphere was defined by one question, i.e. the relationship with the Habsburgs. Since the 16–17th century, Hungarian politicians were divided basically into two groups. In the first group, there were those who believed that any reform could be successful only with the consent and cooperation of the Viennese Court. István Széchenyi said that the transformation of the country should be led by the aristocrats with legal instruments, not by revolution, and with the utmost consideration of Austrian-Hungarian relations.[42] The politicians in the opposition agreed that relations with the crown must be treated carefully but also argued that the interests of the country should come first. In 1847, when both parties (the Conservative Party supported by the Royal Court and the Oppositional Party) presented their political programmes, they were quite like one another – this remained true even if the conservatives had accepted (out of necessity) some of the goals of the opposition.[43] Both wanted to modernize their country; the only real question was how far they were willing to go against the will of the crown.[44]

---

39   ECKHART: *op. cit.*, 346.
40   József RUSZOLY: *Alkotmány és hagyomány* (*Constitution and Tradition*), JATEPress, Szeged, 1997, 27.
41   DEÁK: *op. cit.*, 26–28.
42   SPIRA: *op. cit.*, 177.
43   DEÁK: *op. cit.*, 74.
44   MEZEY: *Magyar alkotmánytörténet...*, *op. cit.*, 240.

5   Part 3: Constitutional Reform – or Revolution?

In November 1847, when Ferdinand V assembled the last feudal Diet, the political situation had become very tense on the entire continent. Just after the Galician slaughter, a rebellion broke out in France. In England banks had to close because of the economic crisis, and a financial crisis started in Austria at the beginning of 1848, when the Viennese Bank went practically bankrupt.[45] To understand why the events of March and April 1848 are interpreted by most legal historians as a "constitutional revolution" or a "legal revolution" nowadays, I would like to summarize the events that transpired during these two months.

Our journey starts on 1 March, when the news about the February Revolution arrived at Pressburg (today: Bratislava). Two days later, Louis Kossuth presented his petition to the king on the floor of the Diet.[46] He argued in his proposal that the Vienna Government was to blame for the economic and social problems because they governed the country in defiance of Hungarian laws. He added that the only way to solve this crisis was not only to abide by the Hungarian Constitution but also to give a constitution to the Austrian Lands which would mean the end of absolutism in the entire Habsburg Empire.[47] Furthermore, the proposal contained the establishment of responsible government, the compulsory emancipation of serfs and envisioned an independent Hungary. I must emphasize that under this term the contemporary politicians did not mean the enthronement of the Habsburgs and separation from the Empire; instead they wanted a self-governed country within the Empire which had to be ruled by its own laws.[48] There was only one problem, i.e. the upper chamber[49] was not in session, and its chair, the palatine, was in Vienna at the time so no one could assemble its members. Therefore, they could not send the motion to the King. Nevertheless, both the speech and the proposal became well-known in Austria and played a great role in the events of 13 March, when the Vienna Uprising broke out.[50]

Meanwhile, the current of events also accelerated in Buda-Pest. This city was Hungary's second most important political centre, where some members

---

45 DEÁK: *op. cit.*, 82.
46 Ibid., 84.
47 ECKHART: *op. cit.*, 347.
48 MEZEY: *Magyar alkotmánytörténet...*, *op. cit.*, 246.
49 The Hungarian Diet consisted of two chambers: the upper chamber, where the aristocrats were seated together with the prelates, while seated in the lower chamber were the representatives of the counties and the royal free cities.
50 DEÁK: *op. cit.*, 84.

of the opposition under the orders of Kossuth reached out to the Company of Ten.[51] The members of this society were radically thinking poets and writers who drafted a document which became famous under the name "Twelve Points". The demands in this petition went beyond those which Kossuth had presented at the Parliament a week earlier. They demanded freedom of the press, union with Transylvania etc., and it concluded with three words: "Equality, Liberty, Fraternity" – an unmistakable reference to the French Revolution. These intellectuals wanted to present this document to the Diet on 15 March. A day earlier however, when they received word about the Vienna Uprising,[52] they decided to proclaim the Twelve Points in Pest. Doing so, the Hungarian Revolution broke out on 15 March.

A day earlier, the palatine returned to Pressburg to assemble the members of the upper chamber, who accepted Kossuth's proposal without any objections. On the morning of 15 March, 72 delegates of the Hungarian Parliament boarded a ship to Vienna to present the motion to the king. On the way, Kossuth proposed to amend the motion with the appointment of a Prime Minister and the establishment of a Hungarian cabinet accountable to Parliament. At that time, nobody knew about the events of 15 March in Pest, so their decision was influenced solely by the Vienna Uprising. When they arrived in the capital, the king declined their demands. On 16 March, when the members of the Court learned about the Revolution in Pest, and even more worrying news reached the capital,[53] the State Conference accepted Kossuth's proposal with two changes: they left out the appointment of Batthyány and the promise that the king would give his royal assent to the enacted bills without amendments. This did not satisfy the Hungarian politicians, and even the moderate Széchenyi insisted upon the acceptance of the original proposal. The palatine circumvented the State Conference and went personally to the king, who gave him the authority to appoint the first Prime Minister of Hungary on 17 March.[54]

A day later, the last Diet began to enact the laws which changed the form of government. Some of the goals were simple to articulate, since from the mid-1840s there had been a consensus among the noblemen about universal and equal taxation, union with Transylvania, freedom of the press, and the abolition of serfdom. All in all, however, the statesmen of 1848 had to undertake a very difficult job. They had to lay down the foundation of a civil state, abolish

---

51　His goal was to put the members of the Diet under political pressure, in order to maintain the support for his proposal.
52　*Ibid.*, 87–88.
53　There was a false report about Petőfi staging a revolt with tens of thousands of serfs.
54　*Ibid.*, 91.

the remnants of the medieval law and order and, furthermore, enact laws guaranteeing the fundamental rights of citizens – in a very short amount of time.

In the end we can state that the lesser nobility, especially Louis Kossuth,[55] played the most important role in shaping the country's future but in doing so, he relied on those aristocrats who supported the reforms, and – even, if somewhat indirectly and for just a moment – the intellectuals were also instrumental in the birth of the constitutional monarchy. However, the leaders of the Revolution in Pest did not have a say in the framing of the constitutional monarchy.[56] Those events started on 15 March and basically ended on the next day. The decisions were made in Pressburg, on the floor of the last feudal Diet, where the nobility in essence triumphed over itself. They enacted laws regarding the establishment of a government responsible to Parliament, enacted parliamentary reform, introduced popular representation, realized the union with Transylvania, and abolished the entailment, the manorial courts and the taxes gathered by the Catholic Church. They also declared the principles of universal taxation, religious liberty and freedom of the press.[57]

6   Part 4: The Enactment of the April Laws

Even if we assume that these Acts had to be enacted in haste, the timetable by which the Diet had to work seems almost surreal. The proposal regarding government responsible directly to Parliament was drafted by a committee of three just in about twenty-four hours,[58] and both chambers of the Assembly enacted the law within the following two days. This happened on 21 March, just four days after the appointment the first prime minister. Kálmán Ghyczy, who drafted the proposal, expressed his dissatisfaction about the haste.[59] One time the debate even went on without him, even if it was his job to forward the decisions from one chamber to the other.[60] It is important to note that the proposal

---

55   For more information, cf. István Széchenyi's Diary, who wrote to Antal Tasner on 17 March: "My politics were safe… but slow. Kossuth staked everything on one chance and won at least that much for the fatherland that my politics could not have achieved in twenty years!". Cf.: *Széchenyi István Válogatott művei* (Selected Works of István Széchenyi), György SPIRA (ed.), vol. 2, Budapest, 1991, 405.
56   DEÁK: *op. cit.*, 100.
57   Cf. Act Nr. III, IV, V, VII, XI, XIII, XV of 1848.
58   István SZIGETI: *„Hazámnak hasznos polgára kívánok lenni" – Ghyczy Kálmán élete és politikai pályája (1808–1888)* ["I want to be a useful citizen for my country" – The Life and Political Career of Kálmán Ghyczy (1808–1888)], Budapest, Gondolat Kiadó, 2013, 94.
59   SZIGETI: *op. cit.*, 95.
60   *Ibid.*, 99.

was not only formally enacted by both chambers of the Diet, which of course, was a constitutional requirement for the validity of the law, but during the debates the text of the bill was changed in accordance with the objections of both houses. This remains true even if the upper chamber did not propose any major changes to the proposal, but the lower chamber accepted their modifications nonetheless.

The bill arrived before the Committee of Parliamentary Affairs of the Hungarian Royal Chancery on 24 March. This public body played a great role in law-making, namely they checked every bill from a constitutional perspective. Without their consent, no bill could go to the king for royal assent, but its members served the interests of the Viennese Court. The Committee did not want to vest the exercise of the royal prerogatives in the newly formed Hungarian government, and proposed changes regarding military affairs and the exercise of the power or pardon and the right of patronage. They based their opinion on the rules of the feudal Hungarian constitution and the *Pragmatica Sanctio*, which established a defensive alliance between the territories of the Habsburg Empire. They also proposed that the King should be able to summon any of the ministers to Vienna at any time. The proposal was delivered to the State Conference on 26 March.

The State Conference "approved" the bill only for tactical reasons. They wanted to withdraw these "concessions", once the "storm" had blown over. Even so, they proposed dramatic changes, according to their proposal, the "independent" government would have been in a subordinate position to the Committee of Parliamentary Affairs of the Hungarian Royal Chancery. Financial affairs would have remained at least partially in common between Austria and Hungary, and military affairs, even the appointment of officers, would have been reserved solely for the king.[61]

These proposals were made public to the Diet on 29 March, when they received the ordinance of the king. The lower chamber was extremely dissatisfied with the answer, and Batthyány announced that under these circumstances he could not accept the office of prime minister. Kossuth said the following on the district session: "The goal is (...) for the hated bureaucracy to remain in Vienna, and therefore the Hungarian government would be nothing more than a low-ranking post office".[62] He also noted that the king gave his word regarding establishment of a national government responsible to the Parliament, and now his advisors wanted to break his promise to the nation. Kossuth held Apponyi, Jósika and Wirkner responsible (all of whom were high ranking

---

61 RUSZOLY: *op. cit.*, 31.
62 *Ibid.*

conservative Hungarian politicians serving in the Viennese Court), and argued that they should be charged with treason.[63] The lower chamber passed a motion which made it clear that the Parliament would not defer from the idea of an independent government. The upper chamber agreed to it without delay.

István (the palatine) went with the resolution to Vienna the next day. His main goal was to get an invitation for Batthyány, Deák, Széchenyi and Eötvös. The debating parties reached an agreement that same night, thanks to reports about the situation in Pest and renewed revolutionary movements in Vienna. The Royal Court was afraid that without any changes the situation would take a turn for the worse. An idea began to spread about the coronation of István that of course would have meant the separation of Hungary. The Court's conditions were as follows: first, the declaration of the palatine's inviolability would apply only to the current palatine. Second, the King would have the right to appoint the high dignitaries of the land (both ecclesiastical and secular), but his decision would require the countersignature of one of the ministers. Third, these cases were to be debated in the presence of a minister in addition to the king and his advisors.[64] Fourth, some temporary decisions were to be made about financial affairs and finally, military decisions would be vested in the king but the countersignature of the minister for military affairs would be required. The Hungarian Diet accepted the conditions and modified the bill on 2–3 April.[65] The king gave his royal assent on 5 April.

The official records show us in the case of the bill about the parliamentary reform that on the floor of the upper chamber there was an intense debate about the motion by the lower chamber. They dealt with the issue of royal assent, the election of parliamentary officers and the right of dissolution. Antal Ocskay questioned the very goal of the bill when he debated the need for annual sessions – even if the Act about the government specifically stated that the cabinet must present the Finance Bill to the Parliament every year. The upper chamber voted for the proposal after the debate, with some amendments. The lower chamber accepted these modifications on 21 March other than the idea that the Diet should be able to make decisions in closed sessions. The prelacy and the aristocrats agreed.[66] The Committee of Parliamentary Affairs published its proposal on 31 March, in which it recommended some

---

63 Ibid., 32.
64 This position was established by Act Nr. 3 of 1848. This person served as the Hungarian "foreign minister" in Vienna. His legal authority was somewhat weaker compared to the other members of the Cabinet, for example he could not countersign the ordinances of the King.
65 Act III of 1848 § 2, §§ 7–8.
66 RUSZOLY: op. cit., 33.

amendments to the bill. A day later, the State Conference accepted the originally proposed bill and therefore made it possible for the king to give his royal assent, which happened on 2 April.

The bill about universal suffrage was clearly influenced by the historical-political situation. In the 1840s, the liberal side of the lesser nobility did not want to treat emancipated serfs as members of another estate, but instead they wanted to incorporate their representatives in the traditional counties. The enactment of universal suffrage was not on the agenda until the French Revolution broke out. Previously, this issue was considered only in the debate about the bill regarding the cities, and even then, only in regard to the parliamentary representation of the cities, intellectuals and the free villages.[67] After the political decision was made in the Spring of 1848, the bill was passed by the Diet, even if the upper chamber opposed the proposal at first. The draft was made by the same three people (Ghyczy-Kossuth-Szemere), who drafted the bill on government. The Hungarian Royal Chancery gave its blessing even before the upper chamber had enacted the bill because the Viennese Court thought that the feudal representative system was unsustainable as did the State Conference. The king gave his assent to the bill shortly thereafter.[68]

It is important to note that these acts were enacted by strictly fulfilling the requirements of the constitution then in effect, i.e. they were enacted by both chambers of the Diet, then accepted by the Committee of Parliamentary Affairs of the Hungarian Royal Chancery and by the State Conference in Vienna.[69] Lastly, they were promulgated by the king as laws of the land on 11 April. Consequently, the 31 Articles of the April Laws were enacted through legal and not by revolutionary means.

Another unique feature of these Acts was that the concept of human rights, representative government and the idea of equality under the law were interpreted by noblemen, and therefore, we can find some differences in their enactment. In contrast to the French Revolution of 1789, when the members of the French National Constituent Assembly abolished all the privileges of the First and Second Estate, the Hungarian Parliament expanded the privileges of noblemen to the general population.[70] For example, when the right to vote was expanded, it was guaranteed that anyone who had possessed this right

---

67   Ibid., 10, 59.
68   Ibid., 68.
69   Árpád KÁROLYI: Az 1848-diki pozsonyi törvénycikkek az udvar előtt (The Acts of 1848, before the Court). Magyar Történelmi Társulat, Budapest, 1936, 62–75; also MEZEY: Magyar alkotmánytörténet..., op. cit., 243.
70   MEZEY: Magyar alkotmánytörténet..., op. cit., 245.

before 1848 could vote afterwards – even if someone did not meet the legal requirements. Consequently, seven to ten percent of the population gained active suffrage.[71] The right of habeas corpus, which had previously belonged to the privileged, became a fundamental right as well. Among the delegates, nobody felt the need to abolish the old medieval historical constitution, instead they saw the events of 1848 as an evolutionary step for the Hungarian constitution.

Why did the members of the Hungarian political elite oppose the idea of revolution so strongly? First, they rightfully thought that the Viennese Court would be more willing to accept the changes if they are seen as being of an evolutionary nature. Secondly, it is important to note that the transformation of the medieval state was done by the same statesmen who safeguarded the institutions of the Hungarian constitution, so abolishing it would have been contrary to their principles.[72] Their respect towards constitutionalism was shown in the Fall of 1848, when the relations between the Viennese and Hungarian governments worsened and the War of Independence broke out. When the king did not want to appoint a new cabinet and unlawfully dissolved the Parliament, the members of the legislative body temporarily appointed a committee with the task of defending the country in the absence of the executive branch of government. They did not form a new cabinet, nor did they try to abolish the prerogatives of the crown.[73]

7   Part 5: Critique of the April Laws

The lack of time contributed greatly to certain inadequacies. Some fundamental human rights were not regulated by these laws (for example the freedom of assembly), in some cases the rules were temporary (like suffrage), and some Acts were only declarative in nature (like the abolishment of the entailment). The greatest deficiency was the regulation of the Austrian-Hungarian relationship. The makers of these laws envisioned an independent Hungary, which would have resulted in a personal union between Hungary and the rest of the Empire. This, however, was unacceptable to the dynasty.

The complexity of the situation from the side of the Austrian Imperial Court can be described as follows: as the waves of the Revolutions of 1848 reached

---

71   Ibid., 319.
72   RUSZOLY: op. cit., 8.
73   MEZEY: Magyar alkotmánytörténet..., op. cit., 370.

the Habsburg Empire, the eleven nationalities and the head of state had to find an answer to the a number of questions. Should the Austrian Empire unite with the then non-existent Germany, or should it remain alone? If the Greater German Solution came to pass, what would happen to the rest of the Habsburg Empire? If Austria stood alone and the Habsburg Monarchy continued to exist, should it be constitutional or absolutist? Should it be reformed into a federalist state or should it remain centralized? If it was federalist, would it need a unified army? What about the minorities? Should they remain within the borders of the Empire or could they form their own states? Who should be the King of Hungary? Should Transylvania unite with Hungary? Should Vajdaság (Vojdovina) be united with Croatia? Should the Czechs gain the right of self-government? Should the Slovaks join them or remain in Hungary? What about the important social, economic reforms, who should execute them? I think, by just looking over these questions, we can understand the words of István Deák, who wrote that two things were common in people's heads, confusion and perplexity.[74]

8 Conclusion and the Impact on National Identity

The delegates of the Assembly in Pressburg circumvented these questions when they framed the April Laws, considering the great political risks. This proved to be a mistake, because it angered the Austrian government and gave them a way to turn the minorities against the Revolution. Some elements of the April Laws (like the one that required the command of the Hungarian language in order to become an elected member of Parliament) gave cause for apprehension. Furthermore, some decisions of the Hungarian Government during Spring 1848 that aimed to strengthen the national identity also widened the rift between Hungarians and the minorities. Most notably, members of the government embraced the concept of the so-called Hungarian political nation that included all national minorities regardless of their ethnicity. At the same time, the very same laws reunited Transsylvania with Hungary, and by doing so, fulfilled a goal that was on the agenda since the beginning of the Ottoman occupation in 1541. The acts regarding the Hungarian University, the establishment of an independent Hungarian army or the law that reinstated the use of the national coat of arms also aimed to strengthen the national identity. When the war broke out to defend these achievements against the Habsburg army, the most important aspect was lost i.e. the bloodlessness of

---

74   DEÁK: *op. cit.*, 18

the transformation.[75] Not only that, when the Hungarian forces surrendered in 1849, according to the Imperial Constitution of Olmütz, Hungary lost its sovereignty and became a part of the Austrian Empire. The decade-long absolute rule of Francis Joseph ended with the October Diploma. In 1860, he tried to transform his empire into a federalist state. The constitutionality of Hungary would have been partially restored, but most of the reorganised Hungarian counties declared that they wanted to restore the effects of the April Laws,[76] which were withdrawn by the Emperor in the fall of 1848 without the consent of the Hungarian Parliament. Even so, years later, when negotiations started between the parties, the April Laws served in many ways as the foundation upon which Hungary's constitutional structure stood after the Austro-Hungarian Compromise.

Bibliography

Judit BEKE-MARTOS: *Állami legitimációs eljárások és államfői jogkör 1867–1918 között* [Public Legitimisation Procedures and the Head of State between 1867–1918], Kossuth Kiadó, Budapest, 2012.

John BOWRING: *Translations from Alexander Petőfi*, Trübner & Co., London, 1866.

István DEÁK: *A törvényes forradalom: Kossuth Lajos és a magyarok 1848–1849-ben* [The Lawful Revolution: Louis Kossuth and the Hungarians (1848–1849)], Gondolat Kiadó, Budapest, 1994.

Ferenc ECKHART: *Magyar alkotmány- és jogtörténet* [Hungarian Constitutional and Legal History], Osiris, Budapest, 2000.

András GERGELY: *Magyarország története a 19. században* [Hungarian History in the 19th Century], Osiris, Budapest, 2005.

Mária HOMOKI-NAGY: *Hűtlenségi perek a reformkorban* [The Crime of Infidelity in the Reform Age], Rubicon, 27(2015)/10, 75–81.

Árpád KÁROLYI: *Az 1848-diki pozsonyi törvénycikkek az udvar előtt* [The Acts of 1848, before the Court], Magyar Történelmi Társulat, Budapest, 1936.

Barna MEZEY: *Magyar alkotmánytörténet* [Hungarian Constitutional History], Osiris, Budapest, 2003.

Barna MEZEY: *Magyar jogtörténet* [Hungarian Legal History], Osiris, Budapest, 2007.

---

75 Judit BEKE-MARTOS: *Állami legitimációs eljárások és államfői jogkör 1867–1918 között* [Public Legitimisation Procedures and the Head of State between 1867–1918], Kossuth Kiadó, Budapest, 2012, 65.

76 *Ibid.*, 70.

Barna MEZEY: *Szuverenitáskérdések* [The Issue of Sovereignty], Jogtörténeti Szemle 3(2015)/3, 52–60.

Pallas Nagy Lexikona, Pillera-Simon (eds.), Pallas Irodalmi és Nyomdai Rt., Budapest, 1897. Source: http://mek.oszk.hu/00000/00060/html/095/pc009589.html (15.3.2017).

József RUSZOLY: *Alkotmány és hagyomány (Constitution and Tradition)*, JATEPress, Szeged, 1997 György SPIRA (ed.): *Széchenyi István* Válogatott művei (Selected Works of István Széchenyi), II., Budapest, 1991.

György SPIRA: *A negyvennyolcas nemzedék nyomában (Following the generation of 1848)*, Magvető Kiadó, Budapest, 1973.

György SPIRA (ed.): *Széchenyi István* Válogatott művei (Selected Works of István Széchenyi), II., Budapest, 1991.

Peter F. SUGAR, Péter HANÁK, Tibor FRANK: *A History of Hungary*. Indiana University Press, Bloomington and Indianapolis, 1994.

István SZÉCHENYI: Hitel. Neumann Kht., Budapest, 2002. Available online at: http://mek.oszk.hu/06100/06132/html/.

István SZÉCHENYI: Világ. Neumann Kht., Budapest, 2002–2003. Available online at: http://mek.oszk.hu/11800/11842/11842.htm.

István SZIGETI: *„Hazámnak hasznos polgára kívánok lenni" – Ghyczy Kálmán élete és politikai pályája (1808–1888) ("I want to be a useful citizen for my country" – The Life and Political Career of Kálmán Ghyczy (1808–1888))*, Budapest, Gondolat Kiadó, 2013.

Levente VÖLGYESI: *Városi kegyúri jogok az újkori Magyarországon (The right of representation in the royal free cities in Hungary in the modern times)*, Iustum Aequum Salutare, 6(2010)/1. 125–129.

CHAPTER 4

Restoring the Hungarian Historical Constitutional Order with a Coronation in 1867

Judit Beke-Martos

1   Introduction

The thesis of this chapter is that the last element in the restoration of the Hungarian constitutional order was the coronation in 1867. In order to prove that, we need to examine two separate issues: first, the constitutional order of Hungary prior to 1867 (Part 1), and second, the coronation as a legally relevant event and not solely one of pomp and circumstance (Part 2). Having demonstrated that the constitutional order had been suspended and needed to be restored and that a coronation was able to restore said constitutional order, we need to examine the event of 1867 to see how, in that case, the coronation re-established the constitutional order (Part 3). From this we may draw the conclusion that the thesis is proven, the Hungarian constitutional order was indeed restored by the coronation of 1867 as its last constitutive element, and that in this particular constitutional struggle, it was the national ceremony, the adherence to the traditions coupled with political events that reinforced and strengthened the national identity (Part 4). Throughout this chapter, the coronation is considered a legal instrument that took on an additional role in 1867. No conclusion could therefore be drawn without the chronological comparison of this very institution represented in this writing, as well as without adjusting weight to the international context, which the 19th century presented in the delicate balance between the Austrian Empire and Hungary.

2   Part 1: The Constitutional Order of Hungary Prior to 1867

Hungary's history as a monarchy in Europe dates back to 1000 AD, when the state was founded and the first king, Stephen I was crowned. The country's development, all the way until the Turkish occupation in the 16th–17th centuries, was more or less in unison with its western counterparts.[1] The occupation

---

1   There are numerous differences in the early history of Hungary when compared to other countries in Western Europe, but the serious delays can rather be observed after the Turkish

© KONINKLIJKE BRILL NV, LEIDEN, 2020 | DOI:10.1163/9789004417359_005

lasted for more than a century and a half. When in 1686, the castle of Buda was liberated with the help of Habsburg troops, it seemed more than logical for Hungarians to show their gratitude to their allies, the Habsburgs, by elevating their respective males to be the hereditary heirs of the Hungarian throne.[2] Since the coronation of Joseph I in 1687 until 1740,[3] it was always the male heir, who was the next in line for the succession and became the King of Hungary. Based on the *Pragmatica Sanctio*,[4] in 1740, the first female heir, Maria Theresa was crowned queen of Hungary, and the hereditary monarchy proceeded accordingly for as long as Hungary had a monarch.[5] Though ruled by one of the most important and influential dynasties in Europe, Hungary's constitutional and legal development, after the Turkish occupation, showed significant delays in comparison to its Western counterparts.[6] Maria Theresa's son, Joseph II – in fact another example of the suspended constitution in the sense of his refusing his coronation – as a ruler of the Enlightenment, he wished to implement rapid changes in Hungary, but the country was not prepared for these reforms, which was, in part, the reason for their failure. As a result of Joseph II's refusal to be crowned, the Hungarian assembly in 1790–1791 enacted

---

occupation. In 1526, the Hungarians lost the battle at Mohács against the troops of the Ottoman Empire, thereby allowing the Turks into the middle of the country. This is when Hungary was separated into two parts, whereas in 1541, having lost the castle of Buda, the country became divided into three parts. The Kingdom of Hungary remained towards the western part of the original territories, which was ruled by the Habsburg king on a hereditary basis; the occupied territories in the middle of the country, where the Ottoman Empire set up its own public administration; and the Transylvanian Territories, which became domestically independent while paying a tax to the Ottoman ruler.

2 Act number I, II and III of 1687.
3 This meant in essence Joseph I (who was crowned in 1687 but ascended the throne upon the passing of his father, Leopold I in 1705) and his brother, Charles III from 1711–1740. Please note that the enumeration of the kings mentioned here follows the Hungarian model.
4 During the assembly of 1722–1723, the Hungarians accepted the female heirs of the Habsburgs to the Hungarian throne (Act number II of 1723), in exchange for the king's declaration that the territories of the Hungarian crown had been inseparable and non-dividable. This was a promise every monarch crowned after the Pragmatica Sanctio entered into force had to include in his or her *diploma inaugurale* as well as in the secular oath delivered upon it.
5 With the exception of the Revolution in 1848–1849 and the so-called democratic attempts in 1918–1919 and 1945, respectively, Hungary's form of state remained a monarchy until 1946, even though it had no king after 1918. Accordingly, the monarchs were: Maria Theresa (1740–1780), Joseph II (1780–1790), Leopold II (1790–1792), Franz I (1792–1835), Ferdinand V (1835–1848), Franz Joseph (1848–1916) and Charles IV (1916–1918).
6 On the Habsburg rule in Hungary see Jenő Barsi RÓNAY: *A Habsburgok Magyarországon*, Bartos Nyomda, Szeged, 1934; Imre GONDA, Emil NIEDERHAUSER: *A Habsburgok – Egy európai jelenség*, Pannonica Kiadó, Budapest, 1998; János SÁRA, Dr.: *A Habsburgok és Magyarország 950–1918*, Athenaeum Kiadó, Budapest, 2001.

new legislation, which imposed a six-month moratorium on the heir apparent within which he had to have been crowned.[7] King Leopold II, Franz I and Ferdinand V all respected these rules and had been crowned within the prescribed timeframe.[8] The difficulty came in 1848, with the unilateral abdication of Ferdinand V.

Hungary, at this time in the middle of the 19th century, had no written constitution. It had a well-developed constitutional order and a number of landmarks in constitutional development that are called today the "achievements of the historical constitution".[9] As sources of law, during the early centuries of Hungarian history, the king's decrees were supported by local customary law. Roman law was only a subsidiary means in the adjudication of Hungarian courts.[10] Due to the Turkish occupation, the urbanisation process characteristic of Western European countries after the Renaissance, did not start in Hungary. On the contrary, a second wave of serfdom started in the 16th century and held on until 1848. The landmarks, which can be categorized as the legal documents providing the foundation of the Hungarian constitutional order, are the Golden Bull of 1222 providing privileges to the nobility, which remained in effect until 1848; the laws of 1351, establishing and enshrining first and foremost the system of land ownership in Hungary, which also remained in effect until 1848; the Tripartitum of 1514, a collection of local customary laws systematically organised with the aim to enact it as a unified code but only ending up being published and distributed among practitioners; the 1723 *Pragmatica Sanctio* guaranteeing the inseparability and non-dividability of the Hungarian crown's territories; and the April Laws of 1848, which in essence realized the Hungarian transition from an absolute monarchy into a constitutional monarchy without any bloodshed. This list of documents is not – as it cannot be – exhaustive.

---

7   Act number III of 1790–1791.
8   In fact, King Ferdinand V was already crowned in 1830 during the reign of his father. On coronations taking place in Bratislava see Stefan HOLCIK: *Pozsonyi koronázási ünnepségek 1563–1830*, Európa Könyvkiadó, Bratislava-Budapest, 1986.
9   The new Fundamental Law of Hungary, which was enacted in 2011 and entered into force on 1 January 2012, elevates these undefined "achievements of the historical constitution" into the current constitution. Fundamental Law of Hungary, National Avowal of Faith and Article R (3).
10   The development of the Hungarian courts was also fairly slow. Serfs were adjudicated upon by their respective landlords for centuries. *Magyar jogtörténet*, Barna MEZEY (ed.), Osiris Kiadó, Budapest, 2007, 298, 324. Following the Turkish occupation, the restored adjudication of the courts relied heavily upon the Tripartitum, the collected and organised book of customs which did not reach the status of promulgated law but was used in the practice of judges.

In addition to the landmarks of the Hungarian constitutional order, there were multiple other laws contributing to the structure and functioning of the Hungarian state, including regulation of the monarch. The head of state, his passing and the succession on the Hungarian throne were regulated in 1848 through the laws of 1687, 1723 and 1791. Accordingly, it was the heir in the Habsburg line of succession who had the right to the Hungarian throne, (primarily male but lacking such an heir, it could also be a female), who had to be crowned within six months of his predecessor's passing. As an inherent part of the coronation's preparatory process, the heir apparent had to issue a document known as the *diploma inaugurale*, in which he promised to uphold and protect the laws and constitutional order of Hungary, and he had to take a secular oath upon this document as a type of security. Although the succession of the heir apparent was regulated by law, the Hungarian assembly had to acknowledge the heir's right to the throne and his accession to it. This can be recognized as the formal legitimisation of the heir. The ceremonial legitimisation followed in the form of the coronation. In order to transfer the totality of power onto the new monarch, both the formal and the ceremonial legitimisation processes had to be completed.[11]

The dichotomy of the legitimisation process – formal and ceremonial – can easily be explained through the origin of the king's power. At the very beginning of any European monarchy, the monarch's power derived solely from God. In order to transfer said power onto the monarch, the Church – as God's representative on Earth – had to celebrate the coronation mass and acknowledge that the monarch was the head of state. In exchange for performing said religious ceremony, the king took a religious oath, the *iuramentum iustitiae et pacis*, and with that promised to protect the Church. As time progressed and the idea of sovereignty appeared, the source of the king's power no longer seemed to be singular, but rather dual as in while it still derived from God, it also derived from the people.[12] The religious transfer of power took place during the coronation. The secular transfer, the relegation of the people's power

---

[11] For more detail on the power-transferring procedure of the head of state see Judit BEKE-MARTOS: *Állami legitimációs eljárások és államfői jogkör 1867–1918 között*, Kossuth kiadó, Budapest, 2012.

[12] Please note that the term people is used for the purposes of this chapter to represent members of the Hungarian population. These were, however, unlike in most Western European countries, the representatives of the nobility since, prior to and during the Turkish occupation, the vast majority of the population were serfs, while following the Turkish occupation, the second wave of serfdom blocked social progress and civil society did not develop. The term people, therefore, here stands for those who were participating in the political life of the country, and those were the nobility.

onto their monarch, could follow in various forms, primarily, however, through acknowledgement by the country's representative body. It was therefore clear that the heir had to be acknowledged and accepted as the heir by the assembly (the legitimisation formally, through the people) and then crowned at a coronation mass (the ceremonial and religious legitimisation including the divine blessing).[13]

The question as to what the procedure would be when a living monarch abdicated the throne did not arise in Hungary until the situation presented itself in 1848. If we look at and accept the dual source of the monarch's power (i.e. from God and from the people), we also need to see that the king or queen entered into a bilateral contract with the representatives of the Church as well as with those of the people, respectively. Regarding the Church, the monarch had to be crowned by the representatives of the Church, who fulfilled their duties in exchange for a promise (the religious oath) that the monarch would protect them. Regarding the people, they transferred their sovereignty to the monarch in exchange for various promises – including protection as well as inseparability and non-dividability of the crown's territories – the king or queen made towards the people. Both of these relationships, between king and Church and between king and the people, can be regarded as contractual agreements. A bilateral contractual agreement could not be terminated unilaterally – especially if there was no justifiable cause. This was the seemingly unresolvable situation in Hungary in 1848, as the Hungarian people – represented through the assembly – had a monarch with whom they entered into a contract, through the issuance of the *diploma inaugurale* secured by the oath. The only way to terminate this contract would have been by mutual agreement. Termination by mutual agreement could have taken the form of the Hungarian assembly's acknowledgement of Ferdinand v's abdication. After that, the assembly would have had to determine the heir apparent, acknowledge said heir's right to the throne and prepare a new contract with the new monarch in the form of a *diploma inaugurale*.

In 1848, as Ferdinand v unilaterally abdicated the Hungarian throne, multiple problems arose. First, the House of Habsburg claimed that a unilateral

---

13   This dichotomy received additional emphasis in Hungary, where, between 1301 and 1526, the country had an elective monarchy. Upon the passing of a monarch, the main political actors elected a new monarch to the throne. During this time, the crown of Saint Stephen, the Holy Crown of Hungary already began to symbolize the sovereignty of the Hungarian people, which was transferred during the coronation process upon the respective monarch. This symbol remained vital all throughout the Hungarian monarchy and every king or queen had to be crowned with the Hungarian Holy Crown. On the Holy Crown, see Ferenc ECKHART: *The Holy Crown of Hungary*, Athenaeum, Budapest, 1941.

abdication and an appropriate succession to the Austrian Emperor's throne would suffice for the change on the Hungarian throne.[14] The succession to the Hungarian throne had been governed at that time by the Hungarian constitutional order and the country's laws. Therefore, relying on a foreign regulation was absolutely unjustified. Second, the news of the change on the Austrian Emperor's throne only reached Hungary with three days delay, on 5 December 1848.[15] There were multiple members of the Hungarian assembly, who – in order to avoid any serious conflicts – suggested that the *de facto* change be acknowledged by the Hungarian assembly as well, but many, led by Lajos Kossuth, thought otherwise.[16]

Therefore, from 2 December 1848, Hungary had a *de jure* king who refused the crown and a *de facto* king, who would not be crowned. The situation was difficult to resolve and – as history shows us – it was not resolved by means of regulation. The factual situation persisted, but its interpretation changed over time. On a hypothetical level, and for a moment accepting that despite the reasoning above, it would have been possible for a monarch to unilaterally dissolve the bilateral contract he entered into with his people, the new king, Franz Joseph, would have had six months to be crowned – in accordance with Act number III of 1790–1791 – as Hungary's legitimate head of state. In order to be crowned, the monarch would have had to approach the Hungarian assembly and request their acknowledgement of his title to the throne as an indirect heir to the still living Ferdinand v.[17] Franz Joseph, having been chosen for the succession precisely because of his lack of contact and relationship with the subjects all around the Habsburg territories, had absolutely no such intention. Relying on his military strength and the assistance of the Russian troops, Franz Joseph defeated the Revolution and the subsequent Hungarian War of Independence and established absolute rule in all territories of the Hungarian crown. Had it not been for the Constitution of Olmütz, we may even conclude that until the expiration of the six-month moratorium, that is until 2 June 1849, no breach happened other than that a living monarch, through a unilateral declaration, abdicated the throne to which he had sworn an oath some eighteen years earlier.

---

14 Ferenc ECKHART: *A Habsburg-Lotharingiai Ház családi törvénye*, Magyar Tudományos Akadémia, Karcag, 1930.
15 Zsolt László KOCSIS: *A magyar államfő jogállása, hatásköre és helyettesítése 1000–1944 között*, published by Dr. Zsolt László Kocsis in cooperation with Graf-X Media Consulting, Budapest, 2004, 152; BEKE-MARTOS: *op. cit.*, 66.
16 KOCSIS: *op. cit.*, 152.
17 Ferdinand v had no children, but he had a brother, Franz Charles, who waived his right to the Hungarian throne, passing it on to his son, Franz Joseph, just turning 18 in 1848.

The real rupture in the Hungarian constitutional order occurred with the publication of the Constitution of Olmütz on 4 March 1849. This document, issued by the Emperor as a decree and sealed with the monarch's seal, was a constitution imposed on all Habsburg territories, effectively suspending the Hungarian constitutional order and integrating the territories of the Hungarian crown into the Habsburg Empire as a region of the Austrian Habsburg Crown. Franz Joseph, by refusing to be crowned, refused to have the sovereignty of the Hungarian people thrust upon him through the embodiment of Hungarian sovereignty, the Holy Crown. In addition to that, he imposed, from the outside, a new constitution and, by integrating those territories into the Empire, breached the *Pragmatica Sanctio*. In contrast to such breach it seems nearly meaningless to mention that a monarch who had not been crowned did not have the right to give his royal assent to a law, let alone issue a constitution. What was to be done against a *de facto* ruler? Since the Hungarian king – having derived his power in part from God – was inviolable, the only person responsible for his actions could be the minister signing off on his actions. In this case, however, there was no such minister and even if there had been, the new constitution created a new political order, a new system in which the tools of the old one no longer applied. One could argue that with the expiration of the six-month moratorium for the heir apparent to be crowned, Hungarian subjects were no longer bound by their duties towards the king, who by then officially occupied the Hungarian throne without the necessary formal or ceremonial legitimisation, but not even that would have changed the fact that the actions of the king, and particularly the issuance of a new constitution, were not to be changed retroactively, not even through the legislature. It is therefore clear that the Hungarian constitutional order has been suspended as of 4 March 1849 and, at the latest, starting from 2 June 1849, Franz Joseph was occupying the Hungarian throne as a *de facto* head of state while lacking legitimisation.

3 Part 2: The Coronation is a Legally Relevant Event and Not Solely One of Pomp and Circumstance

Already in the earliest societies, leaders were inducted into their offices through some form of ceremony. This was utterly important for their legitimisation in the respective community. A military leader could rely on his troops and establish his power based on that. Many other non-elected leaders could establish their powers with different forms of justification, for example through majority land ownership or other forms of wealth. Religious support for these leaders was most of the time very important. The underlying premise of these inaugural ceremonies was to demonstrate power, to justify legitimacy as well as, if necessary, to induce fear.

Coronation ceremonies, the induction of crowned heads of state, also date back many centuries. The crown, as an object, probably derives from the victory laurels, which changed in material to metal over time.[18] The crowning on the head, possibly refers to the early marriage rituals, where through the placement of a form of wreath onto the spouses heads represented their shared responsibilities towards each other.[19] The coronation ceremonies joined these two, with a crown being placed onto the head of the monarch and added to it the benediction of the Church. All this took place during a coronation mass, since, as previously mentioned, it was the Church that transferred the divine power of the monarch to the king at a religious event.[20]

In the early hereditary monarchies, it was the coronation mass alone that finalized the process of succession and transferred the totality of power to the new monarch. With the passage of time and the development of countries, the idea of sovereignty and shared sovereignty began to appear in the form of feudal representative assemblies and the like, the forms of power-transferring became more diverse. The coronation mass, as a religious event during which the monarch was crowned on the head with a crown, persisted and retained its importance throughout the history of monarchies (as it still does today).

The question of whether a coronation ceremony can at all restore a constitutional order is an element of the thesis proposed in this chapter. What are the necessary elements of any ceremonial event to have a legal or even constitutional significance? First, such ceremonies have to be clearly defined, either through some form of written regulation or through custom. Second, these defined ceremonies have to be known and accepted in the given society as something that has significance. If these requirements are met, a ceremony has the possibility to be legally relevant. In terms of a coronation ceremony, its elements were developed over time primarily through custom. Those rules were known to the general population and were followed by those in charge of

---

18 János KIRÁLY: *A király-koronázás eredete, egyházi kifejlődés és ordóbeli kialakulása*, Stephaneum Nyomda Rt., Budapest, 1918, 9.
19 *Ibid.*, 35.
20 The role the Church played in the coronation of the new monarch was debated repeatedly over the centuries and these debates were present in every country, as observed by the historian Emma Bartoniek. Emma BARTONIEK: *A magyar király-koronázások története*, Published by The Hungarian Historic Society, Reprint Series of the Akadémiai Kiadó, Budapest, 1987, 27.

the ceremony, therefore the first element is fulfilled. Regarding the second factor, that the society has to attribute a certain result to a given conduct, is also provided as it was well known and accepted that legitimate heirs to the throne had to be crowned and that included participating in the coronation mass, as well as issuing the *diploma inaugurale* together with the secular oath.

In Hungary, the idea of the country's sovereignty objectifying itself, appeared very early, already at the beginning of the 14th century. As the reign of the House of Árpád, the first Hungarian dynasty, ended following the death of Andrew III in 1301, the feudal assembly agreed to elect the next monarch to the throne from one of the surrounding dynasties. This system of elective monarchy was maintained officially until 1687, but in essence it only functioned until 1526, when the Turkish occupation began. During the period of the elective monarchy, it became increasingly important where, when and how the king became the person vested with the totality of monarchical power. Traditionally, it was the Archbishop of Esztergom (the head of the Hungarian Church), who crowned the king in the Basilica of Székesfehérvár with the Holy Crown of Saint Stephen. The Crown, during this time, became the object that represented Hungarian sovereignty. By having it placed on someone's head, that sovereignty was transferred to that individual.

Accordingly, in Hungary, it was especially true that the coronation, which was in any case an indispensable element of the power-transferring process, had legal relevance, being the occasion where the sovereignty of the Hungarian people was transferred to the new monarch through the Holy Crown. The ceremonial legitimisation process, with the appearance of the dual origin of the king's power (from God and from the people), began to include, along with the coronation mass, the issuance of the *diploma inaugurale* and the secular oath taken upon it, as legally necessary elements.

4 Part 3: The Coronation of Franz Joseph on 8 June 1867

Franz Joseph, the *de facto* king of Hungary since 2 December 1848, was crowned – and his rule thereby legalized – on 8 June 1867. The preparation for this coronation started much earlier. The negotiations between the Royal Court and the Hungarian Parliament were initiated more than once, only to break down in the process. The session of the Hungarian Parliament, which started in 1865 with, among others, the aim of having the head of state crowned, finally produced results by early 1867. Accordingly, Franz Joseph appointed the Hungarian government, – responsible to the Hungarian Parliament, – on

17 February 1867.[21] The Deputy Lord Steward, Count Antal Szapáry was appointed on 10 April 1867 by the Hungarian government to be in charge of the coronation ceremony.[22] The Hungarian Prime Minister, Count Gyula Andrássy proposed a Committee for the drafting of the *diploma inaugurale* and the secular oath. This proposition was adopted by the Parliament and the 24-member Committee finished its task by 3 June.[23]

A delegation of both Houses of Parliament led by the Archbishop of Esztergom, János Simor presented the text to Franz Joseph on 4 June 1867.[24] The king's approval of the text was an important requirement for both the *diploma inaugurale* and the oath becoming law.[25] In addition to the legal formalities (the *diploma inaugurale* and the oath), other ceremonial objects and representatives had to be appointed and transferred as well. Thus, Franz Joseph appointed Count György Károlyi and Baron Miklós Vay as keepers of the crown and observed the ceremonial transfer and opening of the sealed boxes containing the crown jewels on 6 June. The jewels were transferred from the castle to the coronation church during the afternoon of 7 June and the two appointed keepers had to safeguard these during the night before the coronation.[26] The upcoming ceremony was clearly signalled to the inhabitants and arriving guests of the Hungarian capital city as during the evening of 7 June, the church bells rang for a whole hour.[27]

8 June 1867 was a Saturday, a very important Saturday in the constitutional history of Hungary. Members of the bicameral Hungarian Parliament started this day at 5:30 am with a brief special session and then went up to the castle

---

21   Mihály LATKÓCZY: *Korona és koronázás*, Published by Divald Károly Fiai, Eperjes and Budapest, 1892.
22   *Adolf Dux* in: *Koronázási emlékkönyv*, Published on 8 June 1867, 37; Magyar Nemzeti Levéltár: K 27 (Minisztertanácsi ülések) 1. cs. 25 April 1867. 8. np. and 7 May 1867. 3. np.
23   The Committee consisted of the following members: Sámuel Bónis, Ferencz Deák, Frigyes Podmaniczky, Pál Nyáry, Kálmán Tisza, Kálmán Ghyczy, Pál Somssich, Antal Csengery, Baron István Kemény, Pál Trifunácz, László Bezerédj, György Joannovics, Imre Szabó, Emil Trauschenfels, Lajos Vadnay, Ede Zsedényi, Count György Apponyi, Elek Dósa, Károly Szász, György Bartal, József Hosszu, István Bittó, József Justh and Ferencz Pulszky. Dénes KOVÁCS, János SZIKLAY: *Konorázási emlékkönyv: A koronázás története; Az előkészületek*, Budapest, 1892, 52–54.
24   Péter SIMON: *Király és korona – Pillantás a múltra és jelenre*, Kormos Műintézet Nyomása, Budapest, 1892. 312. There are conflicting sources, which date this to 6 June. KOVÁCS, SZIKLAY: *op. cit.*, 58.
25   The text of the *diploma inaugurale* and that of the oath were enacted into Act number II of 1867.
26   KOVÁCS, SZIKLAY: *op. cit.*, 58–60. The keepers of the crown had various duties laid down in Act number VI of 1867.
27   SIMON: *op. cit.*, 312.

hill and took their pre-assigned places in the procession,[28] which left at 7 am from the Buda castle and led to the Matthias Church. The order of the dignitaries in the procession was precisely regulated; Franz Joseph rode his horse, while his wife, Elisabeth travelled in a carriage and eight behind him.[29] Hungary at that time had two archbishoprics: Esztergom and Kalocsa. Both archbishops were present at the Matthias Church that Saturday to greet the royal couple and lead them to an adjacent chapel, where they awaited the arrival of all other participants and guests.

The coronation mass, though clearly a religious ritual, entailed some secular elements. Lacking a palatine, the Parliament elected the Prime Minister to act as a representative of the people during the coronation mass.[30] The head of the Roman Catholic Church in Hungary, the Archbishop of Esztergom celebrated the religious ceremony consisting in part of a Holy Mass. First Franz Joseph took the religious oath, the *iuramentum iustitiae et pacis*. Then he was anointed, an element of the ceremony dating back to the earliest times in our history, when religious as well as secular rulers were given blessing and power through the sacred oil.[31] Saint Stephen's robe was placed on the king's shoulders before him being escorted to a seat where he was to sit and observe the Mass. During the later course of the ceremony, the Archbishop handed the King a sword. Franz Joseph inserted this sword into its scabbard in order to be

---

28   KOVÁCS, SZIKLAY: *op. cit.*, 61.
29   LATKÓCZY: *op. cit.*, 33.
30   From as early as the 15th century, it was the Palatine, in essence the deputy of the king, who as the people's representative participated in the coronation ceremony. He had two main tasks: first to ask the question for which the response was considered the acclamation of the king to the throne, and second, to assist the archbishop in placing the Holy Crown of Hungary on the head of the monarch. As the dual source of the king's power (deriving from God and from the people) became more and more acknowledged, the role of the Palatine during the coronation ceremony diminished. Nevertheless, the participation of the people's representative was the materialisation of this ceremony's constitutional and administrative relevance. This was increasingly true in 1867 as lacking a Palatine, the Parliament elected the Prime Minister to fill this role.
31   Regarding Franz Joseph's 1867 coronation, some sources only mention the king having been anointed, LATKÓCZY: *op. cit.*, 34; others claim his shoulders and arms were touched with the oil, Gyula SZENDE: *Királlyá avatás Magyarországon a vegyes korszakban 1301–1526 – Doktori értekezés*, Fried S. Nyomda, Budapest, 1893, 39; again others say it was only the right wrist, the right arm and between the shoulder blades, Ákos MIHÁLYFI, Dr.: *A magyar királykoronázás jelentősége*, M. Kir. Tudományegyetem Nyomda, Budapest, 1917, 11–12; another source mentions his right wrist, his right armpit and between the shoulder blades, János LUTTER, Dr.: *A szent koronával való koronázás alkotmányjogi jelentősége*, Szent-László-Nyomda Részvénytársaság, Nagyvárad, 1917, 23–24; and some even say it was his forehead annointed with oil, Mór JÓKAI: *A királykoronázás* = KOVÁCS, SZIKLAY: *op. cit.*, 8–9.

girded with it. Once this was on his body, he turned towards the audience, drew the sword from its scabbard and cut through the air twice. This was the symbol of protection against any attacks and enemies, which may threaten the Church. The king wiped the blade of the sword and reinserted it into its scabbard. With the robe on his shoulders and the sword on his waist, the king knelt before the Archbishop allowing him, together with the Prime Minister, to place the Holy Crown of Hungary onto his head. The other two crown jewels, the sceptre and the orb were given in his right and left hands, respectively. The crowned king then rose and was led to the throne to be seated on it. The enthronement completed the act of coronation.[32] Since Franz Joseph was married at the time of his coronation, his wife, Elisabeth was crowned during the same ceremony. The royal couple's offer of a gold coin each and their partaking of the sacrament, concluded the Holy Mass.[33]

The day's events were far from over. Following the coronation mass, the newly crowned king conferred the order of the Golden Spurs on exceptional soldiers. Then, in the coronation procession, a prearranged order of participants proceeded on horses from the castle down to the river and crossed over to the other side, to the Parish Church of Pest.[34] Participation in the Coronation Mass, taking of the religious oath and cutting through the air with a sword in church were the elements of the agreement between the king and the Church. What remained, however, were the elements of the agreement with the people. The text of the *diploma inaugurale* had been presented to Franz Joseph prior to his coronation day and was enacted during the coronation ceremony. The king still had to take the secular oath upon the text of the *diploma inaugurale*. This he did in front of the Parish Church of Pest. The Prime Minister handed the text of the oath to the Archbishop, who administered the oath.[35] The king placed his left hand on the oath-cross and held up his right hand while repeating the words.[36] Substantial crowds gathered to witness the taking of the oath, who exploded in joyful cheers after the words were uttered.[37] With this oath the king promised to keep and uphold the constitutional order of Hungary as well as to maintain its unity. The symbolic gesture of protection

---

[32] LATKÓCZY: *op. cit.*, 34–35.
[33] LUTTER: *op. cit.*, 28–31.
[34] This is the church that is currently on the Pest side of the Elisabeth Bridge towards the North. LATKÓCZY: *op. cit.*, 35.
[35] SIMON: *op. cit.*, 323.
[36] It is unclear from the conflicting sources which way the king was facing while taking his oath. Some say he faced towards East, KOVÁCS, SZIKLAY: *op. cit.*, 69; others say he faced the Parish Church, SIMON: *op. cit.*, 323.
[37] JÓKAI: *op. cit.*, 11.

followed at the next location, a little further to the North but still on the Pest side of the River Danube. The so-called coronation hill, consisting of a pile of land arriving from the various (in 1867, it was from 72) counties of the country,[38] was built close to the Parliament building of that time. Franz Joseph rode up this hill on his horse, drew his sword from its scabbard and pointed in all four cardinal directions, thereby promising to protect the country from attacks and enemies.[39]

The King and Queen returned to the castle for a highly symbolic coronation lunch. Only a selected few were invited to this event and strict protocol regulated every element of this meal.[40] Those in charge of the arrangements of the coronation did not forget about the general public, who visited the city to be a part of this historic event. There were oxen roasted in a public park on the Buda side of the Danube at the foot of the Castle Hill. These festivities lasted into the night while the planned premiere in the National Theatre was cancelled along with the Royal Ball in order to observe the mourning over the sudden death of Archduke Albert's daughter, Matilda.[41]

8 June 1867 was the day of the coronation, but the festivities continued for a few more days with various events for dignitaries and the people alike. On 9 June, there was a seated luncheon for 900 invited guests.[42] On the same day the newly crowned king gave his royal assent to various laws, among them those that granted amnesty to a wide range of people, including political prisoners.[43] On 10 June, members of the public could present gifts to their newly crowned couple. The crown jewels were withdrawn from public display to the king's suite and sealed again in his presence. Franz Joseph and his wife left Hungary on 12 June 1867.[44]

5   Part 4: Conclusion and the Impact on the National Identity

The thesis of this chapter was that the final element in the restoration of the Hungarian constitutional order was the coronation in 1867. For that, it was

---

38   BARTONIEK: *op. cit.*, 167.
39   LATKÓCZY: *op. cit.*, 33.
40   SIMON: *op. cit.*, 327–328.
41   *Ibid.*, 310. Matilda was a member of the Bavarian Royal Court. At 18, she tried to hide a lit cigarette but instead lit her dress with it and died following her burn injuries.
42   LATKÓCZY: *op. cit.*, 36.
43   KOVÁCS, SZIKLAY: *op. cit.*, 72.
44   LATKÓCZY: *op. cit.*, 36; KOVÁCS, SZIKLAY: *op. cit.*, 72.

necessary to prove that the Hungarian constitutional order had been suspended and needed to be restored as well as that the coronation was able to restore the constitutional order. On 4 March 1849, the Hungarian constitutional order was suspended by the Constitution of Olmütz. It is difficult to dispute that once another constitution was imposed on Hungary, its own constitutional order no longer prevailed. In the nineteen years leading up to the Compromise of 1867, changes were made, the Constitution of Olmütz was replaced by other, similar documents, but none of the changes even attempted the return to the Hungarian constitutional order. Franz Joseph's first indication of a wish to regulate his relationship with his Hungarian subjects came in 1860, followed by the brief session of the Hungarian Parliament in 1861. The King wished to come to an agreement with the Hungarians, but neither side was ready to take significant steps towards the other. The long negotiation process towards the Compromise began in 1865. The terms of the laws, which ended up constituting the Compromise, had to be negotiated one by one, but it was without question that the suspended constitution of Hungary would only be restored to its previous state and recognition if Franz Joseph was crowned at a coronation mass with the Holy Crown of Saint Stephen. This finally occurred on 8 June 1867 and with that not only the political and formal legitimisation, but also the ceremonial one was complete. The coronation ceremony was meticulously planned with a focus on the traditional elements, protocol and royal hierarchy. A coronation in and of itself is capable of establishing or restoring a constitutional order, as it inducts the head of state into his or her office, vesting this individual with the totality of power the office holds. Thereby it is a constituting act, even it if is only a certain type of conduct performed in a given way. The precise explanation of the coronation of 1867 shows just how much detail was to be taken into consideration in order to have the legally binding force of the coronation take effect. These were all complete in 1867, thereby finalizing the long and arduous process of finding a compromise between the Austrian Empire and the Kingdom of Hungary.

What remains to be done here is first to draw the conclusion that a constituting act was performed on 8 June 1867 finalizing a long legal process with the ceremonial legitimisation of the king. Second is to examine the potential relevance of this specific coronation and this historic situation in light of the Hungarian national identity and the law's role as a factor in the Hungarian development in this particular setting. The existing legal institution included a number of national elements to yield a result so important for the further functioning of the state.

The numerous minor references to Hungary, Hungarian culture, the attire and the military uniforms throughout the coronation of 1867 all show the importance of the national identity and its expression throughout this legal and also constitutional event. The Hungarian crown jewels, the locations through which the coronation procession led, the coronation hill (upon which the king pointed in all four cardinal directions) built from land arriving from 72 counties of the Hungarian territories, all of these references show the presence and relevance of national identity. The objectified embodiment of Hungarian sovereignty in the Holy Crown is perhaps an example on its own that ultimately proves how law and constitutional change can shape a nation. Hungary's status, through the Compromise of 1867 (finalized by the coronation), was restored to independence and it became an equal partner to the Austrian Empire in the Austro-Hungarian Monarchy. The self-esteem of Hungarians was greatly elevated by this change, since not only did they regain their previous status, but through the establishment of the new state, they became a significant force within Europe, a real partner to the other participants on the international stage. As practice later showed, this was more appearance than reality as the European allies considered the Habsburgs their partners and not the Hungarians, but that does not diminish the position that Hungary gained through the Compromise and the coronation of 1867.

The Austrian-Hungarian partnership has been a difficult one over many centuries. Observed from an objective and scientific perspective, this relationship has always been positive for Hungarians, but it is nearly impossible to exclude the emotional factors that diminish these achievements. It might be difficult to understand from the perspective of a reader today why it was so important for the Hungarians to crown a king they may not have liked at all. It seems that throughout the centuries of the Hungarian Monarchy, the subjects took great pride in having a king and they also drew great security from that leader. Accordingly, when this leader was missing, they felt unsafe and insecure. Therefore, the coronation, the restoration of the country's normal everyday life, was of utmost importance. By the middle of the 19th century, the Habsburg dynasty's hereditary right to the Hungarian throne (dating back to 1687) had been so well established that only very few revolutionaries would have questioned a Habsburg heir's entitlement to the throne. Having had an individual to crown, the Hungarian state was first and foremost interested in having that person crowned. This motivation overshadowed any other doubt or potential alternative political thought. The details of the ceremony had to comply with Hungarian traditions. As soon as the common ground was found between the Royal Court and the Hungarian Parliament, it was not debated from the Austrian side that the details of the ceremony would be organised by the Hungarians according to their practices and rituals. Accordingly, the suspended constitutional order was restored in 1867 through the monarch's proper induction into office while strengthening the national identity of a state taking so much pride in its independence.

Bibliography

Archival Sources
Magyar Nemzeti Levéltár [Hungarian National Archives], K 27 (Minisztertanácsi ülések) 1. cs. 25 April 1867. 8. np. and 7 May 1867. 3. np.

Acts and Statutes
Fundamental Law of Hungary (entered into force 1 January 2012.)
Act number I of 1687
Act number II of 1687
Act number III of 1687
Act number II of 1723
Act number III of 1790–1791
Act number II of 1867
Act number VI of 1867

Literature
Emma BARTONIEK: *A magyar király-koronázások története,* Published by The Hungarian Historic Society, Reprint Series of the Akadémiai Kiadó, Budapest, 1987.

Judit BEKE-MARTOS: *Állami legitimációs eljárások és államfői jogkör 1867–1918 között,* Kossuth kiadó, Budapest, 2012.

Ferenc ECKHART: *A Habsburg-Lotharingiai Ház családi törvénye,* Magyar Tudományos Akadémia, Karcag, 1930.

Ferenc ECKHART: *The Holy Crown of Hungary,* Athenaeum, Budapest, 1941.

Imre GONDA, Emil NIEDERHAUSER: *A Habsburgok – Egy európai jelenség,* Pannonica Kiadó, Budapest, 1998.

Stefan HOLCIK: *Pozsonyi koronázási ünnepségek 1563–1830,* Európa Könyvkiadó, Bratislava – Budapest, 1986.

Mór JÓKAI: *A királykoronázás,* = Dénes Kovács, János Sziklay: *Konorázási emlékkönyv: A koronázás története; Az előkészületek,* Budapest, 1892.

János KIRÁLY: *A király-koronázás eredete, egyházi kifejlődés és ordóbeli kialakulása,* Stephaneum Nyomda Rt., Budapest, 1918.

Zsolt László KOCSIS: *A magyar államfő jogállása, hatásköre és helyettesítése 1000–1944 között,* published by Dr. Zsolt László Kocsis in cooperation with Graf-X Media Consulting, Budapest, 2004.

Dénes KOVÁCS, János SZIKLAY: Konorázási emlékkönyv: A koronázás története; Az előkészületek, Budapest, 1892.

Mihály LATKÓCZY: Korona és koronázás, Published by Divald Károly Fiai, Eperjes and Budapest, 1892.

János LUTTER, Dr.: A szent koronával való koronázás alkotmányjogi jelentősége, Szent-László-Nyomda Részvénytársaság, Nagyvárad, 1917.

Magyar jogtörténet, Barna MEZEY (ed.), Osiris Kiadó, Budapest, 2007.

Ákos MIHÁLYFI, Dr.: A magyar királykoronázás jelentősége, M. Kir. Tudományegyetem Nyomda, Budapest, 1917.

Jenő Barsi RÓNAY: A Habsburgok Magyarországon, Bartos Nyomda, Szeged, 1934.

János SÁRA, Dr.: A Habsburgok és Magyarország 950–1918, Athenaeum Kiadó, Budapest, 2001.

Péter SIMON: Király és korona – Pillantás a múltra és jelenre, Kormos Műintézet Nyomása, Budapest, 1892.

Gyula SZENDE: Királylyá avatás Magyarországon a vegyes korszakban 1301–1526 – Doktori értekezés, Fried S. Nyomda, Budapest, 1893.

CHAPTER 5

The Privy Council Appeal and British Imperial Policy, 1833–1939

Thomas Mohr

1   Introduction

The late sixteenth century saw the beginning of the extraordinary expansion of the British Empire that converted the appellate court of the Privy Council from an obscure medieval institution into a court whose jurisdiction extended to all the continents of the globe and one quarter of the world's population. By the early nineteenth century it was clear that this final appellate court of the British Empire required reform and restructuring to cope with its greatly expanded responsibilities. Lord Brougham made this apparent in a famous 1828 speech in which he told the House of Commons that the Privy Council appeal needed to be reformed to achieve justice for the 'countless millions whom you desire to govern all over the world'.[1]

Brougham proved to be the driving force in creating a restructured 'Judicial Committee of the Privy Council' that came into being in 1833.[2] This chapter will examine the evolution of the Privy Council appeal as an instrument of British Imperial policy during the nineteenth and early twentieth centuries. Nationalists from diverse parts of the Empire often accused the Privy Council of upholding policy objectives championed by governments in London. Some nationalists did not hesitate to accord the Privy Council with the worst insult that can be levelled against any court of law, that of not being independent from the dictates of the government in power.[3] No convincing evidence has yet emerged to support these claims. Yet it is possible to argue that the judges of the Privy Council held similar values and attitudes towards the British Empire as the politicians who led successive British governments. It should be

---

1   P.A. Howell: *The Judicial Committee of the Privy Council 1833–1876*, Cambridge University Press, Cambridge (UK), 1979, 15.
2   The appeal was placed on a statutory basis with the passage of the Judicial Committee Act 1833. This was later amended by the Judicial Committee Act 1844.
3   Cf. Thomas Mohr: *Guardian of the Treaty – The Privy Council Appeal and Irish Sovereignty*, Four Courts Press, Dublin, 2016, 155–159.

remembered that many of these judges had once been politicians themselves and some had even enjoyed ministerial responsibility.

The first policy objective that will be the examined by this chapter concerns the role of the Privy Council in maintaining Imperial unity. This was a policy that was shared by all exponents of Empire. The second policy objective concerns the perceived need for an independent and external adjudicator to act as arbiter of the divisions of power within the federal systems that existed in parts of the Empire. This role was of particular importance with respect to Canada and Australia where the appeal could be presented as a means of keeping these federations together.[4] Tensions between the two linguistic communities in Canada, that were particularly acute within the province of Quebec, were seen as a constant threat to unity. In 1933 the state of Western Australia actually voted in a referendum to secede from the Commonwealth of Australia, although the absence of support from London ensured that the secessionist movement ultimately foundered.[5] Other federal systems of government would later emerge in the Empire in the middle of the twentieth century, for example the Federation of Malaya, the Federation of Rhodesia and Nyasaland and the West Indies Federation. The Privy Council was promoted as the potential arbiter of divisions of power within these federations and in devolved systems of government within the Empire.[6]

Another policy objective examined by this chapter concerns the Privy Council's role in retaining London's powers of oversight over key economic policies followed by self-governing parts of the Empire. This was a policy objective that was widely shared in British political and judicial circles in the late nineteenth and early twentieth centuries. Finally, this chapter will examine the emergence of the Privy's Council's involvement in the development of human rights. This could be presented as bringing the values of an enlightened metropolis to the peripheries of Empire. The latter included the dependent colonies but also, on occasion, included the self-governing colonies of white settlement known as the 'Dominions'.[7]

---

4 Cf. e.g. A.B. KEITH: *Dominion Autonomy in Practice*, Oxford University Press, London, 1929, 46.
5 Thomas MUSGRAVE: *The Western Australian Secessionist Movement*, Macquarie Law Journal, 3(2003), 95–129.
6 Second Schedule, Section 83, Federation of Malaya Order in Council, 1948, 1948/108; Sections 61–63, Federation of Rhodesia and Nyasaland (Constitution) Order in Council, 1953, 1953/1199 and Sections 87–9, The West Indies (Federation) Order in Council, 1957, 1957/1364.
7 The use of a capital 'D' when referring to the 'British Dominions' was required by the British government in order to avoid confusion with the wider term 'His Majesty's dominions' which

The role of the Judicial Committee of the Privy Council as an instrument of British Imperial policies had a profound impact on the history and development of the British Empire. Many of these policies remained relevant after the tide of Empire receded as the Privy Council continued to act as a final appellate court for many of the independent states in the new Commonwealth of Nations. Some policies were directly responsible for the decline of the Privy Council's area of jurisdiction in the twentieth century on the basis of claims that they were incompatible with the interests and values of individual parts of the Commonwealth. This aspect of the history of the Privy Council appeal may prove instructive for international courts in the twenty first century who bear the responsibility of hearing cases from multiple jurisdictions with differing histories and cultures.[8]

The policy objectives examined by this chapter are closely connected with the common themes of legal instrumentalism, modernisation and national identity that run through this book. The first theme is reflected in the development of a legal institution that began life in medieval England and later served as a vital source of unity within a global British Empire. The use of the institution of the Privy Council appeal as an instrument of economic oversight and as a means of safeguarding human rights is also relevant to this theme and to the theme of modernisation. Finally, the theme of national identity, and the related assertion of local values, is critical in understanding the slow decline of a court that once heard appeals from diverse legal systems from many different parts of the world.

An important barrier to revealing connections between the actions of the Judicial Committee of the Privy Council and key policies concerning the British Empire is the absence of any published work examining this court in its global context. Existing histories of this court tend to focus on single jurisdictions, on a few chosen jurisdictions or on a region within the British Empire.[9] In addition, legal textbooks from jurisdictions that, at the time of writing,

---

referred to the British Empire as a whole. Cf. the National Archives of the United Kingdom (TNA) HO 45/20030. This chapter will follow this convention.

8 Cf. e.g. the analogies drawn between the Judicial Committee of the Privy Council and the World Trade Organisation in Jacqueline D. KRIKORIAN: *International Trade Law and Domestic Policy – Canada, the United States and the WTO*, UBC Press, Vancouver, 2012, xvii–xix.

9 This tendency to focus on a single jurisdiction is shared by the author of this chapter. Cf. MOHR: *Guardian of the Treaty..., op. cit.* David SWINFEN provides a history of political debates in the Dominions concerning the Privy Council Appeal in *Imperial Appeal – The Debate on the Appeal to the Privy Council, 1833–1986*, Manchester University Press, Manchester, 1987. An account of the appeal in the British colonies in Africa is provided by Bonny IBHAWOH: *Imperial Justice – Africans in Empire's Court*, Oxford University Press, Oxford, 2013.

maintained the appeal to the Judicial Committee of the Privy Council often devoted considerable attention to the merits of whether or not the appeal should be abolished and tended to examine its decisions through this narrow prism.[10] These considerations have hampered attempts to examine the practical impact of the appeal to the Judicial Committee of the Privy Council on key issues that spanned many or all of the jurisdictions of the British Empire. The purpose of this chapter is to provide a few useful signposts in initiating analysis of these important aspects of the legal history of the British Empire. A broad approach, such as that taken by this chapter, is risky in an era of scholarship that encourages increased specialisation at the expense of wider perspectives. This is a barrier that must be overcome as it is also an inhibiting feature in the creation of a general history of the Privy Council appeal. This chapter advocates greater emphasis on thematic and comparative studies of the appeal to the Judicial Committee of the Privy Council in place of the national and regional studies that continue to dominate scholarship in this area.

2 The Privy Council Appeal as a Pillar of Imperial Unity

The Privy Council was widely perceived as a vital pillar upholding the unity of the British Empire. It was often described as the 'golden link' or 'sheet-anchor' of the Empire and was compared to the Royal Navy and the monarchy as a source of Imperial unity.[11] Yet the role of this Imperial court went beyond symbolism. The appeal to the Privy Council was also perceived as maintaining uniformity in the interpretation of key aspects of statute law drafted in similar terms in the self-governing parts of the Empire.[12] It was also credited with maintaining uniform interpretation of the unwritten common law between the parts of the Empire that belonged to the common law legal tradition.[13] Supporters of greater autonomy for the self-governing Dominions sometimes asked why it was necessary to maintain this cherished uniformity in these

---

10 A good example is the work of the Irish barrister Hector HUGHES: *National Sovereignty and Judicial Autonomy in the British Commonwealth of Nations*, PS King, London, 1931.

11 National Archives of Ireland (NAI), Department of Foreign Affairs, file 3/1, draft speech on *Abolition of Appeals to the Privy Council*, undated 1933; The Times, 14 August 1933 and Norman BENTWICH: *The Judicial Committee of the Privy Council as a Model of an International Court of Human Rights*, International Law Quarterly 2(1948)/3, 392–401.

12 For example, cf. A.B. KEITH: *Dominion Autonomy...*, op. cit., 46.

13 For example, cf. J.W. HARRIS: *The Privy Council and the Common Law*, Law Quarterly Review, 106(1990), 574–600.

areas of law, a task that was often seen as 'superhuman' in dimension.[14] In addition, the Privy Council was sometimes criticised for taking laws and precedents made in a particular part of the Empire and applying them in another part of the Empire in which very different conditions prevailed. One notable example concerns a precedent set in India on a point of Islamic law that was later applied in East Africa on the mistaken assumption that the values and conditions of these regions were similar or identical.[15]

Some critics concluded that it might be preferable to allow the colonies and Dominions to adapt the common law and statute law according to their own particular needs.[16] Nevertheless, the role of the Privy Council in maintaining legal unity was often promoted as an important aspect of maintaining the political unity of the British Empire. A.F. Pollard compared the unification of medieval England by 'the hammering out in the Courts of a common English law' to the unification of the British Empire in the modern era through the work of the Judicial Committee of the Privy Council.[17] More recent scholarship has focused on the Privy Council appeal as an agent of globalisation.[18]

Although the role of the Privy Council appeal as a 'sheet-anchor of Imperial unity' was widely publicised, it was not without critics in the early twentieth century as the self-governing Dominions grew in power and confidence.[19] Some commentators concluded that if uniformity in the sphere of law was really desirable it would be better to achieve this by means of consultation than to have it imposed by a judicial body.[20] This source of criticism was particularly relevant in relation to the body of statute law known as 'Imperial legislation' that was passed by the parliament at Westminster for the colonies and Dominions of the British Empire.[21] This Imperial legislation enjoyed superior

---

14   HUGHES: *op. cit.*, 101–102.
15   Cf. G.W. BARTHOLOMEW, J.A. ILIFFE: *Decisions*, International and Comparative Law Quarterly, 1(1952)/3, 392–399, J.N.D. ANDERSON: *Waqfs in East Africa*, Journal of African Law, 3(1959)/3, 152–164 and Kenneth ROBERTS-WRAY: *Commonwealth and Colonial Law*, Stevens, London, 1966, 461.
16   HUGHES: *op. cit.*, 101–102.
17   A.F. POLLARD: *The Commonwealth at War* quoted in H. Duncan HALL: *The British Commonwealth of Nations*, Methuen, London, 1920, 266–267.
18   For example, cf. IBHAWOH: *op. cit.*
19   National Archives of Ireland, Department of Foreign Affairs, file 3/1, draft speech on *Abolition of Appeals to the Privy Council*, undated 1933.
20   HUGHES: *op. cit.*, 102.
21   Analysis of the different types of Imperial statutes in existence in the early twentieth century can be found in Thomas MOHR: *British Imperial Statutes and Irish Law – Imperial Statutes passed before the creation of Irish Free State*, Journal of Legal History, 31(2010)/3, 308–309.

status to local colonial or Dominion laws. A Canadian legal commentator concluded, 'the value of the appeal to the Privy Council does not lie so much in the enforcement of a common view ... as in its special power to enforce the supremacy of Imperial legislation'.[22]

The supremacy of Imperial legislation over local laws was maintained by common law and by an important Imperial statute known as the Colonial Laws Validity Act 1865. The Judicial Committee of the Privy Council maintained this position of supremacy by invalidating local laws on the basis of incompatibility with Imperial statutes that extended to the relevant colony or Dominion. By the dawn of the twentieth century the Privy Council proved increasingly reluctant to use this legal sledgehammer in relation to the self-governing Dominions. Yet reluctance should not be confused with obsolescence. For example, in 1926 the Privy Council enforced the supremacy of Imperial legislation in the controversial Canadian case of *Nadan v. The King* which resulted in a provision of the Canadian Criminal Code being declared void and inoperative.[23] This court also acted as guardian and final arbiter of the 1921 'Articles of Agreement for a Treaty' that underpinned the foundation of the Irish Free State.[24] The Privy Council was empowered to strike down any Irish law that violated these 'Articles of Agreement for a Treaty' which were enshrined in an Imperial statute.[25] Some commentators have even argued that the practice of judicial review in many parts of the former British Empire has its roots in the function of the Judicial Committee of the Privy Council in striking down local laws that were inconsistent with Imperial legislation.[26]

The role of the Judicial Committee of the Privy Council as a pillar of Imperial unity was often publicised by colourful descriptions of the diversity of litigants that appeared before this Imperial court. In the early twentieth century Lord Haldane described entering the court chamber 'in company with white men, some of whom look as if they had come from the far West, and may be of American appearance; yellow men, some of whom come from Hong Kong; Burmese, who come from Burma; Hindus and Mohammedans from

---

22 E.R. Cameron, quoted in The Republic of Ireland, 3 April 1922. A.B. Keith wrote that the Privy Council 'possesses the highest authority on the prerogative of the Crown and it upholds the supremacy of Imperial legislation over Dominion enactments'. Quoted in HUGHES: *op. cit.*, 12.
23 [1926] 2 DLR 177 and [1926] AC 482.
24 Cf. MOHR: *Guardian of the Treaty...*, *op. cit.*
25 See Preamble, Irish Free State Constitution Act 1922 (UK) and Section 2 of the Constitution of the Irish Free State (Saorstát Éireann) Act 1922 (Irl).
26 Edward MCWHINNEY: *Judicial Review in the English-Speaking World*, University of Toronto Press, Toronto, 1956, 14, 58–59.

India; Dutch from South Africa; a mixed race from Ceylon-all sorts of people may be straying in there, and you will feel yourself in good Imperial company'.[27] The question of whether Imperial unity might be bolstered by a corresponding diversity among the judges who sat on the Judicial Committee of the Privy Council proved to be more difficult. Successive British governments and the Judicial Committee itself did make determined efforts throughout the nineteenth and twentieth centuries to create greater diversity in terms of judicial representation. Nevertheless, a number of considerations, including formidable barriers of distance and expense, ensured that the Judicial Committee of the Privy Council was always dominated by judges from the United Kingdom. Distance and expense were not the only barriers in a multi-racial Empire that included the populous sub-continent of India. The governments of the self-governing Dominions, many of which severely limited non-white immigration, had little enthusiasm for seeing significant numbers of Asian judges hearing appeals from their courts. For example, Sir Robert Borden, prime minister of Canada from 1911 to 1920, made it clear to British officials that Canada could not accept a court that heard Canadian appeals in which Hindus or Muslims held equal status with the other judges.[28]

In 1909 Syed Ameer Ali became the first native Indian judge to sit on the Judicial Committee of the Privy Council.[29] Although the multi-racial nature of the litigants who appeared before the Judicial Committee was often celebrated, a multi-racial judiciary was an entirely different matter.[30] In the case of Ameer Ali religion proved to be a greater barrier than race. Ameer Ali, a Muslim, was privately accused of judicial bias in favour of other Muslims who found themselves engaged in litigation with persons of other faiths.[31] These allegations are worthy of further investigation, but the large number of appeals from India ensured the continuation of appointing Indian judges to the Judicial Committee of the Privy Council. For example, Dinshah Fardunji Mulla was appointed to the court in 1930. He, along with Ameer Ali, has been praised for playing a crucial role 'in bringing indigenous perspectives to the jurisprudence of the JCPC, particularly in terms of their expertise and interpretations of Hindu and Islamic law'.[32] However, Mulla himself was neither a Hindu nor a Muslim but a Parsi. It would be fascinating to learn more about reactions to his

---

27 R.B. HALDANE: *The Work for the Empire of the Judicial Committee of the Privy Council*, Cambridge Law Journal 1(1922)/2, 144.
28 TNA, LCO 2/3464, memorandum by Claud Schuster, 10 July 1923.
29 IBHAWOH: *op. cit.*, 151–152.
30 HALDANE: *op. cit.*, 144.
31 TNA, LCO 2/533, Claud Schuster to George Coldstream, 7 Dec. 1954.
32 IBHAWOH: *op. cit.*, 152.

appointment in India and reactions to his interpretations of law among Hindus and Muslims. By contrast to India, the relatively small number of African appeals to the Judicial Committee of the Privy Council ensured that no African judge, with the exception of white South Africans, sat on the court until 1962 by which time most African colonies had achieved or were on the way towards achieving independence.[33] In short, the composition of the Judicial Committee of the Privy Council, local reactions to particular appointments and lack of representation from large parts of the Empire all merit further investigation.

The policy of Imperial unity was sometimes seen as underpinning one of the Judicial Committee's most notable idiosyncrasies as a court of law. This was a rule established in the seventeenth century that only a single unified judgment could be delivered, while any dissenting judgments could not be made public.[34] The votes of the judges on every decision were carefully recorded, although many of these records were lost during German bombing in the Second World War.[35] This policy had the great advantage of ensuring that differences of opinions between judges from different parts of the Empire were not vulnerable to use by nationalist interests. Nevertheless, despite a regime of strict secrecy, dissenting judgments did leak out on a number of occasions and caused considerable embarrassment.[36] The policy itself was a cause of division and some judges even refused to sit on Privy Council appeals as long as this rule was maintained.[37]

3 The Privy Council as Overseer of Systems of Federal and Devolved Government

Perceptions of the Privy Council appeal as a source of Imperial unity were complemented by claims that it also acted as a source of local unity. For

---

[33] In 1962 Adetokunbo Ademola, a Nigerian judge, was appointed to the Judicial Committee of the Privy Council. *Ibid.*

[34] This rule was established by Order in Council of 22 February 1627 and confirmed by Order in Council of 4 February 1878. A.B. KEITH: *Responsible Government in the Dominions*, vol. 3, Clarendon Press, Oxford, 1912, 1376.

[35] HOWELL: *op. cit.*, 203–204. Cf. also Alan C. CAIRNS: *The Judicial Committee and its Critics*, Canadian Journal of Political Science, 4(1971)/3, 331–332, 345.

[36] HOWELL: *op. cit.*, 201–203.

[37] HOWELL: *op. cit.*, 222–223. Cf. also Sir Josiah H. SYMON: *Australia and the Privy Council*, Journal of Comparative Legislation and International Law, 4(1922)/4, 147. On the perceived disadvantages of the practice of delivering a single judgment cf. A.B. KEITH: *Responsible Government in the Dominions*, 2nd ed., vol. 2, Clarendon Press, Oxford, 1928, 1104–1105. Cf. also SWINFEN: *op. cit.*, 221–246.

example, one of the leading historical accounts of the Privy Council appeal in North America concludes that the appeal was an important source of unity between the colonies that would later form the United States of America.[38] The Privy Council appeal was, after all, one of the few institutions held in common by the thirteen colonies before the declaration of independence in 1776. Historical accounts of the appeal in British India often credit it as being an important source of internal unity. One Indian commentator concludes 'the Privy Council gave national character to our law in contradiction to local character which differed from place to place in different parts of the country'.[39] Another commentator adds 'At a time when there was no link between the various Sadar Courts, Supreme Courts, and the High Courts in India, and when they could interpret the law differently from one another, the Privy Council provided a unifying force, a connecting link between them'.[40] The image of the Judicial Committee of the Privy Council as a 'great unifying force' has proven to be an important counterweight to less complementary assessments of its place in the legal history of India.[41]

The theme of maintaining unity also proved important with respect to maintaining the integrity of the federal unions that existed within the Empire. One of the key features of the Privy Council appeal in the late nineteenth and early twentieth centuries was its role in interpreting the division of powers between the provincial and Dominion governments and legislatures in Canada after 1867 and the state and federal governments and legislatures in Australia.[42] Analogies were often drawn between the positions of the Privy Council and the US Supreme Court which continues to perform a similar function in the United States of America.[43]

The Privy Council was also intended to serve as the arbiter of the limits of autonomy under the bills of 1886 and 1893 and the acts of 1914 and 1920 designed to give Ireland a devolved parliament within the United Kingdom,

---

38   Loren P. BETH: *The Judicial Committee of the Privy Council and the Development of Judicial Review*, American Journal of Comparative Law, 24(1976)/1, 42.
39   Mahendra P. SINGH: *Outlines of Indian Legal & Constitutional History*, Universal, New Delhi, 2006, 103.
40   S.S. SHILWANT: *Legal and Constitutional History of India*, Sanjay Prakashan, New Delhi, 2003, 221–222.
41   Cf. SINGH: *op. cit.*, 104 and SHILWANT: *op. cit.*, 220–222.
42   Lord Haldane, a leading judge of the Judicial Committee of the Privy Council, admitted that the court followed a policy of granting leave to appeal more freely with respect to parts of the Empire that adhered to a federal model than the strict approach taken with respect to unitary states. *Hull v. McKenna* [1926] IR, 405.
43   BENTWICH: *op. cit.*, 394.

a policy known as 'home rule'.[44] In the early twentieth century Irish home rule was sometimes mooted as the first stage in a federal settlement that would see the creation of new parliaments in England, Wales and Scotland in addition to Ireland.[45] Irish home rule never became reality and instead the island was divided between two self-governing entities by 1922. Northern Ireland became an autonomous part of the United Kingdom while the Irish Free State, located in the south and west of the island, became a self-governing Dominion within the Empire.[46] Proposals for Irish unification based on a federal settlement were mooted in the 1920s and 1930s, with the Privy Council serving as the final arbiter of the division of powers, but these never became reality.[47] However, the Judicial Committee did become the arbiter of devolution settlements within the United Kingdom itself in the late twentieth century. In the 1990s the Privy Council was empowered to hear appeals relating to the devolution of powers to legislative assemblies in Scotland, Wales and Northern Ireland before this power of jurisdiction was eventually transferred to the new Supreme Court of the United Kingdom in 2009.[48]

The role of the Privy Council as the overseer of federal settlements damaged the appeal in the eyes of some Canadians and Australians in the nineteenth and twentieth centuries. The perception that the Privy Council tended to favour the provinces in Canada and the states in Australia at the expense of the federal institutions proved to be an important consideration in campaigns to abolish the Privy Council appeal from these Dominions.[49] An early attempt at

---

44 Sections 25 and 36 of the Irish Government Bill 1886; Sections 22 and 23 of the Irish Government Bill 1893; Sections 28, 29 and 30 of the Government of Ireland Act 1914 and Sections 49 to 53 of the Government of Ireland Act 1920 (UK).
45 John KENDLE: *Ireland and the Federal Solution – The Debate over the United Kingdom Constitution, 1870–1921*, McGill-Queen's University Press, Kingston, 1989.
46 Articles 1 and 2 of the Articles of Agreement for a Treaty between Great Britain and Ireland. See Schedule, Irish Free State (Agreement) Act 1922 (UK).
47 Cf. e.g. Irish Times, 19 February 1929.
48 Scotland Act 1998; Government of Wales Act 1998 and Northern Ireland Act 1998 (UK). The Supreme Court of the United Kingdom was established under Part 3 of the Constitutional Reform Act 2005 (UK).
49 For example, cf. McWHINNEY: *op. cit.*, 51–52, 64–75. In Canada this perception of the appeal as a safeguard for minorities was augmented by Privy Council decisions that supported provincial autonomy. For example, *Attorney General for Ontario v. Attorney General for Canada* [1896] AC 348 and *Attorney General for Ontario v. Attorney General for Canada* [1937] AC 326. Many of the most notable decisions in this area were made by Lord Watson whose role in shaping Canadian constitutional law is discussed in David SCHNEIDERMAN: *A. V. Dicey, Lord Watson, and the Law of the Canadian Constitution in the Late Nineteenth Century*, Law and History Review, 16(1998)/3, 495–523. The Canadian experience appears to have influenced opinions in Australia on the Privy Council appeal. For

abolition in Canada in the 1870s proved unsuccessful[50] while a similar effort in Australia in 1900 was also defeated.[51] In both cases the provinces and states threw their political weight behind the Privy Council appeal and so ensured its continuation in Canada and Australia for decades to come. The Privy Council appeal was finally abolished in Canada in 1949 and in Australia in 1986.[52]

The role of the Privy Council as the arbiter of federal settlements even extended to settling boundary disputes between the constituent parts of the Empire. For example, the Privy Council settled boundary disputes between Victoria and New South Wales in 1872[53] and between Manitoba and Ontario in 1885.[54] This role inevitably rendered the Privy Council vulnerable to condemnation and resentment by those unhappy with the final determination made on the location of the border. A good example is the Privy Council's 1927 determination of the Labrador boundary between Canada and Newfoundland.[55] This was not a federal matter at the time of this decision because Newfoundland was a separate self-governing Dominion in 1927 and would not become the 10th province of Canada until 1949. This boundary remains controversial as th final determination by the Privy Council heavily favoured the interests of Newfoundland at the expense of the French-speaking Canadian province of Quebec.[56]

The Privy Council also played a minor role in the creation of the boundary commission that was intended to revise the border established between the Catholic-dominated Irish Free State and Protestant-dominated Northern Ireland.[57] The decisions made by the Privy Council in this dispute, coupled with the eventual collapse of the Boundary Commission in 1925, did nothing to

---

example, the High Court of Australia stated that it was 'common knowledge' when the Australian Constitution was being drafted that 'the decisions of the Judicial Committee in Canadian cases had not given widespread satisfaction'. *Baxter v. Commissioners of Taxation, New South Wales* (1907) 4 CLR 1087 at 1111. Cf. also HOWELL: *op. cit.*, 81–87.

50   SWINFEN: *op. cit.*, 27–28, 45–49.
51   MOHR: *Guardian of the Treaty...*, *op. cit.*, 14–15.
52   *Ibid.* 13–15. Cf. also Act to Amend the Supreme Court Act 1949 (Can) and the Australia Act 1986 (Aus).
53   W. Harrison MOORE: *The Case of Pental Island*, Law Quarterly Review, 20(1904)/3, 236–244. The Privy Council also heard a boundary dispute between South Australia and Victoria but this was an appeal from the Australian High Court and not a reference under Section 4 of the Judicial Committee Act 1833 (UK). *South Australia v. Victoria* [1911] 12 CLR 667.
54   A.B. KEITH: *The Constitutional Law of the British Dominions*, Macmillan, London, 1933, 275.
55   (1927) 43 TLR 289.
56   Cf. e.g. Patrick MCGRATH: *A Layman's view of the Privy Council*, Dalhousie Review, 3(1927)/7, 291–301.
57   Cmd. 2214. Cf. also Cmd. 2155, 2166 and 2264.

enhance its reputation among Irish nationalists.[58] The Irish border remained unchanged, a position that remains controversial to this day.

4 Oversight of Economic Policy

The Privy Council was also seen as promoting British Imperial policy in the economic sphere in the nineteenth and early twentieth centuries. Key areas of economic activity such as merchant shipping and copyright were considered matters exclusively within the field of Imperial competence. These areas were regulated by special Imperial statutes passed at Westminster with the Judicial Committee of the Privy Council acting as final arbiter.[59]

It was often argued that the Privy Council appeal provided necessary reassurance for British firms to invest in the colonies and, in particular, in the self-governing Dominions.[60] It was argued that the court acted as a safeguard of British investors in Dominion securities or Dominion business undertakings by shielding them from reckless or irresponsible actions by local governments. Colonial secretary Joseph Chamberlain promoted this safeguard in 1900 while facing an initiative to abolish the Privy Council appeal from the embryonic Commonwealth of Australia. Chamberlain, in resisting the Australian move to abolish the appeal, argued that the British government felt obliged to consider this issue 'from the point of view of the very large class of persons interested in Australian securities or Australian undertakings who are domiciled in the United Kingdom'.[61]

The argument that the Privy Council appeal gave confidence to British investors by providing a measure of oversight over Dominion affairs by London was mirrored in other areas of law. For example, regulations made by the British Treasury under the authority of the Colonial Stock Act 1900 provided that a Dominion could only have its stocks admitted to the list of trustee securities in the United Kingdom on condition of formally agreeing that the British government had the right to exercise the power of 'disallowance', a special form of veto, over any Dominion legislation that could adversely affect the security.[62]

---

58   MOHR: *Guardian of the Treaty...*, op. cit., 52–54.
59   Cf. the Merchant Shipping Act 1894 and the Copyright Act 1911 (UK). Cf. also *Graves v. Gorrie* [1903] AC 496 and *Performing Right Society v Bray UDC* [1930] IR 509.
60   This resulted in claims from some quarters that the Privy Council favoured British moneyed interests over Dominion interests. For example, cf. HUGHES: *op. cit.,* 9, 94–100, 104–105, 126.
61   *Ibid.*, 99.
62   *British Parliamentary Papers, 1930*, Cmd. 3479, paragraph 25.

The Irish Free State, Canada and South Africa objected to this provision in 1929 on the basis that this aspect of Imperial policy was unwarranted and profoundly insulting to the Dominions.[63] The Irish Free State proposed replacing London's power of disallowance with an agreement that Dominion legislatures would guarantee by means of statute that they would not legislate to the detriment of stockholders.[64] Although individuals in the British government proved sympathetic to this argument,[65] the Treasury was adamant that the existing conditions remain in place.[66] The Treasury argued that the United Kingdom was free to insert any conditions she pleased when granting a financial privilege. Imperial oversight in this area remained intact.[67]

Critics argued that Imperial policies in the economic sphere, as reflected in the Colonial Stock Act and in perceptions of the economic role of the Privy Council appeal, created damaging impressions. These policies suggested that the United Kingdom could not trust the legislatures and courts of the self-governing Dominions to act responsibly. In addition, the image of the Privy Council as the protector of sectional interests damaged its reputation in some quarters. H. Duncan Hall, a noted Australian authority on Imperial and Commonwealth affairs, asserted that one of the main reasons behind the decision of the Australian Labour Party to campaign for the abolition of the Privy Council appeal 'was the desire to secure for the Australian people greater equality in matters of justice; and to enable them to exercise a firmer control over the absentee capitalist'.[68] Similar sentiments were evident in the Irish Free State where the controversial decision of the Privy Council in the 1926 case of *Lynham v. Butler* was widely, though inaccurately, perceived as being influenced by the desire to protect the interests of Irish landlords.[69] Further controversy followed in Canada in the 1930s when the Privy Council struck down key parts of the Canadian 'New Deal' designed to mitigate the impact of the Great Depression.[70]

---

63   Cf. also National Archives of Canada (NAC), Oscar Skelton Fonds, MG30 D33, Vol. 4, 4–1.
64   TNA, CAB 32/69, DL 3rd Meeting.
65   The attorney general Sir William Jowitt declared that he would be happy to see the disappearance of a power that might prove a source of political embarrassment. TNA, CAB 32/69, DL 3rd Meeting.
66   National Archives of Canada, Oscar Skelton Fonds, MG30 D33, Vol. 4, 4–1.
67   This area of law was finally reformed in the Colonial Stock Act 1934 (UK).
68   HALL: *op. cit.*, 270.
69   HUGHES: *op. cit.*, 99.
70   Cf. e.g. W.P.M. KENNEDY: *The British North America Act: Past and Future*, Canadian Bar Review, 15(1937)/6, 393–400; Vincent C. MACDONALD: *The Canadian Constitution Seventy Years After*, Canadian Bar Review, 15(1937)/6, 401–427; F.R. SCOTT: *The Consequences of the Privy Council Decisions*, Canadian Bar Review, 15(1937)/6, 485–494.

5   The Privy Council Appeal and Human Rights

By the early twentieth century a number of important decisions indicated a new role for the Privy Council in pushing a 'progressive' agenda from the centre to the peripheries of Empire. A good example is the 1920s case of *Attorney General for British Columbia v. Attorney General for Canada* in which the Privy Council invalidated immigration legislation passed by British Columbia that discriminated against Japanese migrants.[71] Another example is the Privy Council's decision in the Kenyan case of *R v. Kuruma*, which is often seen as laying the foundations of the principle of excluding prejudicial evidence in criminal trials throughout much of the former territories of the British Empire, although this falls slightly outside the time period of this analysis.[72]

The most celebrated instance of the Privy Council advancing a human rights agenda in the early twentieth century concerns the Canadian case of *Edwards v. Attorney General of Canada*, better known as the 'Persons Case'.[73] This case concerned whether the term 'persons' used in the British North America Act 1867 in the context of eligibility to sit in the Canadian senate could be interpreted to include women. The Judicial Committee of the Privy Council overruled the Canadian Supreme Court to hold that women could be considered 'persons' in this context and so could sit in the Canadian senate.[74] This case is celebrated in legal circles for establishing what is known as the 'living tree doctrine', that the interpretation of a constitution should adapt to the circumstances and values of the present.[75] This image of the Privy Council propagating a 'progressive doctrine' is reflected in impressive memorials to this decision in several parts of Canada including Olympic Plaza, Calgary and Parliament Hill, Ottawa. The decision was also commemorated on a Canadian $50 bill that circulated between 2004 and 2012.

The perceived role of the Privy Council as the protector of minority communities was celebrated throughout the nineteenth and twentieth centuries.

---

71   [1924] AC 203.
72   [1955] AC 197. Other important appeals concerning the development of the law of evidence include *Mahlikilili Dhalamini v. The King* [1942] AC 583 and *R v. Ndembera* (1947) 14 EACA 85.
73   [1930] AC 124.
74   The reality that the word 'person' could not be interpreted to implicitly include males and females in the period is evident in the provisions of Article 3 of the 1922 Constitution of the Irish Free State which provides 'Every person, without distinction of sex, domiciled in the area of the jurisdiction of the Irish Free State …'.
75   BENTWICH: *op. cit.*, 394.

These included the French-speaking population of Canada, the English-speakers of South Africa, the Protestant population of the Irish Free State and the New Zealand Maoris. The Judicial Committee of the Privy Council was also perceived as the guarantor of the rights of vulnerable majorities. This was of particular relevance to native communities living in parts of southern Africa that were ruled by white minorities.

The role of the Privy Council as a neutral arbiter in internal colonial and Dominion conflicts could be used to bolster claims that this Imperial court was an essential pillar in maintaining Imperial unity. However, the perception of this Imperial court as the 'protector' of minority or vulnerable communities did create hostile reactions among the dominant communities that threatened the survival of the Privy Council appeal. For example, the governments of the Irish Free State protested in the 1920s and 1930s that there was no real necessity for the Privy Council to safeguard the rights of the Protestant minority living in its territory. Successive Irish governments circulated unconvincing and self-interested arguments that only a tiny portion of the Protestant minority really desired the appeal.[76] In addition, the very idea of minority protection enforced by an external court was deemed offensive to the majority Catholic community who wished to abolish the appeal. W.T. Cosgrave, the first prime minister of the Irish Free State, deplored a situation in which 'a minority of 7½ per cent should be entitled to prevent the wishes of the remaining 92½ from being realised'.[77] Nevertheless, attempts made by Irish governments to enlist support from Canada in initiatives aimed at limiting or abolishing the Privy Council appeal in the 1920s and 1930s proved unsuccessful. This surprised many Irish statesmen as Canada had supported the Irish Free State in other important proposals aimed at enhancing Dominion autonomy.[78] Nevertheless, Canadian governments were unwilling to identify themselves with moves to abolish the Privy Council appeal as long as this institution was supported by its French-speaking minority.[79]

The Irish Free State abolished its appeal to the Privy Council in the 1930s and became the first Dominion to take this fateful step.[80] The consequences

---

76 Thomas MOHR: *The Privy Council appeal as a minority safeguard for the Protestant community of the Irish Free State, 1922–1935*, Northern Ireland Legal Quarterly, 63(2012)/3, 365–395.
77 National Archives of Ireland, Department of the Taoiseach S4285B, Cosgrave to Granard, 8 November 1930.
78 MOHR: *Guardian of the Treaty...*, op. cit., 92–97.
79 Cf. e.g. A.B. KEITH: *Responsible Government...* (1928), op. cit., vol. 2, 1230.
80 Constitution (Amendment No. 22) Act 1933 (Irl) and *Moore v. Attorney-General for the Irish Free State* [1935] IR 472 and [1935] AC 484.

facing the Privy Council appeal when seen as threatening the interests of a dominant community were also illustrated after the conclusion of the Second World War. For example, the prospect of the Privy Council adjudicating on laws concerning racial status in South Africa proved to be a rallying cry for those in the white community who wished to abolish the appeal.[81] The aftermath of the 1948 South African election saw the official adoption of the policy of apartheid. It was no coincidence that the abolition of the Privy Council appeal followed less than two years later.[82] The Privy Council was also perceived as the protector of the black majority living in the British colony of Southern Rhodesia, particularly after 1965 when the dominant white minority unilaterally declared the independence of the colony under the name of 'Rhodesia'.[83] The role maintained by the Privy Council in the years that followed, in delivering decisions seen as favouring the position of the black majority in addition to its non-recognition of Rhodesian independence, led the Rhodesian government to officially abolish the appeal in 1969.[84]

6 Conclusion

No global history of the Privy Council appeal can be written without a considerable expansion of secondary sources on which a potential author or authors can build. One approach is to call for more accounts of the operation of the appeal in the context of particular jurisdictions or regions of the world. Such works are useful but this approach would be slow when dealing with entities as vast and diverse as the British Empire and Commonwealth and uneven coverage is likely to remain for some time to come. A black letter approach, that explores the appeal in terms of particular law subjects, has merits but is likely to miss political considerations that cannot be divorced from the wider history of the appeal. It may be that explorations of key themes in terms of policy and

---

81   TNA, LCO 2/3465 WH Clark, High Commissioner to J.H. Thomas, 25 Mar. 1935.
82   Privy Council Appeals Act 1950 (SA).
83   This should not be seen as suggesting that native litigants were always successful before the Privy Council. The Ndebele and Shona tribes were unsuccessful in asserting land rights in *In re Southern Rhodesia* [1919] AC 211. Lord Sumner's conclusions as to the land rights of indigenous peoples ([1919] AC 211 at 233) can be contrasted with a more recent Australian judgment in *Mabo v. Queensland (No. 2)* [1992] HCA 23; (1992) 175 CLR 1.
84   Section 62 of the Rhodesia Act 1969 (Rhod). Cf. Thomas MOHR: *A British Empire Court: An Appraisal of the History of the Judicial Committee of the Privy Council*, Anthony MCELLIGOT et al. (eds.), *Power in History: Historical Studies XXVII*, Irish Academic, Dublin, 2011, 130–132.

perception would prove to be a particularly useful approach in providing firm foundations for a general history. This chapter has attempted to identify some key themes that merit further investigation in their own right in addition to building solid foundations for wider scholarly works. These policy objectives are closely connected with the common themes of legal instrumentalism, modernisation and national identity that run through this book. A number of conclusions can be presented with respect to the role of the Judicial Committee of the Privy Council in maintaining and enforcing key Imperial policies in the nineteenth and early twentieth centuries. Conclusions and proposals for future exploration relating to policies concerning Imperial unity, federalism, economic policy and human rights will be examined in turn.

The perceived role of the Privy Council as an instrument of maintaining Imperial unity declined, at least with respect to the self-governing Dominions, in the aftermath of the enactment of the 1931 Statute of Westminster. This statute saw the British government abandon the longstanding policy of enforcing the supremacy of Imperial statutes over Dominion laws.[85] Dominion nationalists had long attacked the need to retain substantial uniformity of laws within the Empire. Nevertheless, most supporters of greater Dominion autonomy acknowledged the desirability of maintaining uniformity in some key areas of law, for example in the field of maritime law. They argued that uniformity in such important areas of law should, on principle, be maintained by means of consultation rather than being enforced by an Imperial court.[86] This new approach was reflected in the Commonwealth Merchant Shipping Agreement of 1931, a voluntary agreement that replaced the supremacy of Imperial legislation in this area of law.[87] The enactment of the Statute of Westminster in 1931 was not intended to reverse the policy of retaining legal uniformity, at least in those areas of law in which uniformity was deemed essential, but did reverse the policy of using the Judicial Committee of the Privy Council as a means of enforcing such uniformity.

The abandonment of an overall policy of retaining legal uniformity after 1931 did not have immediate effect thanks to the reluctance of most of the Dominions to accept the full impact of the Statute of Westminster.[88] Yet this

---

[85] Section 2, Statute of Westminster Act 1931 (UK).
[86] HUGHES: *op. cit.*, 102.
[87] Section 5 of the Statute of Westminster had removed certain limitations on the power of the Dominion Parliaments to legislate in relation to merchant shipping. These limitations were reflected in Sections 735 and 736 of the Merchant Shipping Act 1894 (UK).
[88] The most important provisions of the Statute, Sections 2 to 6, were not adopted by Australia until 1942 and New Zealand until 1947. See Statute of Westminster Adoption Act 1942 (Aus.) and Statute of Westminster Adoption Act 1947 (NZ). These provisions never

gradual transition only exacerbated the sense of uncertainty in this area. In the decades that followed the Privy Council found itself attempting an awkward balancing act in enforcing uniformity in some areas of law while tolerating diversity in others.[89] The court has received praise in Australia for adroitly maintaining this balancing act. It would be interesting to learn how this unenviable position was maintained in other parts of the world.

The long-standing rule that the Judicial Committee of the Privy Council deliver a single judgment while keeping any dissenting opinions away from public scrutiny was finally abandoned in 1966.[90] This rule was the subject of sustained debate throughout the nineteenth and early twentieth centuries and provides considerable potential for future scholarship. Regional differences of opinion on this rule are of particular interest. For example, consultation on the possibility of removing the single judgment rule in 1912 revealed that there was a lack of consensus even within particular Dominions. In Canada the provinces of Ontario, Quebec, Prince Edward Island, New Brunswick and Saskatchewan favored the publication of dissenting judgments while British Columbia and Alberta had no objection to the change. However, Nova Scotia and Manitoba supported the continuance of the single judgment rule. The absence of consensus between the provinces on reform ensured that the Canadian government favored the maintenance of the status quo and the single judgement rule survived for another half century.[91] The reasons behind these differences of opinion are worthy of greater attention.

The association of national identity with judicial sovereignty played a key role in the decline of the jurisdiction of the Judicial Committee of the Privy Council in all regions of the world during the twentieth century. In 1965 the

---

applied to Newfoundland as a separate Dominion. Newfoundland ceased to be self-governing as a consequence of a financial serious crisis in 1933. Canada agreed that its Constitution, at that time composed of Imperial legislation, would remain unaffected by the provisions of the Statute. See Section 7(1) of the Statute of Westminster Act 1931. South Africa passed a parliamentary resolution that attempted to protect certain entrenched provisions within its Constitution, the South Africa Act, 1909, from the impact of the Statute. Manley O. HUDSON: *Notes on the Statute of Westminster, 1931*, Harvard Law Review 46(1932), 266. No equivalent action to exempt the 1922 Irish Constitution, or key aspects of it, from the impact of the Statute was ever untaken by the Irish parliament. Cf. Thomas MOHR: *The Statute of Westminster, 1931 – An Irish Perspective*, Law and History Review 31(2013)/1, 749–791.

89 Oliver JONES: *Public Prosecutor v Oie Hee Koi (1968): Not so Humbly Advising? Sir Garfield Barwick and the Introduction of Dissenting Reasons to the Judicial Committee of the Privy Council = Great Australian Dissents*, Andrew LYNCH (ed.), Cambridge University Press, Cambridge (UK) 2018, 121.

90 Judicial Committee (Dissenting Opinions) Order, 1966 (S.I. 1966, No. 1100).

91 TNA, LCO 2/3464, Report of the Privy Council of Canada, 8 Oct. 1912.

attorney general of Kenya, Charles Njonjo, acknowledged this reality when he stated 'Although the Judicial Committee of the Privy Council is a court of very high legal standing, it is not our court ... it is my personal view that continuing appeals to the Judicial Committee of the Privy Council would not be in keeping with the dignity of our Republic'.[92] This rise in nationalist sentiment could be seen as the primary reason for the decline in the jurisdiction of the Judicial Committee of the Privy Council.[93] Yet, the utility of a comparative approach to examining the relationship between the Privy Council appeal and national identity goes beyond local reasons for abolishing the appeal. Additional areas of further study in this area include examination of national and regional reactions to appointments to the Judicial Committee of the Privy Council. Proposed reforms such as making the Judicial Committee of the Privy Council an itinerant court also merit further investigation.[94] The failure of proposed alternatives to the Privy Council appeal, for example the attempt to create a Commonwealth Tribunal at the 1930 Imperial Conference, might also deserve some attention.[95] Comparisons with other courts inevitably meet challenges based on the comparison of very different legal systems. However, the longevity of the Judicial Committee of the Privy Council ensures that comparisons over differing periods of time are not a barrier. This ensures that the Privy Council appeal can be compared with the courts of other European colonial powers and with post-colonial regional courts such as the East African Court of Justice, the Court of Justice of the Economic Community of West African States and the Caribbean Court of Justice.

Those who argued that the decisions of the Privy Council tended to hamper the emergence of strong central governments in the Dominions of Canada and Australia often condemned its role as overseer of federal settlements within the Empire. However, the role of the Privy Council as guardian of the rights of the Canadian provinces and, in particular, in safeguarding the rights of the French-speaking province of Quebec has also been credited with maintaining the unity of the Dominion of Canada. Pierre Trudeau, prime minister of

---

92 Quoted in Oliver JONES: *A worthy predecessor? The Privy Council on appeal from Hong Kong, 1853–1997* = *Hong Kong's Court of Final Appeal*, Simon N.M. YOUNG, Yash P. GHAI (eds.), Cambridge University Press, Cambridge (UK), 2013, 102.

93 E.g., MOHR: *Guardian of the Treaty...*, op. cit., 150–155.

94 Cf. e.g. SWINFEN: op. cit., 178–220. Cf. also Rohit DE: *A Peripatetic World Court' Cosmopolitan Courts, Nationalist Judges and the Indian Appeal to the Privy Council*, Law and History Review, 32(2014)/4, 821–851.

95 Cf. Report of the Conference on the Operation of Dominion Legislation and Merchant Shipping Legislation, 1929, Cmd. 3479, para. 125 and Imperial Conference 1930, Cmd. 3717, 22–24.

Canada, argued that without the Privy Council's support for provincial autonomy 'Quebec separation might not be a threat today; it might be an accomplished fact'.[96]

The attitudes of minority communities in the British Empire and later in the Commonwealth towards the Privy Council appeal represent an important field for future research. Even if hard evidence of these attitudes proves elusive the perceptions of majority communities as to the attitudes of their respective minority communities are themselves worthy of investigation. The wealth of material on the attitudes of the Protestant community of the Irish Free State towards the appeal has ensured that it has already attracted some attention.[97] Similar analyses of the attitudes of the Maori community of New Zealand might yield interesting results. The perceived support of this community for the appeal is often credited as an important factor that extended the longevity of the appeal in New Zealand, which only moved to abolish the appeal in 2003.[98] The importance of Canada in the history of the British Empire and Commonwealth ensures that attitudes among the French-Canadian population in the nineteenth and twentieth centuries are of particular interest. This community included the veteran nationalist Henri Bourassa (1868–1952) who always denied the argument that the appeal represented a real minority safeguard and insisted that 'the Judicial Committee of the Privy Council is not primarily a tribunal, but a semi-political, semi-judicial body'.[99] This community also contained Louis-Philippe Brodeur (1862–1924), a judge of the Canadian Supreme Court, who once praised the appeal by admitting that 'litigants prefer sometimes to come before the Privy Council rather than go before the Supreme Court of Canada'.[100] Did the attitude of most French-Canadians in this period fall somewhere between these two extremes?

The policy arguments that saw the promotion of the Privy Council appeal in the Dominions as an instrument that provided necessary reassurance for British investment had unfortunate consequences. They created an image of

---

96 Peter W. HOGG: *Canada: From Privy Council to Supreme Court* = *Interpreting Constitutions: A Comparative Study*, Jeffrey GOLDSWORTHY (ed.), Oxford University Press, Oxford, 2006, 76.

97 MOHR: *Guardian of the Treaty...*, op. cit.

98 Sections 42 and 50, Supreme Court Act 2003 (NZ). Cf. e.g. Megan RICHARDSON: *The Privy Council and New Zealand*, International and Comparative Law Quarterly, 46(1997), 908–918 and John William TATE: *Hohepa Wi Neera: Native Title and the Privy Council Challenge*, Victoria University of Wellington Law Review, 35(2004), 73–115.

99 W.P.M. KENNEDY: *The Imperial Conferences, 1926–1930*, Law Quarterly Review, 48(1932), 207.

100 TNA, CO 886/5B, meeting of 12 June 1911.

the Judicial Committee of the Privy Council as 'the representative and protector of either large vested interests or monied interests, particularly in England'.[101] This policy argument was also used to support accusations, particularly in the Irish Free State, that the Privy Council was biased in favour of British firms and creditors.[102] Similar impressions of bias towards British commercial interests were also evident when an Australian judge, Sir Ninian Stephen who would later become Governor General of Australia, accused the Privy Council of acting 'in the interests of the great fleet-owning nations' in merchant shipping cases.[103] If such impressions existed among the white self-governing Dominions there is surely a case for examining similar attitudes within the British colonies of the nineteenth or twentieth centuries where the potential for complaint was far greater.

The perceived role of the Judicial Committee of the Privy Council as a progressive and modernising human rights court in the early twentieth century years gained new prominence with the growth of interest in this field after the horrors of the Second World War. The Privy Council was even promoted as a model of an international court of human rights in the immediate aftermath of the conflict.[104] There is no doubt that this court became more and more concerned with the maintenance of human rights as the twentieth century progressed, a concern that outlived its role as a pillar of Imperial unity and outlived the very existence of the British Empire itself. Yet, the emergence of the Privy Council appeal as a perceived instrument of modernisation in the sphere of human rights has resulted in accusations that its decisions are out of touch with local values that are claimed to be integral aspects of national identity. It cannot be denied that the fortunes of the Privy Council have suffered in recent decades as a direct consequence of this role.

A good example of this trend is the decision in the Singaporean case of *Jeyaretnam v. Law Society of Singapore* that was delivered in 1988.[105] This appeal to the Privy Council followed a long series of hearings before local courts concerning criminal charges levelled against the sole opposition MP in Singapore.[106] The initial trial and a number of retrials before the Singaporean courts resulted in the imposition of a number of sanctions against the accused, but these did

---

101   HUGHES: *op. cit.*, 99.
102   *Ibid.*, 9, 94–100, 104–105, 126.
103   *Port Jackson Stevedoring v. Salmond and Spraggon* (1978) 139 CLR 231 at 258. Cf. also HALL: *op. cit.*, 269–270.
104   BENTWICH: *op. cit.*, 394.
105   [1989] AC 608 at 631–632.
106   Cf. JONES, *op. cit.*, 114–117.

not disqualify him from continuing to sit in parliament under Singaporean law. An additional retrial finally imposed a penalty that disqualified the accused from sitting in parliament and from continuing his previous profession as a solicitor. The case was finally appealed to the Judicial Committee of the Privy Council which expressed 'deep disquiet' and condemned the perceived abuses of process that had preceded the final decision of the Singaporean courts. Singapore reduced the scope of its appeal to the Privy Council in the aftermath of this decision and complete abolition soon followed.[107]

Engagement with human rights issues also undermined the Privy Council appeal in many of the island nations of the Caribbean in the 1990s. The decision in *Pratt and Morgan v. Attorney General of Jamaica*,[108] which placed limits on the imposition of capital punishment, was met with widespread complaints that the Privy Council was out of touch with the values of Caribbean nations where the death penalty enjoys significant support. The stance adopted by the Privy Council on this matter has resulted in many Caribbean nations initiating the process of abolishing the appeal.[109]

The beginning of a phased introduction of sharia law in the small East Asian county of Brunei in 2014 is likely to create new challenges for the Judicial Committee of the Privy Council as its final court of appeal. The jurisdiction of the Privy Council in relation to Brunei is limited to civil cases. Nevertheless, the potential for decisions based on human rights principles that are vulnerable to accusations of being out of touch with local values and conditions remains acute. In this context, the continuation of the Privy Council appeal in relation to Brunei may soon come under strain.

Accusations of being out of touch with local values were also evident during the heyday of the appeal in the late nineteenth and early twentieth centuries and were even made in the former Dominions in which the majority or a substantial part of the population were of British descent.[110] For example, the decision of the Privy Council to consider granting leave to appeal to Louis Riel, the messianic leader of the Métis rebellion in Saskatchewan in 1885, provoked outrage in English-speaking Canada. Riel was refused leave to appeal his conviction for treason, but the Canadian parliament still responded by attempting

---

107 Judicial Committee (Amendment) Act 1989 (Sing).
108 [1993] 4 All ER 769.
109 Cf. MOHR: *Guardian of the Treaty...*, op. cit., 136–137.
110 For example, cf. J.S. EWART: *Appeals to the Judicial Committee of the Privy Council – The Case for Discontinuing Appeals*, Queen's Quarterly 37(1930), 456–461.

to abolish criminal appeals to the Privy Council in an 1888 criminal code.[111] Criticism of the institution of the Privy Council appeal tended to reach new heights in the immediate aftermath of unpopular decisions and accusations of being a 'colonial relic' typically followed. The occasional delivery of an unpopular decision together with accusations of incompetence or being out of touch are, of course, the fate of any court of law. Yet it is unlikely that identical decisions by a local court would have provoked similar calls for abolition.

The outrage that followed unpopular decisions by the Privy Council and resulting accusations of incompetence or being out of touch were heightened by its nature as a court sitting in another jurisdiction and staffed by foreign judges. Decisions by the European Court of Human Rights demanding that the right to vote be provided to prisoners together with opposition to the extradition of clerics Abu Hamza and Abu Qatada have led to calls for the withdrawal of the United Kingdom from the jurisdiction of that court.[112] Before the 2016 Brexit referendum Theresa May, then home secretary, declared 'If we want to reform human rights laws in this country, it isn't the EU we should leave but the ECHR and the jurisdiction of its court'.[113] It should be remembered that the Judicial Committee of the Privy Council was promoted as a model for an international human rights court long before the creation of the European Court of Human Rights, the Council of Europe and many international human rights treaties.[114] This ensures that future analysis of the Privy Council appeal's role in promoting and enforcing human rights would not be limited to the historical sphere but would retain considerable contemporary relevance. The increasingly volatile circumstances of the early twenty first century render it prudent that international human rights institutions and courts be aware of the fate of the Privy Council appeal in many parts of the world.

Yet, the Judicial Committee of the Privy Council has always shown an ability to adapt and continuously reinvent itself that has allowed it to survive against all odds. Its impending doom has now been predicted by legal and political

---

111 *Riel v. The Queen* (1885) 10 AC 675. Section 1025, Canadian Criminal Code 1888, which purported to abolish appeals to the Privy Council in criminal cases, was eventually declared void on the grounds of incompatibility with Imperial legislation. *Nadan v. The King* [1926] 2 DLR 177 and [1926] AC 482.

112 Cf. Daily Telegraph, 25 April 2016 (telegraph.co.uk/news/2016/04/25/eu-referendum-uk-eu-migration-free-for-all-michael-gove-brexit/#update-20160425–1203, accessed 7 June 2016).

113 bbc.com/news/uk-politics-eu-referendum-36149798, accessed 10 May 2018.

114 BENTWICH: *op. cit.*, 392.

commentators for almost a century.[115] The Privy Council made a seamless transition from its role as pillar of the political and economic unity of the British Empire to acting as a neutral arbiter in a free Commonwealth and a champion of human rights values. This history is not yet complete and its evolution continues. As the appeal becomes increasingly limited to the British oversea territories, which have mostly become tax havens, it may further evolve into a court responsible for curbing the worst excesses of such regimes. Perhaps the most engaging study of all is the examination of the ability of the Judicial Committee of the Privy Council to thwart successive prophets predicting its imminent demise.

Bibliography

Archival Sources

National Archives of Canada, Oscar Skelton Fonds, MG 30 D33, Vol. 4, 4–1.
National Archives of Ireland, Department of Foreign Affairs, file 3/1.
National Archives of Ireland, Department of the Taoiseach S4285B.
National Archives of the United Kingdom, CAB 32/69.
National Archives of the United Kingdom, HO 45/20030.
National Archives of the United Kingdom, LCO 2/533.
National Archives of the United Kingdom, LCO 2/3464.
National Archives of the United Kingdom, LCO 2/3465.
National Archives of the United Kingdom, CO 886/5B.

Literature

J.N.D. ANDERSON: *Waqfs in East Africa*, Journal of African Law, 3(1959)/3, 152–164.
G.W. BARTHOLOMEW, J.A. ILIFFE: *Decisions*, International and Comparative Law Quarterly, 1(1952)/3, 392–399.
Norman BENTWICH: *The Judicial Committee of the Privy Council as a Model of an International Court of Human Rights*, International Law Quarterly, 2(1948)/3, 392–401.
Loren P. BETH: *The Judicial Committee of the Privy Council and the Development of Judicial Review*, American Journal of Comparative Law, 24(1976)/1, 22–42.
Alan C. CAIRNS: *The Judicial Committee and its Critics*, Canadian Journal of Political Science, 4(1971)/3, 301–345.
Daily Telegraph, 25 April 2016.

---

115 Cf. e.g. A.B. KEITH: *War Government in the British Dominions*, Clarendon Press, Oxford, 1921, 285–288.

Rohit DE: *A Peripatetic World Court' Cosmopolitan Courts, Nationalist Judges and the Indian Appeal to the Privy Council*, Law and History Review, 32(2014)/4, 821–851.

J.S. EWART: *Appeals to the Judicial Committee of the Privy Council – The Case for Discontinuing Appeals*, Queen's Quarterly, 37(1930), 456–461.

R.B. HALDANE: *The Work for the Empire of the Judicial Committee of the Privy Council*, Cambridge Law Journal, 1(1922)/2, 143–155.

H. Duncan HALL: *The British Commonwealth of Nations*, Methuen, London, 1920.

J.W. HARRIS: *The Privy Council and the Common Law*, Law Quarterly Review, 106(1990), 574–600.

Peter W. HOGG: *Canada: From Privy Council to Supreme Court = Interpreting Constitutions: A Comparative Study*, Jeffrey GOLDSWORTHY (ed.), Oxford University Press, Oxford, 2006, 55–105.

P.A. HOWELL: *The Judicial Committee of the Privy Council 1833–1876*, Cambridge University Press, Cambridge (UK), 1979.

Manley O. HUDSON: *Notes on the Statute of Westminster, 1931*, Harvard Law Review, 46(1932), 261–289.

Hector HUGHES: *National Sovereignty and Judicial Autonomy in the British Commonwealth of Nations*, PS King, London, 1931.

Bonny IBHAWOH: *Imperial Justice – Africans in Empire's Court*, Oxford University Press, Oxford, 2013.

Irish Times, 19 February 1929.

Oliver JONES: *Public Prosecutor v Oie Hee Koi (1968): Not so Humbly Advising? Sir Garfield Barwick and the Introduction of Dissenting Reasons to the Judicial Committee of the Privy Council = Great Australian Dissents*, Andrew LYNCH (ed.), Cambridge University Press, Cambridge (UK) 2018, 116–130.

Oliver JONES: *A worthy predecessor? The Privy Council on appeal from Hong Kong, 1853–1997 = Hong Kong's Court of Final Appeal*, Simon N.M. YOUNG, Yash P. GHAI (eds.), Cambridge University Press, Cambridge (UK), 2013, 94–118.

A.B. KEITH: *The Constitutional Law of the British Dominions*, Macmillan, London, 1933.

A.B. KEITH: *Dominion Autonomy in Practice*, Oxford University Press, London, 1929.

A.B. KEITH: *Responsible Government in the Dominions*, vol. 3, Clarendon Press, Oxford, 1912.

A.B. KEITH: *Responsible Government in the Dominions*, 2nd ed., vol. 2, Clarendon Press, Oxford, 1928.

A.B. KEITH: *War Government in the British Dominions*, Clarendon Press, Oxford, 1921.

John KENDLE: *Ireland and the Federal Solution – The Debate over the United Kingdom Constitution, 1870–1921*, McGill-Queen's University Press, Kingston, 1989.

W.P.M. KENNEDY: *The Imperial Conferences, 1926–1930*, Law Quarterly Review, 48(1932), 191–216.

W.P.M. KENNEDY: *The British North America Act: Past and Future*, Canadian Bar Review, 15(1937), 393–400.

Jacqueline D. KRIKORIAN: *International Trade Law and Domestic Policy – Canada, the United States and the WTO*, UBC Press, Vancouver, 2012.

Vincent C. MACDONALD: *The Canadian Constitution Seventy Years After*, Canadian Bar Review, 15(1937)/6, 401–427.

Patrick MCGRATH: *A Layman's view of the Privy Council*, Dalhousie Review, 3(1927)/7, 291–301.

Edward MCWHINNEY: *Judicial Review in the English-Speaking World*, University of Toronto Press, Toronto, 1956.

Thomas MOHR: *A British Empire Court: An Appraisal of the History of the Judicial Committee of the Privy Council*, Anthony MCELLIGOT et al. (eds.), *Power in History: Historical Studies* XXVII, Irish Academic, Dublin, 2011, 125–145.

Thomas MOHR: *British Imperial Statutes and Irish Law – Imperial Statutes passed before the creation of Irish Free State*, Journal of Legal History, 31(2010)/3, 61–85.

Thomas MOHR: *Guardian of the Treaty – The Privy Council Appeal and Irish Sovereignty*, Four Courts Press, Dublin, 2016.

Thomas MOHR: *The Privy Council appeal as a minority safeguard for the Protestant community of the Irish Free State, 1922–1935*, Northern Ireland Legal Quarterly, 63(2012)/3, 365–395.

Thomas MOHR: *The Statute of Westminster, 1931 – An Irish Perspective*, Law and History Review, 31(2013)/1, 749–791.

W. Harrison MOORE: *The Case of Pental Island*, Law Quarterly Review, 20(1904)/3, 236–244.

Thomas MUSGRAVE: *The Western Australian Secessionist Movement*, Macquarie Law Journal, 3(2003), 95–129.

Megan RICHARDSON: *The Privy Council and New Zealand*, International and Comparative Law Quarterly, 46(1997), 908–918.

Kenneth ROBERTS-WRAY: *Commonwealth and Colonial Law*, Stevens, London, 1966.

David SCHNEIDERMAN: *A.V. Dicey, Lord Watson, and the Law of the Canadian Constitution in the Late Nineteenth Century*, Law and History Review, 16(1998)/3, 495–523.

F.R. SCOTT: *The Consequences of the Privy Council Decisions*, Canadian Bar Review, 15(1937)/6, 485–494.

S.S. SHILWANT: *Legal and Constitutional History of India*, Sanjay Prakashan, New Delhi, 2003.

Mahendra P. SINGH: *Outlines of Indian Legal & Constitutional History*, Universal, New Delhi, 2006.

David SWINFEN: *Imperial Appeal – The Debate on the Appeal to the Privy Council, 1833–1986*, Manchester University Press, Manchester, 1987.

Josiah H. Symon: *Australia and the Privy Council*, Journal of Comparative Legislation and International Law, 4(1922), 137–151.

John William Tate: *Hohepa Wi Neera: Native Title and the Privy Council Challenge*, Victoria University of Wellington Law Review, 35(2004), 73–115.

The Times, 14 August 1933.

CHAPTER 6

Direct Impact on Hungarian Migration Policy of the 1870 Agreement on Citizenship between the United States and Austria-Hungary (1880s–1914)

Balázs Pálvölgyi

1 Introduction

The question of the national identity and the creation of a modern nation state became more and more crucial for Hungary and for the Hungarian elite in the framework of Austria-Hungary. After 1867, the Reconciliation with Vienna, the modernisation of the Hungarian legal system was of first importance. Of course, during the intensive legislation work, the codification activity the government had to take into account the new issues and challenges as constituted the migration for the country.

In the late 1860s the first non-political migrants departed for overseas destinations from Hungary, and it was not clear to the politicians of that time whether a new period of mass migration was imminent.[1] In the following decades the number of immigrants to the United States multiplied, which pushed all players towards a more comprehensive regulation of the issue. Of course, there were some points in the area, such as questions of citizenship, which attracted more attention than others from the interested governments. This issue was intertwined with other crucial problems such as the question of migrants' military service or, as a more general factor, the problem of state control over the flow of migration. The migration movement put in a special light the codification of the law on citizenship or in wider sense, all problems relating to the citizenship question. Due to the main migration destination, the US, it seems as if the settlement of the problem became a three-players-game between Budapest, Vienna and Washington. The direct interaction between the three parties' policy and legal solutions is clear.

---

1 Gusztáv THIRRING: *A magyarok kivándorlása Amerikába* [Migration of Hungarians to America] Közgazdasági Szemle 20(1896), 36, 49. Dénes JÁNOSSY: *A Kossuth-emigráció Angliában és Amerikában, 1851–1852* [The Kossuth-emigration in England and in the USA, 1851–1852], I. kötet, Magyar Történelmi Társulat, Budapest, 1940, 2.

2 Steps for Settling the Citizenship Questions between the US and the Migration Countries – the Bancroft Treaties

From the middle of the 19th century onward, coinciding with the steamship boom, companies offered a cheap, smooth and quick journey to overseas destinations and this contributed to a constant flow of transatlantic migration from European countries.[2] Seeing that a hefty part of the migrants was made up of young males, emigration countries considered the phenomenon a threat to their military interests.[3] Therefore, they intended to block the emigration of those who were of compulsory military service age and to protect the interests of their army.[4] Finally, this led to cases in which the immigrants' former home countries took steps for the enforcement of the obligation of military service for return migrants, which triggered disputes between the United States and important European migration countries, first and foremost the United Kingdom and Prussia.[5] The immigrants' citizenship constituted a constant problem in the United States. The whole issue was more complicated, as those persons who arrived in the United States as children, were regarded by their old home country as citizens and could have appeared as involuntary absentees.[6] Consequently, when returning to their old country, they were often punished,

---

[2] Günter MOLTMANN: *Steamship Transport of Emigrants from Europe to the United States, 1850–1914: Social, Commercial and Legislative Aspects* = *Maritime Aspects of Migration*, Klaus FRIEDLAND (ed.), Böhlau, Köln-Wien, 1989, 316; Raymond L. COHN: *The Transition from Sail to Steam in Immigration to the United States*, The Journal of Economic History, 65(2005)/2, 472.

[3] *Abstracts of reports of the Immigration Commission : with conclusions and recommendations, and views of the minority*, William P. DILLINGHAM (ed.), GPO, Washington, 1911, vol. 1, 58–59; *Immigrants, by age classification: 1820–1997* (table ad 226–230) = *Historical Statistics of the United States, Earliest Times to the Present: Millennial Edition*, Susan B. CARTER, Scott Sigmund GARTNER, Michael R. HAINES, Alan L. OLMSTEAD, Richard SUTCH, Gavin WRIGHT (eds.), Cambridge University Press, New York, 2006.

[4] Dierk WALTER: *A Military Revolution? Prussian Military Reforms before the Wars of German Unification*, Forsvarsstudier/Defence Studies 2(2001), 7–10; Alan FORREST: *The Legacy of the French Revolutionary Wars. The Nation-in-Arms in French Republican Memory*, Cambridge University Press, Cambridge (UK), 2009, 110; Kristofer ALLERFELDT: *Beyond the Huddled Masses: American Immigration and the Treaty of Versailles*, I.B.Tauris&Co, London, 2006, 54.

[5] Paul QUIGLEY: *The American Civil War and the Transatlantic Triumph of Volitional Citizenship* = *The Transnational Significance of the American Civil War*, Jörg NAGLER, Don H. DOYLE, Marcus GRÄSER (eds.), Palgrave Macmillan, Cham, 2016, 35–36; Peter J. SPIRO: *At Home in Two Countries. The Past and Future of Dual Citizenship*, New York University Press, New York, 2016, 16–18; Torrie HESTER: *Deportation. The origins of U.S. Policy*, University of Pennsylvania Press, Philadelphia, 2017, 39.

[6] Karen SCHNIEDEWIND: *Migrants Returning to Bremen: Social Structure and Motivation, 1850 to 1914*, Journal of American Ethnic History, 12(1993)/2, 50.

sentenced for evasion of military service or inducted into the army by force. In practice, the European countries did not take into account the changes in the migrants' nationality, or they acted under the assumption that the migrants' former citizenship provided sufficient grounds for the enforcement of military service, in other words, they maintained military obligations. As a consequence, American citizenship in practice could not be taken into account on the territory of former home countries, so the practice of the interested European states limited the protection provided by American citizenship.[7] Although Washington was aware of the problem and the European countries' practices affected ultimately American citizenship, initially it showed a careful and reserved attitude which slowly changed from the middle of the 19th century onward. The vicissitudes of American citizens in Europe came to light; newspapers reported the controversial approach by European countries in relation to compulsory military service for their former citizens. Due to theese developments, Washington changed its position concerning the effects of naturalisation, and stressed that it would cut all ties between the new American citizen and the old home country. Consequently the United States had to protect their new citizens against these states in the same way as it did natural born ones.[8] Together with these changes, the United States reformed its citizenship law as well and in addition to the points in relation to naturalisation, it built into its legal framework the right to emigration and release from citizenship.[9] In order to settle the citizenship questions in the context of migration, the United States initiated the conclusion of treaties with the important European emigration countries in the 1860s. These treaties, named after the United States ambassador in Berlin, were subsequently called "Bancroft-treaties", constituting a model for the treaty concluded with Austria-Hungary as well.[10]

---

7   George H. YEAMAN: *Allegiance and citizenship. An inquiry into the claim of European governments to exact military service of naturalized citizens of the United States*, Møller, Copenhagen, 1867.
8   E.g. New York Times 10 May 1867; New York Daily Tribune 11 July 1872, 2; Árpád KIRÁLYFI: *Az 1871:XLIII. t.cz.-be iktatott államszerződés*. [International Agreement implemented by the 1871 Law], Különlenyomat a „Jogállam" XII. évfolyamának 7–10. füzetéből, Franklin, Budapest, 1913, 4.
9   Prentis WEBSTER: *A treatise on the law of citizenship in the United States. Treated historically*, M. Bender, Albany New York, 1891, 151.
10 Oscar S. STRAUS: *The United States doctrine of citizenship and expatriation*. Georg H. Ellis, Boston, 1901, 6, 16; New York Times 16 July 1868; Edward W.S. TINGLE: *Germany's Claims upon German-Americans in Germany. A Discussion of German Military and other Laws which may affect German-Americans temporarily in Germany together with some comment upon existing Treaties*. T&J. W. Johnson &Co., Philadelphia, 1903, 95–110; David Jayne HILL:

3 Accord on Citizenship between the United States and Austria-Hungary

Although in the 1860s migration from Austria-Hungary hadd not yet reached a critical level, Vienna was also approached by Washington for the conclusion of an agreement on citizenship, which was signed finally in 1870.[11] Budapest had no special remarks concerning the document, apart from a few points deemed to be misleading concerning the constitutional relationship between Austria and Hungary within the framework of the Empire.[12] Seeing that after the Compromise between Austria and Hungary in 1867 the possibility of a common citizenship instead of separate Austrian and Hungarian ones – which could be concluded from the Agreement's text – would question the Hungarian constitutional position, namely the country's sovereignty within the framework of Austria-Hungary, the Hungarian political elite attacked the document's terms.[13]

While the Hungarian parliament debated the formulation of the Agreement, it seems as that its real essence and importance went unnoticed. On the one hand, this Agreement brought new solutions into the Hungarian citizenship law, namely it referred to the loss of Hungarian citizenship (through residence on American soil), the cases and process of re-naturalisation and finally ensured impunity for acts in relation to the migrants' compulsory military service.[14] The Agreement in fact opened a loophole for those who left the country before starting their military service with the possibility of naturalisation after five years' dwelling on American soil. These persons, as new American citizens, while remaining free from military service, could not be punished for neglect

---

Dual Citizenship in the German Imperial and State Citizenship Law, The American Journal of International Law 12(1918)/2, 359; John M. MAGUIRE: *Naturalization of Alien*, Harvard Law Review, 32(1918)/2, 162; John Palmer GAVIT: *Americans by choice*, Harper&Bros, New York, 1922, 55–59; Michael WALTER: *The Bancroft Conventions: Second-Class Citizenship for Naturalized Americans*, International Lawyer 12(1978)/4, 826; Alfred M. BOLL: *Multiple Nationality and International Law*, Martinus Nijhoff Publishers, Leiden-Boston, 2007, 185.

11   Képv. Ir. 1869–72. X. köt. 28–29; Peter J. SPIRO: *At Home in Two Countries. The Past and Future of Dual Citizenship*, New York University Press, New York, 2016, 59.

12   Gejza FERDINANDY: *Magyarország közjoga* [Constitutional Law of Hungary], Politzer, Budapest, 1902, 248.

13   Árpád KIRÁLYFI: *A magyar állampolgárság kizárólagossága* [The exclusiveness of Hungarian citizenship], Különlenyomat a Concha-emlékkönyvből, Franklin, Budapest, 1913, 44; Ulrike VON HIRSCHHAUSEN: *From imperial inclusion to national exclusion: citizenship in the Habsburg monarchy and in Austria 1867–1923*, European Review of History/Revue européenne d'histoire, 16(2009)/4, 553.

14   GAVIT: *op. cit.*, 56.

of their administrative obligations and no investigation could be made in relation to this service. Seeing that there was no compulsory military service in the United States, migrants could count on a double gain: they could evade both their old country's military and the American army as well. All in all, through the solutions of the 1870 Agreement they could be free from any military service, which made the United States as a migration destination even more attractive.[15]

Execution of the Agreement seemed to be problematic like in other European countries. The Hungarian authorities could not manage the cases of return migrants appropriately; they tended not to take into account the migrants' real legal situation.[16] The Interior Minister even had to order the lower level authorities to handle these cases accurately and legally.[17] By that time, the Hungarian government had grown cautious in the cases which could affect the relationship with the United States.

The most important problem of the Agreement, namely that it could have a real effect on the migration of those of military service age, became clear only after its had been concluded. When the discussions started over the migration issue in Hungary, among the points raised, the question of military age migrants appeared immediately.[18] It seemed that this problem constituted a crucial issue, which pushed the government toward elaboration of a quick and simple solution. Faced with increasing migration, Budapest decided to take measures in order to slow down the flow.

The Agreement, as an international legal act, had of course a special position in the Hungarian legal system. Since the Agreement was concluded by the United States and Austria-Hungary, it did not seem to be at all easily amendable. The government had to regard the agreement as in effect an untouchable element within Hungarian legal system which had a strong effect not only on issues of migration but also on the evolution of the Hungarian citizenship law. The solutions provided by the Agreement diverged from those of the 1879 Law on Citizenship, duplicating the legal framework in a controversial way. While the 1879 Law intended to preserve the migrants' Hungarian citizenship and did not regulate the loss of citizenship, thereby admitting the existence of dual nationality, the Agreement excluded this possibility.[19] All in all, there were different solutions to the questions citizenship and naturalisation for those who

---

15   AT-OeStA HHStA MdÄ AR F57-49-1.
16   MNL OL K150-2643-1896-I-10-768; HESTER: *op. cit.*, 36–40.
17   BM 28.933/1898.
18   MNL OL K150-1476-1886-VII-14-2382; MNL OL K150-1693-1888-VII-14-14733.
19   KIRÁLYFI: *A magyar állampolgárság kizárólagossága...*, *op. cit.*, 63; KN 1869–72. XVII. k. 1869–355; FERDINANDY: *op. cit.*, 248.

migrated to the United States and for those to other destinations which interfered with the basic aims of the government.

As it became quite clear that the points of the Agreement affected the country's interests, the government tried to manage the situation, and in 1895 informed the Common Ministry of Foreign Affairs that it would opt for either a radical reform or denunciation of the agreement.[20]

Meanwhile, due to intensive immigration, American migration policy changed, as well. Migration from Central and East Europe continuously grew, constituting a new wave of migration into the United States from the 1880s onward. The newcomers had a different strategy than those of the settlers of the previous decade: it was based rather on a limited period of work in the United States, in other words most of them planned a return to their old home country and some returned again to America.[21] In light of this return and circular migration, the Agreement's points providing additional protection against the authorities in the former home country became crucial. First of all, because of the constant waves of "new migration" a clear anti-immigrant trend had appeared in the United States, pushing the government towards a restrictive policy.[22] In relation to the issues of citizenship, Washington faced problem of the fraudulent naturalisation, i.e. that a number of immigrants,

---

20 AT-OeStA HHStA MdÄ AR F57-50-1.

21 *A Magyar Szent Korona országainak kivándorlása és visszavándorlása. 1899–1913* [Migration and return migration of the Hungarian Holy Crown's countries], M. Kir. Közp. Statisztikai Hivatal, Budapest, 1918, 66–67.,74; *Report of Frank Dyer Chester = Special Consular Reports. Emigration to the United States*, GPO, Washington, 1904, 8; *Reports of the Immigration Commission. Abstracts of reports of the Immigration Commission. With conclusions and recommendations and views of the minority*, vol. 1, William P. DILLINGHAM (ed.), GPO, Washington, 1911, 181; Günter MOLTMANN: *American-German Return Migration in the Nineteenth and Early Twentieth Centuries*, Central European History, 13(1980)/4, 381; Neil Larry SHUMSKY: *"Let No Man Stop to Plunder!" American Hostility to Return Migration, 1890–1924*, Journal of American Ethnic History, 11(1992)/2 56–75; Mark WYMAN: *Round-Trip to America. The immigrants return to Europe, 1880–1930*. Cornell University Press, Ithaca-London, 1993, 6; Timothy J. HATTON, Jeffrey G. WILLIAMSON: *The Age of Mass Migration. Causes and Economic Impact*, Oxford University Press, New York-Oxford, 1998, 95–98.

22 Prescott F. HALL: *The Recent History of Immigration and Immigration Restriction*, Journal of Political Economy, 21(1903)/8, 736; John HIGHAM: *Origins of Immigration Restriction, 1882–1897: A Social Analysis*, The Mississippi Valley Historical Review, 39(1952)/1, 78–79; Hans P. VOUGHT: *The Bully Pulpit and the Melting Pot. American Presidents and the Immigrant, 1897–1933*. Mercer University Press, Macon, 2004, 11–13, 18–20; Catherine COLLOMP: *Labour Unions and the Nationalisation of Immigration Restriction in the United States, 1880–1924 = Migration Control in the North Atlantic World. The Evolution of State Practices in Europe and the United States from the French Revolution to the Inter-War Period*. Andreas FAHRMEIR, Oliver FARON, Partick WEIL (eds.), Berghahn, New York-Oxford, 2005, 237–252, 245–246.

having acquired United States citizenship returned home and abused their new legal status.[23] Although the problem appeared in diplomatic correspondence as well, the two parties did not decide to modify the problematic points of the agreement.[24] Austria-Hungary hesitated in denouncing the treaty and finally phased out the whole issue, while the United States launched a reform of the naturalisation regulation right after the turn of the century.[25] Nevertheless, with the 1906 law on naturalisation with the possibility of *de facto* withdrawal of American citizenship from returnees, Washington created an even more ambiguous situation for the Austro-Hungarian authorities.[26] Thus, the situation became even more complex after the American reforms and it seems that the steps by the two parties contributed to further ambiguity.

4 Quest for Solutions Counterbalancing the Legal and Economic Pull Factors

From the 1880s onwards, having realised the limits of its room for manoeuvre, the Hungarian government sought both an effective and simple tool to push back the migration and it seemed that migration agents could form a primary target. These persons provided various services for migrants: first of all, they sold tickets for the journey, helped them with practical information and sometimes worked as guides from the migrants' home right up to embarkation. For the public and for the political elite as well this player in the migration business constituted the most unsavoury element, against which hard measures were to be introduced.[27] Therefore, with actions against this group the government could prove to the public its resolve in managing the situation while the real roots of increasing migration remained untouched. Even the government admitted that Hungarian migration was based mainly on economic factors,

---

23 *Report to the president of the Commission on Naturalization appointed by executive order March 1 1905*, GPO, Washington, 1905, 13.
24 AT-OeStA HHStA MdÄ AR F57-50-1.
25 George M. STEPHENSON: *A History of American Immigration 1820–1924*, Ginn, Boston, 1926, 246; Irene BLOEMRAAD: *Citizenship Lessons from the Past: The Contours of Immigrant Naturalization in the Early 20th Century*, Social Science Quarterly, 87(2006)/5, 941–942; Patrick WEIL: *The sovereign citizen: denaturalization and the origins of the American Republic*, University of Pennsylvania Press, Philadelphia, 2013, 4–7.
26 Act of June 29 1906. *United States. Naturalization laws and regulations*, GPO, Washington; GAVIT: *op. cit.*, 81–82.
27 Torsten FEYS: *The Battle for the Migrants the Introduction of Steamshipping on the North Atlantic and its Impact on the European Exodus*, Liverpool University Press, Liverpool, 2013, 88.

namely on wage differences an on the limited economic prospects in agriculture, but there was no real chance for a general land reform.[28] All in all, the government had to handle both the general migration problem and the special problem of migration of those of military age, mainly with administrative tools.

These factors left their mark on the elaborated solutions, first of all the 1880 Law on Migration Agents, which ultimately made the activity of migration agents illegal. After that, most governmental efforts focused on those agents deemed to be responsible not only for the growth in problem numbers, but also for most illegal migration cases. Those who were not authorised to leave the country would try to cross the borders often with the help of these agents. Therefore, local authorities together with the police made efforts to discover the hidden migration routes in order to dampen the flow. Of course, as these local agents sold tickets on the big steamship companies, the strategy of the big players defined the developments in Hungary in the end. Seeing the dynamically increasing migration, the Hungarian market was of prime importance for the interested companies. Therefore, a system was built with which the companies and the agents could easily evade the Hungarian authorities' control and could ensure the smooth migration business.[29] They sent advertising materials by post and could create sales and information points, small offices on the other side of the Hungarian borders.[30] Thus, the authorities'

---

28   *A korlátolt forgalmú birtokok kimutatása és Magyarország területének mivelési ágak szerinti megoszlása* [Statistics of bound plots], A Földmivelésügyi Magy. Kir. Minister rendeletéből összeállította és kiadja a Ministerium Mezőrendőri és Statisztikai Osztálya, Budapest, 1893, 5; *Mezőgazdasági munkabérek Magyarországon 1896-ban* [Wages in agricultural sector in Hungary], Kiadja a Földművelésügyi M. Kir. Minister, Budapest, 1898; *A kivándorlás. A Magyar Gyáriparosok Országos Szövetsége által tartott országos ankét tárgyalásai* [Migration], Pesti Lloyd-Társulat ny., Budapest, 1907, 7, 20, 27; *Egán Ede a „hegyvidéki akció" miniszteri biztosának jelentése Darányi Ignác földművelésügyi miniszternek a ruszin hegyvidékről kivándorolni szándékozó helyi földtulajdonosok földjeinek megvásárlása és ruszin földműveseknek részletfizetés formájában való eladása tárgyában.* [Report of the minister's commissioner ...] = Gábor G. KEMÉNY: *Iratok a nemzetiségi kérdés történetéhez Magyarországon a dualizmus korában,* vol. 2, 1892–1900, Tankönyvkiadó, Budapest, 1956, 846–848; Lajos BECK: *A magyar földbirtok megoszlása* [Repartition of the Hungarian agricultural domains], Pallas, Budapest, 1918, 37; Bertalan NEMÉNYI: *A magyar nép állapota és az amerikai kivándorlás* [Situation of the Hungarian population and the American migration], Athenaeum, Budapest, 1911, 24; Gyula RÁCZ: *A magyar földbirtokosság anyagi pusztulása* [Decline of the Hungarian landowners], Deutsch Zsigmond és Társa, Budapest, 1906, 62; István RÁCZ: *Parasztok, hajdúk, cívisek*[Peasants, haiduks, townees], Társadalomtörténeti tanulmányok, Debreceni Egyetem, Debrecen, 2000, 117.

29   HALL: *op. cit.,* 26–27.

30   E.g. MNL OL K150-2770-1896-VII-14-44556; Pesti Hírlap 22 February 1892.

actions brought only modest results: after repeated governmental actions, arrests and information campaigns the ticket selling network quickly recovered, and the government had to admit by the turn of the century that all its efforts were effectively in vain.

5 Comprehensive Migration Policy – Within the Borders

Given the unsuccessful efforts, the government launched a new program to create a coherent migration policy instead of a pile of measures. Moreover, by that period migration problems had developed into a complex group of problems growing more and more dangerous for Budapest. Around the turn of the century tens of thousands were leaving the country each year. This constituted an economic question of course; furthermore, the whole migration problem was more and more coupled with the question of ethnic minorities in Hungary. Meanwhile, the migration of the military age group, of those who did not fulfil their military obligations or even had escaped from service constituted a constant problem as well, so it became absolutely urgent to provide a more feasible solution than the previous one which targeted almost exclusively migration agents.

Besides the hidden steps focusing on ethnic minorities, important measures aiming to reduce illegal migration were taken in a more visible way.[31] That was not easy either, because only a short section of the Hungarian borders were at the same time external borders of the Monarchy and the "internal" borders in practice weren't controlled at all. Furthermore, seeing that the external borders were under-controlled as well, illegal border crossing remained a widespread phenomenon in the entire period.[32] The migrants did not declare themselves as overseas migrants to the authorities, and in the true illegal cases they crossed the borders evading the checkpoints and could continue their journey with the help of agents until embarkation. As a result, a new system of border control was set up starting at the turn of the century, in order to create a safeproof system for blocking the illegal crossings.[33] To ensure the possibility

---

31   MNL OL K26-574-1903-XVI-79-3047.
32   Barna BUDAY: *A pool-szerződés és a kivándorlás* [The Pool Agreement and migration], Athenaeum ny., Budapest, 1911, 2.
33   ME 1905/5692; BM 1905/91.000; József PARÁDI: *A dualista Magyarország határőrizete a migráció tükrében*[Border control vis-a-vis migration in the dualist Hungary] = *Migráció, Tanulmánygyűjtemény, I. kötet.*, Sándor ILLÉS, Pál Péter TÓTH (eds.), KSH Népességtudományi Kutató Intézet, Budapest, 1998, 57–72; Csaba CSAPÓ: *A magyar királyi csendőrség története* [History of the Hungarian gendarmerie], Pro Pannonia, Pécs, 1999, 119.

of a more effective control system, the government reformed the migrant passport as well and prescribed the compulsory migration route via Fiume, the only Hungarian port for embarkation.[34] With these measures Budapest expected a decrease in illegal border crossing and a decline in migration among those of military age as well. The obligatory route through Fiume triggered an intensive debate at the national and international level, and the reactions of Washington showed the sensitivity of the whole question in which the states' migration policies clashed. By the turn of the century, the "new immigration" issue constituted a more and more acute question, vexing not only the political elite but also public opinion as well. It became clear that the open door policy of Washington was set to be changed and the government intended to create a more controlled immigration system. In this context, the Hungarian government's actions attracted attention and the investigation launched by Washington covered the Hungarian situation as well.[35]

On the other hand, in the first decade of the 20th century, the Hungarian government found itself caught in the crossfire of the big steamship companies. That period was hallmarked by the intensive competition between the most important players in the sector, which became important to the interested states as well.[36] Among the most influential groups the Atlantic pool cartel maintained first place in the Hungarian migration business, and intended to cooperate with the Hungarian government only in a limited way. Due to this situation Budapest was not able to control embarkation at the main German ports.[37] Consequently, the government had to find a partner to ensure the

---

34 BM 1904/64.041; FEYS: *op. cit.*, 170–173.
35 Marcus BRAUN: *Immigration abuses: glimpses of Hungary and Hungarians: a narrative of the experiences of an American immigrant inspector while on duty in Hungary, together with a brief review of that country's history and present troubles*, Pearson Advertising Co., New York, 1906; *United States. Certain reports of Immigrant Inspector Marcus Braun: letter from the secretary of commerce and labor, transmitting, in response to the inquiry of the House, certain reports made by Immigrant Inspector Marcus Braun*, Washington, GPO., 1906, 4.
36 Eugene Tyler CHAMBERLAIN: *The New Cunard Steamship Contract*, The North American Review, 177(1903)/563, 533–543; John MOODY: *The masters of capital. A chronicle of Wall Street*, Yale University Press, New Haven (CT), 1920, 110; Gerhard A. RITTER: *Der Kaiser und sein Reeder. Albert Ballin, die HAPAG und das Verhältnis von Wirtschaft und Politik im Kaiserreich und in den ersten Jahren der Weimarer Republik*, Zeitschrift für Unternehmensgeschichte/Journal of Business History, 42(1997)/2, 137–162; Drew KEELING: *Transatlantic Shipping Cartels and Migration between Europe and America, 1880–1914*, Essays in Economic and Business History, 17(1999), 200–201.
37 Cf. e.g. Kivándorlási Ellenőr 15.02.1908; Ulf BRUNNBAUER: *Emigrants, America, and the State since the Late Nineteenth Century*, Lexington, London, 2016, 80–81.

control measures for filtering out the illegal migrants in Fiume. Having negotiated with Cunard, the government could work out an acceptable framework for the company concession to launch a Fiume – New York line.[38] Nevertheless, as quickly became obvious, this solution could not bring a breakthrough in the realisation of the governmental plans for control. All in all, neither the efforts to ensure a controlled Fiume – New York line with Cunard, nor the negotiations with the members of the pool could create a situation generally acceptable for Budapest. Thus, the unauthorized migration of those of military age continued and it became clear that Budapest had to elaborate with Vienna a common solution to the problem.

It seems that the Austrian government focused only later on the question. Although migration was of a similar volume as in Hungary, the legal regulation of the issue remained basically modest. Although the Austrian part of the Empire ranked among the strongest emigration domains in the American statistics, there was not a migration legislation program comparable to the Hungarian half of the Empire.[39] Of course, the legal framework relating to the military obligations could provide a clear directive for the (common) management of the flow and for filtering out illegal migration; it seems that cooperation was not strong enough between the two parts of the Monarchy to solve the Hungarian concerns. Having realised the limits of its migration policy, Budapest launched negotiations with its Austrian counterpart in order to create, or rather to strengthen the control system at the external borders of the Monarchy and to cause the Austrian government introduce control measures concerning migrants from Hungary.[40]

Of course, the complex structure of Austria-Hungary constituted a factor which made the possibility of a common solution quite uncertain. In some cases even the implementation of clauses of Austrian decrees relating to migrants – to Hungarian citizens as well – departing from Austria became unclear.[41] Furthermore, the elaboration of a common solution was slowed not only by constitutional questions but also by Hungarian political events, namely by the changes in the ruling parties and the Cabinet crisis at that time.

---

38   MNL OL K150-3609-V-20; Mihály SINGER: *A Cunard vonal és a kivándorlás Magyarországból* [The Cunard Line and Hungary], s.n., New York, 1904, 10.
39   Hans CHMELAR: *Höhepunkt der österreichischen Auswanderung*, Verlag der Österreichischen Akademie der Wissenschaften, Wien, 1974, 46.
40   MNL OL K150-3609-1910-V-20-22489.
41   MNL OL K150-3609-1904-V-20-59393.

Consequently, after the first steps toward cooperation between the authorities of Austria and Hungary a longer interval blocked the elaboration of an effective system. The main question of the negotiations was how the authorities could enforce special rules on the group military age individuals in relation to the other's citizens. It seems as if both governments' efforts remained paralysed by some divergences in the details. The most problematic point of the issue, interestingly enough, was the age limit for the control measures, which differed in the two halves of the Monarchy: in Austria it was 50, while in Hungary 36 years.[42] For the effective settlement of the question the two governments continued negotiations until 1913 without a breakthrough. Although an agreement was elaborated, because of administrative hurdles and manoeuvres it did not enter into force, and the two governments merely exchanged messages, letters and information on the issue until the outbreak of World War I.[43]

6 Conclusion

Migration constituted a crucial problem for the Hungarian government from the 1880s until the outbreak of World War I. While the necessity of a comprehensive migration policy was clear to Budapest, the real room for manoeuvre was limited by various factors. Although there were stronger pull factors for Hungarian migration than the benefits of 1870 the Agreement on Citizenship, it is also true that its most important effect on migration appeared in the migration discussions and constituted a solid basis for the increasingly restrictive migration policy.

The developments of the early 1900s show that the policies of all interested governments remained suffocated by the 1870 Agreement, elaborated to the situation of the 1860s. From the late 1880s, the migration from Austria-Hungary boomed, constituting a hard problem to both parties, the United States, and Hungary as well. The existing regulations of the parties formed a puzzle which pieces did not fit together perfectly, however it gave a functioning net. Nevertheless, the two, or rather three parties, seeing the fact that Vienna elaborated its regulation too, the slight changes of the system and the finetune of the migration rules remained a common area of the parties in which they intertwined.

---

[42] MNL OL K150-3609-1910-V-20-22489.
[43] MNL OL K150-3609-1912-V-20-116261; MNL OL K150-3609-1914-V-20-4197-9473.

Moreover, citizenship questions and domains connecting to the issue, first of all the nation-building policies became more and more crucial to the parties. It seems as if the importance of the national identity question would block the ways of the migration problem's common solution which led to the development of the separate solutions, in Washington and in Budapest as well.

Seeing the volume and character of the migration, Washington had finally to revise its immigration policy, and it became evident that citizenship and naturalisation questions must constitute a crucial part of the reform. Concerning Austria-Hungary, the special system of the Monarchy formed an additional problem in the issue, i.e. the two parts of the Empire would have to elaborate a genuinely common solution to manage the most acute problems. Without that, Hungary had to act virtually on its own and having accepted the situation, launched a programme to ensure at least control over the flow of migration. Budapest had to conduct its migration policy in a narrow band without encroaching on the 1870 Agreement, the special relationship with Austria, and taking into account the reality of the big steamship companies' power and interests, as well. Among the above external factors the 1870 Agreement constituted a solid, constant element which became outdated and problematic almost at the very moment of its conclusion, having a visible effect on the development of Hungarian migration policy. On the other hand, being a country of destination, there remained more tools, first of all, the immigration control in the hands of Washington. Seeing the fact that the 1870 Agreement served initially rather more the American interests than those of Austria-Hungary, the divergence between the two parties' position remained. Finally, the 1870 Agreement simultaneously gave a push to the Hungarian modernisation and hindered the elaboration of a coherent and comprehensive citizenship and migration law.

Bibliography

Archival Sources

Magyar Nemzeti Levéltár [National Archives of Hungary], K26-574-1903-XVI-79-3047.
Magyar Nemzeti Levéltár, K150-1476-1886-VII-14-2382.
Magyar Nemzeti Levéltár, K150-1693-1888-VII-14-14733.
Magyar Nemzeti Levéltár, K150-2643-1896-I-10-768.
Magyar Nemzeti Levéltár, K150-3609-1904-V-20-59393.
Magyar Nemzeti Levéltár, K150-3609-1910-V-20-22489.

Magyar Nemzeti Levéltár, K150-3609-1912-V-20-116261.
Magyar Nemzeti Levéltár, K150-3609-1914-V-20-4197-9473.
Österreichisches Staatsarchiv, Haus-, Hof- und Staatsarchiv, Ministerium des Äußern, Administrative Registratur, F57-49-1.
Österreichisches Staatsarchiv, Haus-, Hof- und Staatsarchiv, Ministerium des Äußern, Administrative Registratur, F57-50-1.

Literature

Abstracts of reports of the Immigration Commission: with conclusions and recommendations, and views of the minority, William P. DILLINGHAM (ed.), Washington, 1911, GPO, vol. 1, 58–59.

Act of June 29 1906. *United States. Naturalization laws and regulations,* GPO, Washington.

Kristofer ALLERFELDT: *Beyond the Huddled Masses: American Immigration and the Treaty of Versailles,* I.B.Tauris&Co, London, 2006.

Lajos BECK: *A magyar földbirtok megoszlása,* Pallas, Budapest, 1918.

Irene BLOEMRAAD: *Citizenship Lessons from the Past: The Contours of Immigrant Naturalization in the Early 20th Century,* Social Science Quarterly, 87(2006)/5, 927–953.

Alfred M. BOLL: *Multiple Nationality and International Law.* Martinus Nijhoff Publishers, Leiden-Boston, 2007.

Marcus BRAUN: *Immigration abuses: glimpses of Hungary and Hungarians: a narrative of the experiences of an American immigrant inspector while on duty in Hungary, together with a brief review of that country's history and present troubles,* New York: Pearson Advertising Co., 1906.

Marcus BRAUN: *United States. Certain reports of Immigrant Inspector Marcus Braun: letter from the secretary of commerce and labor, transmitting, in response to the inquiry of the House, certain reports made by Immigrant Inspector Marcus Braun,* [Washington, GPO, 1906].

Ulf BRUNNBAUER: *Emigrants, America, and the State since the Late Nineteenth Century,* Lexington, London, 2016.

Barna BUDAY: *A pool-szerződés és a kivándorlás* [The Pool Agreement and migration], Athenaeum ny., Budapest, 1911, vol. 2.

Eugene Tyler CHAMBERLAIN: *The New Cunard Steamship Contract,* The North American Review, 177(1903)/563, 533–543.

Hans CHMELAR: *Höhepunkt der österreichischen Auswanderung,* Verlag der Österreichischen Akademie der Wissenschaften, Wien, 1974.

Raymond L. COHN: *The Transition from Sail to Steam in Immigration to the United States,* The Journal of Economic History, 65(2005)/2, 469–495.

Catherine COLLOMP: *Labour Unions and the Nationalisation of Immigration Restriction in the United States, 1880–1924* = *Migration Control in the North Atlantic World. The Evolution of State Practices in Europe and the United States from the French Revolution to the Inter-War Period*, Andreas FAHRMEIR, Oliver FARON, Partick WEIL (eds.) Berghahn, New York-Oxford, 2005, 237–252.

Csaba CSAPÓ: *A magyar királyi csendőrség története*, Pro Pannonia, Pécs, 1999.

Egán Ede a „hegyvidéki akció" miniszteri biztosának jelentése Darányi Ignác földművelésügyi miniszternek a ruszin hegyvidékről kivándorolni szándékozó helyi földtulajdonosok földjeinek megvásárlása és ruszin földműveseknek részletfizetés formájában való eladása tárgyában = Gábor G. KEMÉNY: *Iratok a nemzetiségi kérdés történetéhez Magyarországon a dualizmus korában*, vol. 2: 1892–1900, Tankönyvkiadó, Budapest, 1956, 846–848.

Gejza FERDINANDY: *Magyarország közjoga*, Politzer, Budapest, 1902.

Torsten FEYS: *The Battle for the Migrants the Introduction of Steamshipping on the North Atlantic and its Impact on the European Exodus*, Liverpool University Press, Liverpool, 2013.

Alan FORREST: *The Legacy of the French Revolutionary Wars. The Nation-in-Arms in French Republican Memory*, Cambridge University Press, Cambridge (UK), 2009.

John Palmer GAVIT: *Americans by choice*. Harper&Bros, New York, 1922.

Prescott F. HALL: *The Recent History of Immigration and Immigration Restriction*, Journal of Political Economy, 21(1903)/8, 735–752.

Timothy J. HATTON, Jeffrey G. WILLIAMSON: *The Age of Mass Migration. Causes and Economic Impact*, Oxford University Press, New York-Oxford, 1998.

Torrie HESTER: *Deportation. The origins of U.S. Policy*, University of Pennsylvania Press, Philadelphia, 2017.

John HIGHAM: *Origins of Immigration Restriction, 1882–1897: A Social Analysis*, The Mississippi Valley Historical Review, 39(1952)/1, 77–88.

David Jayne HILL: *Dual Citizenship in the German Imperial and State Citizenship Law*, The American Journal of International Law 12(1918)/2, 356–363.

Immigrants, by age classification: 1820–1997 = *Historical Statistics of the United States, Earliest Times to the Present: Millennial Edition*, Susan B. CARTER, Scott Sigmund GARTNER, Michael R. HAINES, Alan L. OLMSTEAD, Richard SUTCH, Gavin WRIGHT (eds.), Cambridge University Press, New York, 2006.

Dénes JÁNOSSY: *A Kossuth-emigráció Angliában és Amerikában, 1851–1852* [The Kossuth-emigration in England and in the USA, 1851–1852], I. kötet, Magyar Történelmi Társulat, Budapest, 1940.

Drew KEELING: *Transatlantic Shipping Cartels and Migration between Europe and America, 1880–1914*, Essays in Economic and Business History, 17(1999), 195–213.

Árpád KIRÁLYFI: *A magyar állampolgárság kizárólagossága*, Különlenyomat a Concha-emlékkönyvből. Franklin, Budapest, 1913.

Árpád KIRÁLYFI: *Az 1871:XLIII. t.cz.-be iktatott államszerződés*, Különlenyomat a „Jogállam" XII. évfolyamának 7–10. füzetéből, Franklin, Budapest, 1913.

Kivándorlási Ellenőr 15.02.1908.

A kivándorlás. A Magyar Gyáriparosok Országos Szövetsége által tartott országos ankét tárgyalásai, Pesti Lloyd-Társulat ny., Budapest, 1907.

A korlátolt forgalmú birtokok kimutatása és Magyarország területének mivelési ágak szerinti megoszlása, A Földmivelésügyi Magy. Kir. Minister rendeletéből összeállította és kiadja a Ministerium Mezőrendőri és Statisztikai Osztálya, Budapest, 1893.

John M. MAGUIRE: *Naturalization of Alien*, Harvard Law Review, 32(1918)/2, 160–166.

A Magyar Szent Korona országainak kivándorlása és visszavándorlása. 1899–1913, M. Kir. Közp. Statisztikai Hivatal, Budapest, 1918.

Mezőgazdasági munkabérek Magyarországon 1896-ban. Kiadja a Földművelésügyi M. Kir. Minister, Budapest, 1898.

John MOODY: *The masters of capital. A chronicle of Wall Street*, Yale University Press, New Haven (CT), 1920.

Günter MOLTMANN: *American-German Return Migration in the Nineteenth and Early Twentieth Centuries*, Central European History, 13(1980)/4, 378–392.

Günter MOLTMANN: *Steamship Transport of Emigrants from Europe to the United States, 1850–1914: Social, Commercial and Legislative Aspects = Maritime Aspects of Migration*, Klaus FRIEDLAND (ed.), Böhlau, Köln-Wien, 1989, 309–320.

Bertalan NEMÉNYI: *A magyar nép állapota és az amerikai kivándorlás*, Athenaeum, Budapest, 1911.

New York Daily Tribune 11 July 1872.

New York Times 10 May 1867.

New York Times 16 July 1868.

József PARÁDI: *A dualista Magyarország határőrizete a migráció tükrében*[Border control vis-a-vis migration in the dualist Hungary] = *Migráció, Tanulmánygyűjtemény*, I. kötet., Sándor ILLÉS, Pál Péter TÓTH (eds.), KSH Népességtudományi Kutató Intézet, Budapest, 1998, 57–72.

Paul QUIGLEY: *The American Civil War and the Transatlantic Triumph of Volitional Citizenship = The Transnational Significance of the American Civil War*, Jörg NAGLER, Don H. DOYLE, Marcus GRÄSER (eds.), Palgrave Macmillan, Cham, 2016, 33–48.

Gyula RÁCZ: *A magyar földbirtokosság anyagi pusztulása*, Deutsch Zsigmond és Társa, Budapest, 1906.

István RÁCZ: *Parasztok, hajdúk, cívisek*, Társadalomtörténeti tanulmányok, Debreceni Egyetem, Debrecen, 2000.

Report of Frank Dyer Chester = Special Consular Reports. Emigration to the United States, GPO, Washington, 1904, 8.

Reports of the Immigration Commission. Abstracts of reports of the Immigration Commission. With conclusions and recommendations and views of the minority, vol. 1, William P. DILLINGHAM (ed.), GPO, Washington, 1911.

Report to the president of the Commission on Naturalization appointed by executive order March 1 1905, GPO, Washington, 1905.

Gerhard A. RITTER: *Der Kaiser und sein Reeder. Albert Ballin, die HAPAG und das Verhältnis von Wirtschaft und Politik im Kaiserreich und in den ersten Jahren der Weimarer Republik*, Zeitschrift für Unternehmensgeschichte/Journal of Business History, 42(1997)/2, 137–162.

Karen SCHNIEDEWIND: *Migrants Returning to Bremen: Social Structure and Motivation, 1850 to 1914*, Journal of American Ethnic History, 12(1993)/2, 35–55.

Neil Larry SHUMSKY: *"Let No Man Stop to Plunder!" American Hostility to Return Migration, 1890–1924*, Journal of American Ethnic History, 11(1992)/2 56–75.

Mihály SINGER: *A Cunard vonal és a kivándorlás Magyarországból*, s.n., New York, 1904.

Peter J. SPIRO: *At Home in Two Countries. The Past and Future of Dual Citizenship*, New York University Press, New York, 2016.

George M. STEPHENSON: *A History of American Immigration 1820–1924*, Ginn, Boston, 1926.

Oscar S. STRAUS: *The United States doctrine of citizenship and expatriation*, Georg H. Ellis, Boston, 1901.

Gusztáv THIRRING: *A magyarok kivándorlása Amerikába* [Migration of Hungarians to America] Közgazdasági Szemle 20(1896), 30–52.

Edward W.S. TINGLE: *Germany's Claims upon German-Americans in Germany. A Discussion of German Military and other Laws which may affect German-Americans temporarily in Germany together with some comment upon existing Treaties*. T&J. W. Johnson &Co., Philadelphia, 1903, 95–110.

Ulrike VON HIRSCHHAUSEN: *From imperial inclusion to national exclusion: citizenship in the Habsburg monarchy and in Austria 1867–1923*, European Review of History/ Revue européenne d'histoire, 16(2009)/4, 551–573.

Hans P. VOUGHT: *The Bully Pulpit and the Melting Pot. American Presidents and the Immigrant, 1897–1933*, Mercer University Press, Macon, 2004.

Dierk WALTER: *A Military Revolution? Prussian Military Reforms before the Wars of German Unification*, Forsvarsstudier/Defence Studies 2(2001), 3–34.

Michael WALTER: *The Bancroft Conventions: Second-Class Citizenship for Naturalized Americans*, International Lawyer 12(1978)/4, 825–833.

Prentis WEBSTER: *A treatise on the law of citizenship in the United States. Treated historically*, M. Bender, Albany NY, 1891.

Patrick WEIL: *The sovereign citizen: denaturalization and the origins of the American Republic*, University of Pennsylvania Press, Philadelphia, 2013.

Mark WYMAN: *Round-Trip to America. The immigrants return to Europe, 1880–1930*, Cornell University Press, Ithaca and London, 1993.

George H. YEAMAN: *Allegiance and citizenship. An inquiry into the claim of European governments to exact military service of naturalized citizens of the United States*, Møller, Copenhagen, 1867.

CHAPTER 7

Political Systems in Transition and Cultural (In)dependence: The Limits of a Legal Transplant in the Example of the Brazilian's Court of Auditors Birth

Marjorie Carvalho de Souza

1   Introduction

One of the main discursive tools of legitimacy for a new governement that intends to build its own credibility is to propose legal and institutional reforms. A call for modernisation, mainly by an administration that rose to power banishing the old monarchy, is an important motto for assuring the so-desired political legitimacy. Not by coincidence, that was one of the reasons why, in the aftermath of the Republic proclamation in 1889, a Federal Court of Auditors was created in Brazil to assist the legislative in the exercise of external control over the state budget.

Prior to then, the public budgetary control was still held by an executive agency, devoid of full independence, what reinforced the argument of renovation that embased, only one year after the political system's change, the enactment of the Decree No. 966-A, on 7 November 1890. This statute created the *Tribunal de Contas*, a national court with administrative and financial autonomy in relation to the legislative, executive and judicial bodies to review and adjudicate the acts concerning the Republic's budget.

Nonetheless it was celebrated as a matter of supreme interest for the nation its principal apologist – the finance minister Rui Barbosa, the bill's author – admitted having looked for models among foreing references. In the explanatory memorandum that accompanied the decree, he revealed having taken the French, Italian and Belgian models as guides to create a regulation for the financial service. He even declares a preference by the Italian one, considered the most perfect construction among the three forms.

It was that admitted influence what motivated the problem that this chapter intends to afford: if that was effectively a classical case of legal transplant in an ex-colony or if it was only a rethoric statement for external legitimacy. Even it seems at least incongruous trying to reshape a national identity after the monarchy's fall with institutional reforms that just reproduce foreing models, that can not be a discarded hypothesis in a historical context of long-life cultural dependence.

But that can not be accepted as an immediate conclusion. That's why this chapter is dedicated to put in comparison the Brazilian and Italian contexts of creation of a Court of Auditors and their respective rules to comprehend if the discursive idea of "influence" is reliable in practice. What could be, at first glance, an impressive case of legal transplant, can show, in fact, the limits of this metaphor to explain how law travels across borders.

With this view, this chapter aims to investigate the reception – and its limits – of foreign models in the control of public funds during the construction of this system at the start of the Brazilian Republic. Trying to avoid a diminutive view that merely detects the European influence in the creation of the Court of Auditors in Brazil when the Republic was proclaimed, this chapter emphasizes the role of history in a comparative study underscoring the differences between the Brazilian system and the Italian one – adopted as the main model – from their historical itineraries.

This is why it starts with a discussion about the transition of the political system in Brazil and its relationship with the creation of the Brazilian Court of Auditors, then shifts to the Italian context to make the same comparison in that country, that also saw its Court of Auditors created in a moment of government change. The next section attempts to show the contrasts between these two systems from the specificities of each historical background. The last section will conclude the chapter measuring the real dimension of the promised "influence" in a place where cultural dependence and affirmation of national identity were not automatic incongruent ideals.

2 Political Systems in Transition and the Creation of a Court of Auditors in Brazil and Italy: A Common Background of Institutional Change

Emblematic of moments of transition in the form of government is the adoption of several political reforms to reorganise and suit the structure of administration to the new regime. Brazil became a Republic on 15 November 1889 after a military coup that deposed the Emperor Dom Pedro II[1] and installed a

---

1 Dom Pedro I's son, he was the second and last ruler of the Empire of Brazil, created in 1822 when his father declared Brazilian independence from Portugal. He reigned for over 58 years, after the abrupt abdication of Dom Pedro I on 1831, when he was just a five-years-old boy. For an English version of his historical profile, cf. Lila Moritz SCHWARCZ: *The Emperor's Beard:*

provisional government. Its first act was to issue a decree proclaiming, provisionally, the Federal Republic, converting the old imperial provinces in federal states.²

Among all the reforms undertaken at this time, the one that is of interest in this chapter is the creation of the Federal Court of Auditors as a way to rationalize public expenditures. The enterprise was an initiative of the then finance minister Rui Barbosa,³ who wrote the Explanatory Memorandum of the Decree n° 966 A of 7 November 1890.⁴ He asserted that the most important providence that a well-constituted political society could demand of its representatives was the transformation of the state budget in an inviolable and sovereign institution.

At the same time that the jurist recognized the importance of that instrument – affirming that there was no institution more important to the regular administrative and political mechanism of a people than budgetary law – he showed his prudence and consideration when said that in anyone else there was a greater propensity to more serious and dangerous abuses. He attributes, then, to the Republic with its regenerative power, the task of making the budget subject to scrupulous observation, according to the constitution, in its federal form. The budgetary accounting system then in force was, according to Barbosa, faulty and weak in its execution.

Dom Pedro II and the Tropical Monarchy of Brazil, John GLEDSON (transl.), New York, Hill and Wang, 2004.

2   Other measures could be mentioned: (i) the separation between state and church; (ii) creation of national symbols; (iii) reform of the criminal code; (iv) creation of a commission to prepare a draft of the constitution of the Republic. For a discussion about the place of those reforms inside the republican project, cf. Aliomar BALEEIRO: *A Constituição de 1891. Os pródromos da República, o clima emocional de 1889–1891 = Senado Federal, Constituições Brasileiras (1891)*, Brasília, CEE/MCT/ESAF/MF, 2002.

3   A renowned politician, diplomat, journalist and jurist, Rui Barbosa de Oliveira (1849–1923) was one of the leading intellectuals of his time, who acted to shape several important Brazilian policies, including the direct elections and abolition of slavery campaigns. He highly supported the federative regim and religious freedom during his parliamentarian life. Barbosa was also a famous essayist and was one of the founders (and later president) of the Brazilian Academy of Letters. But his international mark was made during the 1907 Peace Conference at the Hague, where he defended the legal equality among states and became known as "the Eagle of The Hague". He was later elected as a judge to the International Court of Justice at the Hague. For an english profile, cf. José H. Fischel De ANDRADE: *"The Eagle of the Hague": a short historical note on the Peace Palace's Bust of Rui Barbosa*, Perspectivas (Latin American Society of International Law), 3(2008), 1–3.

4   Rui BARBOSA: *Exposição de motivos de Rui Barbosa sobre a criação do TCU*. Revista do Tribunal de Contas da União, 30(1999)/82, 253–262.

The establishment of the Court of Auditors was a fundamental piece to rearrange the system, once it was an intermediate judiciary body between the administration and the legislature, placed in an autonomous position, with attributions of review and judgment and surrounded by guarantees against any threats to the exercise of its vital functions. Thus, ten months after assuming the ministry, Rui Barbosa sent to the head of the Provisional Government, Marechal Deodoro da Fonseca, the text of Decree nº 966-A, dedicated to the establishment of the Court of Auditors. However, only after the promulgation of the Republican Constitution was the Court instituted and was regulated in the next year by Decree nº 1.166, of December 17, 1892.

Before these events, the idea had already been discussed in Brazil, with a bill having even been proposed to the Senate of the Empire. In that period, public income and expenses were supervised by the Court of National Public Treasury that was subordinated to the executive and, in this way, deprived of full independence. The president of this court was the finance minister himself, the only member who had a decisive vote, while the others were just advisory.

The discussions about the creation of a Court of Auditors lasted almost one century, polarized between those who defended its importance – for whom the public accounts should be examined by an independent organ – and those who were against it because they thought that the public accounts could remain under the control by those who already did so. Only the fall of the Empire and the political and administrative reforms of the young Republic could bring this to pass, one of the keystones of its edification.

The model proposed by Minister Rui Barbosa was the fruit, as he said, of research abroad of masters, guides, practical reformers in the financial service branch that in other countries nearly had its own literature, professors and experts, while "among us nothing is known". He said that especially Italy could offer a model. The government should seek there contributions if it wanted a beneficial and compensative reform of the execution of expenses.

Rui Barbosa identifies two systems that in the European context inspired the creation of this kind of institution in the 19th century: the French and the Italian. The first extended beyond France to other important states in Europe, such as Sweden, Spain, Greece, Serbia, Romania and Turkey. The second extended beyond Italy, dominating also in the Netherlands, in Belgium, Portugal, Chile and Japan. In the first system, supervision was limited to prevent expenses from being ordered or paid beyond the capacity of the budget. In the other, the action of the judiciary ranges much further: it anticipates abuse, obstructing from the outset acts of the executive power, which could generate illegal expenses.

The minister asserted that of the two systems, the second was the one that fully met the purpose of the institution in question and provides the necessary elasticity to its creator's mind. It was not enough to judge the administration, to report any excesses committed and to punish the transgression. There should be, between the power that periodically authorizes expenses and the power that executes them daily, an independent mediator, that helps one and the other, communicating with the legislature and intervening in the administration. Yet it was not just to act as a guard, but was to prevent the perpetration of budgetary offenses, through rejection of the acts of the executive when necessary.

In his thought, it was infinitely better to prevent illegal and arbitrary payments than to censure them after they had been made. The subsequent control was sufficient regarding tax agents, because they were to provide guarantees that made them effectively responsible for the defence of the public treasury. But ministers would not provide these themselves, and therefore a preliminary guarantee was necessary, namely the preventive supervision of the Court.

Another point praised by Rui Barbosa – but with one reservation that will be analysed later in this chapter – was that Italian law provideed a much stronger prerogative to authorize the orders of expenses, generalizing the role of the Court of Auditors not only to cover the acts of the executive power related to the state budget that influence public incomes and revenues, but all royal decrees, independent of the ministry from where they came or the object to which they referred. He considered also a important advantage of this model, namely the promptness in liquidating accounts. The Italian Court of Auditors operates regularly, all year, following operations, as they take place, by the accounts of income and expenses that are communicated by the minister. All the reasons above, according to him, argued for the choice of the Italian model.

To understand this supposed standard, it's important to remember that the Kingdom of Italy was unified in 1861 and that there were were already four Courts of Auditors in the pre-unification kingdoms there: one in what had been Sardinia, whose seat was in Turin; another in Florence; another in Naples and the last one in Palermo. In front of the need of approval, for the first time, of a unique balance to the whole kingdom, the government recognized the indispensability of first creating an institution responsible for the control of that balance. This is why the Finance Minister Pietro Bastogi, in November of the same year, hastened to present to the Chamber of Deputies a project for the institution of the Court of Auditors. It was discussed for a long time at the Congress, enduring several modifications. The law n. 800 was passed on 14 August 1862 and simuntaneously the Courts of the pre-unification kingdoms were abolished. The institution started to work in Turin on 1 October 1862.

As Vicario[5] recalled, the Court of Auditors was the first national institution that extended its jurisdiction over the entire kingdom.

Meanwhile, it is necessary to look at Piedmont to understand the decisive steps that led to the creation of the Italian Court of Auditors. The unification law of 1862 was preceded by many projects, but in the end was made "according to the model" – to use an expression of Mastroberti – of the Piedmont law and then extended to the whole of Italy. On 5 November 1852, the Finance Minister Cavour presented to the Congress a project about administrative law, general accounting and the Court of Auditors, in which he affirmed the absolute need of concentrating the preventive and consumptive control in an irremovable judge.[6] The project did not continue, but these concepts were used by the Interior Minister Urbano Rattazi, who presented two other projects in 1854: one about the abolition of the Chamber of Auditors and about administrative contentious; the other about the institution of the Court of Counts. The concepts of these projects were finally formalized in a decree-law about the institution of a new Court of Counts, that were effective in Piedmont and Lombardy for two years, until the arrival of the new law after unification. This "new law", in fact, was very similar to that from 1859, except for small differences, and is is similar to what happened in the entire process of unification in Italy: the prominence of the political hegemony of Piedmont.[7]

In this model, the preventive control is of great importance because of its extension and efficacy. The advantage of the preventive control over the control *a posteriori* is that it hinders patrimonial damage to public revenues, while the control *a posteriori,* in the best scenario, can only obligate repayment. And the most remarkable thing, as all the authors warn, is that this final control is not confined to acts of a strictly financial nature, but also relates to all decrees of the sovereign, whatever the object. The function is consolidated with the *vidimus* and the registration (art. 13 and art. 19 CC): two distinct acts that represent the two purposes that were intended to reach through the control of the Court.

Errico Presutti explains that this idea came from Belgium, that introduced preventive control to its legal system in 1820 establishing the principle that no

---

5 Edoardo VICARIO: *La Corte dei Conti in Italia: Studio teorico pratico*, F. Vallardi, Milano, 1913.
6 Francesco MASTROBERTI: *La Corte dei Conti ieri,* Rivista di diritto amministrativo AMMINISTRATIV@MENTE 2(2012), 1–6.
7 About this argument, an excellent analysis was written by Nelson Moe in a text from 1992 whose title "Altro che Italia! Il Sud dei piemontesi" summarizes his intention: to denounce the representation of the South after unification as an imposition of its protagonists: the politicians from Piedmont. Nelson MOE: *"Altro che Italia!" Il Sud dei piemontesi (1860–61)*, Meridiana: Rivista di storia e scienze sociali 15(1992), 153–189.

provision for paying any expenses of the state could be ordered if it had not been preventively verified, liquidated and registered by the Court of Auditors.[8] Italy took this idea and extended it beyond its original limits. It was extended not only to payment orders, but also to all acts in which contracts were approved or expenses were authorized, independently of its form or nature and to all acts of nomination, promotion or transfer of employees, or to those regarding salaries, pensions and payments in charge of the state.

3 Re-Reading the Standard: Changes and Appropriations of an Institutional Model

The advantage of a comparative study of law for legal historians is well summarized by Alan Watson when he sustains that "comparative law does not only take from legal history, it can also give".[9] This is verifiable whenever foreign legal models are (non) professedly imitated; even if it is just a selective adoption of particular legal institutions or rules. In these hypotheses, it is fundamental to understand not only the "influenced" system, but also the foreign rules and institutions - the one who borrows and the other who creates its own system based in that influence. This is because the borrowed rule does not operate exactly in the same way it did in its original place.

And that was also recognized by the mastermind of the creation of the court himself, Rui Barbosa, who admitted the inadequacy of a full transplant of Italian law to Brazilian reality and makes a reservation in the same Explanatory Memorandum that was mentioned previously.[10] According to him, it seemed that the evolution that was reached in Italy, that brought the inspectorate of the Court of Auditors beyond the boundaries of the acts related to public finances may be vulnerable, and it would have been better if the functions had been limited to the area of the financial acts of the government.

Crossing this boundary, the Court could become an obstacle to the administration, making ministerial action difficult in an unfavourable way, even nullifying initiatives of the government in acts that did not affect the integrity of the budget. It would be better, according to him, to circumscribe the new

---

8   Errico PRESUTTI: *Il controllo preventivo della Corte dei Conti sulle spese pubbliche*, Tipografico Editrice, Torino, 1908.
9   Alan WATSON: *Legal transplants: an approach to comparative law*, 2ª ed, University of Georgia Press, Georgia, 1993. 102.
10 Rui BARBOSA: *op. cit.*

authority in the natural limit of its needs, reducing the prevent supervision of the Court to those government acts that could relate to the incomes or expenses of the public treasury. With this reservation, he confirms that the Italian system is the best model because the preventative jurisdiction is the essential characteristic of this organisation.

Nevertheless, even when a transplanted rule arrives unchanged, its impact in a new social context results in a transformation. This is why the second section of this chapter was dedicated to offer a historical overview of the moments in which the Court of Auditors was installed in Brazil and Italy. It could be seen that in both countries the Court arrived at a moment of transition as an instrument of consolidation of the new regime. But Brazil in 1890 had already been a unified state since 1774, when it was still a colony of Portugal, that had become an Empire with the declaration of independence in 1822.

Then, in 1889 the Proclamation of the Republic changed the form of government and the form of state to a federal state. The creation of the Court of Auditors among the first acts of the Provisional Government was not to unify the country, since there was already a national court – the previously mentioned Court of the Public Treasury – but to make it independent of the executive power, no longer subordinate to the "will of the Empire", and to make the public budget a stable institution.

On the other hand, in Italy, it was one of the first acts of the government with a different main intent: to consolidate the unification of the territory of the country. Before the *Risorgimento* there were, as already mentioned here, four courts of auditors in the different regions, that had even different systems of organisation. It was then necessary to balance the entire kingdom. Thus, while Italy was trying to consolidate the unification, Brazil was trying to consolidate the federation, decentralizing its system.

The form of government also affects the rules of nomination of who would constitute the Court. In the Brazilian Republic, according to Art. 6 of the Decree n° 966-A, the members of the Court would be chosen by a decree of the President of the Republic, that was subject to the approval of the Senate. They had the same guarantees of irremovability as the Federal Supreme Court. In the Italian monarchy, according to Art. 3 of the mentioned law n. 800, the members of the Court were nominated by a royal decree, proposed by the Minister of Finance, after deliberation of the Cabinet Council. In his article for the *Enciclopedia giuridica italiana* from 1902 about the Court of Auditors, Ugo Giovanni Battista affirms that even entrusting the executive power with the nomination of the members, the Court was independent because its president and councillors could not be removed from office except by a royal decree in accordance with the opinion of a commission comprised of the presidents and the vice presidents of the Senate and the Chamber of Deputies (Art. 4).[11]

About the attributions of the courts, in Italy, as already mentioned, examined are all the royal decrees (Art. 13), independent of the ministry from whence they emanated and the object they discuss, all of them are to be submitted to the Court of Auditors to receive the *vidimus* and have their registration effectuated. Next, the Court should approve contracts, authorize expenses and the removal of employees, and all those acts that establish pensions, salaries or other consignments in charge of the state should be presented to the Court of Auditors to receive the *vidimus* and be registered.

In Brazil, the Court should examine just the operations that concern the incomes or expenses of the Republic. Thus, just executive decrees, orders or acts that could potentially constitute an expense or interest the finances of the Republic were submitted to the judgment of the Court of Auditors, that should also give its *vidimus* when they do not violate any law or exceed the means voted by the legislative.

In the case of a negative opinion from the Court, in Italy (Art. 14) it should refuse its *vidimus* throughout a motivated decision. This decision is then transmitted by the President to whom it may concern. In case he persists, the matter would be examined by the Cabinet Council. If they resolve that the act or decree should stand, the Court would be called to deliberate and if it considers still valid the cause of the refusal, it would order the registration, but with a *vidimus* under reservation. According to Art. 18, the Court, every January, should communicate to the Presidency of the Senate and to the Chamber of Deputies the list of the executed *vidimus* under reservation with the respective decision.

In Brazil, the initial procedure is the same, but if the ministers who had an act refused by the Court wishes to persist in its realisation, on its own responsibility, can approve publicity and execution, but then the Court will submit this fact, as soon as possible, to the examination of the Congress, also registering it under reservation, and declaring its opinion to the legislative. The difference is that rejected acts are reported immediately.

The last comparison can be seen in the perspective of the constitutional prevision. In Italy, the fundamental law of the kingdom was the *Statuto*

---

[11] Giovanni Batista UGO: *Cortei dei Conti* = Enciclopedia Giuridica Italiana: esposizione ordinata e complete dello stato e degli ultimi progressi della scienza, della legislazione e della giurisprudenza nel Diritto Civile, Commerciale, Penale, Pubblico, Giudiziario, Costituzionale, Amministrativo, Internazionale, Ecclesiastico, Economico con riscontri di Storia del Diritto, Diritto romano e di Legislazione comparata, vol 3, part 3, Pasquale Stanislao MANCINI (ed.), Milano 1902, 908–996.

Albertino, whose name comes from the king that promulgated it, Carlo Alberto di Savoia Carignano, in 1848 in the Kingdom of Piedmont-Sardinia. From the unification until the end of the Second World War, this was the statute in force in Italy. It did not foresee the Court of Auditors. In Brazil, instead, two years after the proclamation of the Republic by the Provisional Government, the Republican Constitution, Art. 89 formalized the institution of a Court of Auditors directed to verify the legality of the public income and expenses before sending them to the Congress. Its members should be named by the President of the Republic with the approval of the Senate, and they could lose their place by a sentence.

In short, we can not talk about a complete and pure legal reception, not only because of a theoretical and inherent impossibility, but for an empirical discompass between different legal cultures. What is still impressive, meanwhile, it's the rethoric importance attributed by the lawmakers to the foreign paternity of the new institution. The Court of Auditors, created to reinforce the political sovereignty of the newborn Republic and strengthen the national control over the budget, was legitimated as a necessary institution throught its external roots.

4 Conclusion

The methodological approach for comparative law offered by Alan Watson, already mentioned in this paper, anticipates a problem of the conclusions of this kind of legal research: the fragility and the possibility of error is greater than in any other branch of study. However, even without establishing any definitive conclusion, the perspective here adopted led us to some interesting observations about (i) legal transplants, (ii) legal history and (iii) the concept of law itself (iii).

First of all, we are conduced to the necessity of considering the phenomenon of legal transfers between cultures in a plural way, which also considers the effects of their return. In this work, I tried to understand those communicative dynamics of change by considering the inner multilateralism of the contaminations among legal cultures, underlining the difference of contexts as a determinant factor in the (re)interpretation and in the (re)reading of texts.

Meanwhile, it's not meaningless the fact that properly the idea of a legal transplant – that, according to our investigation was not complete and pure – was used to legitimate the creation of the Court of Auditors in Brazil. Not in a moment when the reinforcing of a national identity was so important, after the fall of a long-term element of unification for the nation: the monarchy led by a Portuguese Imperor. Even in this context, the foreing references were still a strong argument of legitimation for any political proposal. Mainly the European models.

That conducts us to the reflection offered by Heikki Pihlajamäki about the common place in comparative histories of rising "the European heartland" as a "standard" to be followed. With this expression he means that the legal history of the peripheries is constantly measured in contrast to the center, forcing the first to look at their legal past with comparative glasses on, telling in which extent it is similar to the center and how their own legal history differs from it.[12]

In South America, this dependence on European legal culture is easily visible, even if presumed importations are, actually, completely new elaborations. Despite political emancipation, the cultural translation process from the "old continent" throughout sea route lines was continuous in the construction of the Latin American legal science, at least in a discursive dimension that constantly celebrated the European literature.

That's why is so important, in a comparative study starting from the south, not only detecting the European influence in the creation of some institution, in a traditional peripheral view that recognizes the ascendancy of the center, but rather to emphasize the differences between them, as we tried to do. This is because the underlying premise of this work is based in the principles established by the methodological approach of Alan Watson: the conviction that a voluntary reception or transplant frequently, perhaps always, involves a change in the law, due to many factors.

The second point I would like to underline is a common thought for legal historians that deserves to be recalled in a comparative study: the continuity of a word does not mean the continuity of its meaning. A word that is repeated in a different context from where it was created, even when it carries something of its original meaning, suffers modifications that are derived from the cultural frameworks in which it is read.

Lastly, all the remarks above are related to a particular conception of law, understood as a local phenomenon, connoted in relation with its context, namely the place, the time and the society. That is an empirical perspective, understood with the help of legal history, that shows the inseparable connection between the rules and the identity of the people to which they are directed. The transportation of law does not change its nature, and even the imported elements are submitted to this logic.

---

12   Heikki PIHLAJAMÄKI: *Comparative Contexts in Legal History: are we all comparatists now?* Sequência, 1(2015)/36, 57–75 (scielo.br/scielo.php?script=sci_arttext&pid=S2177705520150 00100057&lng=en&nrm=iso>, accessed 15.6.2016).

Bibliography

Rui BARBOSA: *Exposição de motivos de Rui Barbosa sobre a criação do TCU.* Revista do Tribunal de Contas da União, 30(1999)/82, 253–262.

Ugo Giovanni BATISTA: *Cortei dei Conti = Enciclopedia Giuridica Italiana: esposizione ordinata e complete dello stato e degli ultimi progressi della scienza, della legislazione e della giurisprudenza nel Diritto Civile, Commerciale, Penale, Pubblico, Giudiziario, Costituzionale, Amministrativo, Internazionale, Ecclesiastico, Economico con riscontri di Storia del Diritto, Diritto romano e di Legislazione comparata,* vol 3, part 3, Pasquale Stanislao MANCINI (ed.), Milano 1902, 908–996.

Francesco MASTROBERTI: *La Corte dei Conti ieri,* Rivista di diritto amministrativo AMMINISTRATIV@MENTE 2(2012), 1–6.

Nelson MOE: *"Altro che Italia!" Il Sud dei piemontesi (1860–61),* Meridiana: Rivista di storia e scienze sociali, 15(1992), 153–189.

Heikki PIHLAJAMÄKI: *Comparative Contexts in Legal History: are we all comparatists now?* Sequência, 1(2015)/36, 57–75.

Errico PRESUTTI: *Il controllo preventivo della Corte dei Conti sulle spese pubbliche,* Tipografico Editrice, Torino, 1908.

Edoardo VICARIO: *La Corte dei Conti in Italia: Studio teorico pratico,* F. Vallardi, Milano, 1913.

Alan WATSON: *Legal transplants: an approach to comparative law, 2nd* ed, University of Georgia Press, Georgia, 1993.

Aliomar Baleeiro: A Constituição de 1891. Os pródromos da República, o clima emocional de 1889–1891. Senado Federal, Constituições Brasileiras (1891), Brasília, CEE/MCT/ESAF/MF, 2002.

José H. Fischel De Andrade: "The Eagle of the Hague": a short historical note on the Peace Palace's Bust of Rui Barbosa, Perspectivas (Latin American Society of International Law), 3(2008), 1–3.

Lila Moritz Schwarcz: The Emperor's Beard: Dom Pedro II and the Tropical Monarchy of Brazil, John Gledson (transl.), New York, Hill and Wang, 2004.

CHAPTER 8

Constitutional Systems of Free European States (1918–1939)

Tadeusz Maciejewski and Maja Maciejewska-Szałas

1   Constitutions of Free Cities in the German Reich in the Weimar Period. Introduction

The Constitution of the German Reich was passed on 11 August 1919 in Weimar.[1] The relationship between the Reich as a whole and its federal constituents was regulated by Chapter I (The System and Tasks of the Reich), in particular Section 1 (The Reich and the States; Articles 1–19) although relevant provisions were to be found in numerous other articles of the constitution.[2]

Unitary tendencies become evident early in the Constitution, i.e. in Article 2 replacing the previously hierarchical order of the members of the First Reich and its successors (the Confederation of the Rhine, the German Confederation, the North German Confederation, the Second Reich) with one, in which each of them was designated as a *Land* (state), instead of the former term *Staat* (country). The states were eighteen in number, with Germany having the capacity to enlarge its territory and create new states within its borders (Article 18). The new division reflected social, economic and cultural traditions rather than historical ones. This was severely criticized by those former German states, such as Prussia or Bavaria, which had played a special role in the past. As a result, each state was obliged to be constituted as a republican "free state" (Article 17). They were all empowered to issue their own constitutions but not

---

1 Tadeusz Maciejewski obtained financial resources for conducting research in the area covered by the article from the National Science Center on Decision No. DEC-2014/15/B/HS5/03321. The article was translated by Sebastian Macieja, Dawid Michalski and Piotr Kitowski.
2 The first project of the constitution (*Vorentwurf zur Verfassung des Deutschen Reichs (Entwurf I) von 3. Januar 1919 (Nicht veröffentlich))*: *Quellensammlung zum deutschen Reichsstaatsrecht*, Heinrich TRIEPEL (ed.), 4th ed., Siebeck, Tübingen, 1926; German text of the constitution: *Reichgesetzblatt* 152(1919), 1383. Polish translation (*Konstytucja Rzeszy Niemieckiej z dnia 11 sierpnia 1919 r.*): *Nowe konstytucje*, Julian MAKOWSKI (ed.), Warsaw, Hoesisck, 1925; cf. also *Dokumente zur Deutschen Verfassungsgeschichte*, Ernst Rudolf HUBER (ed.), vol. 3, Kohlhammer, Stuttgart, 1966, 129–155.

before the enactment of federal basic law so as to ensure compliance. This was contravened by Anhalt, Baden, and Oldenburg, which did so earlier, although in accordance with the constitutional principles agreed upon by the National Assembly and the Committee of the States. The other states were forced to either amend their constitutional drafts (e.g. Bavaria) or settle for provisional work-in-progress (e.g. Prussia). The names of the states varied, in tribute to their historical past despite express provisions to the contrary in Article 17 of the Weimar Constitution. This exemplified the once-prominent differences but left no impact on the substance of the state constitutions.[3]

1.a Hamburg

On 16 March 1919, a special Citizens' Assembly vested with the powers of a constitutional assembly was appointed in Hamburg with a view to enacting a constitution. The Senate joined in the effort in October that year with 67 proposed articles which, compared to subsequent legislation, were of a general nature. These were extended and elaborated to form a new draft in September 1920, serving as the basis for the future constitution. The draft was discussed in a preliminary session of three days and submitted for final debate, which lasted three months. Subsequently, eight successive sessions were held to complete the first reading (20 and 29 October; 5, 10, 12, 19, 26 November; 1 December). The second reading took place on 22 and 29 December. Final editing, which took place between the first and second readings, was carried out behind closed doors under the direction of Wolfgang Brinckmann of the Democratic Party of Germany (DDP). 95 SPD-DDP coalition deputies voted in favour,

---

3   The most important publications about the Constitution of Weimar Republic include: Gerhard ANSCHÜTZ: *Die Verfassung des Deutschen Reichs vom 11. August 1919. Ein Kommentar für Wissenschaft und Praxis*, Stilke, Berlin, 1933; Willibalt APELT: *Geschichte der Weimarer Verfassung*, Biederstein Velt, München, 1946; Johann Viktor BREDT, *Der Geist der deutschen Reichsverfassung*, Stilke, Berlin, 1924; August FINGER: *Das Staatsrecht des Deutschen Reichs. Der Verfassung vom 11. August 1919*, Enke, Stuttgart, 1923. In Polish literature the highest value has monograph by Jan WĄSICKI: *Rzesza a kraje niemieckie 1914–1949*, Wydawnictwo Poznańskie, Poznań, 1977. In German textbooks about the Constitution of 1919: Ernst FORSTHOFF: *Deutsche Verfassungsgeschichte der Neuzeit*, vierte Auflage, Stuttgart, Kohlhammer, 1972, 164–191; Fritz VON HARTUNG: *Deutsche Verfassungsgeschichte vom 15. Jahrhundert bis zur Gegenwart*, sechste Auflage, Koehler, Stuttgart, 1954, 315–342; Werner FROTSCHER, Bodo PIEROTH: *Verfassungsgeschichte*, vierte Auflage, C.H. Beck, München, 2003, 275–302; Otto KIMMINICH: *Deutsche Verfassungsgeschichte*, Nomos, Frankfurt a. M., 1970, 484–540; Christian-Friedrich MENGER: *Deutsche Verfassungsgeschichte der Neuzeit*, fünfte Auflage, Müller Juristicher Verlag, Heidelberg, 1980, 167–174; Hans FENSKE: *Deutsche Verfassungsgeschichte. Vom Norddeutschenbund bis heute*, Copress, Berlin, 1981, 46–54.

while forty opposition deputies voted against. The Senate promulgated the constitution on 7 January 1921, effective as of the same day.[4]

The constitution consisted of a preamble and seventy-one articles grouped in nine chapters entitled as follows: State and Nation, Citizens' Assembly, Senate, Legislative, Administration, Commercial and Occupational Association, Municipalities, and Final and Interim Provisions.[5]

The constitution laid down the city's political system as a republican state under the name of "The Free Hanseatic City of Hamburg" within the Reich (Article 1). Power was held by the people and exercised pursuant to the above-mentioned Constitution of Hamburg and other acts (Article 2). In contrast to the other states, the constitution did not define the state's relationship to the Reich, merely designating it as a member.

The legislative was traditionally named the Citizens' Assembly – *Bürgerschaft* – consisting of 160 members (deputies) elected by democratic, five-point (universal, equal, direct, secret and proportional) suffrage. These were to be regulated by a future act on elections. The elections could only be held on a Sunday or another holiday (Article 3). Active voting rights extended to all citizens of the Reich who had reached twenty years of age and had been living the Hamburg state (*Staatsgebiet*) (Article 4).

The Assembly's term was three years (Article 13) with the possibility of earlier dissolution. A motion to dissolve had to be proposed by ¼ of the members, recorded on the agenda a week prior to the session and notice provided to all deputies and senators. Dissolution required the consent of a majority of deputies (Article 17) with the type of majority unspecified, though presumably a simple majority (Article 14) in line with Article 32 of the Federal Constitution. In the case of dissolution, the Senate would hold new elections within sixty

---

4 Text of the constitution: *Die Verfassung der Freien und Hansestadt Hamburg. Vom 7. Januar 1921*, Hamburgisches Gesetz und Verordnungsblatt 5(1921), 9; Otto RUTHENBERG: *Verfassungsgesetze des deutschen Reichs und der deutschen Länder nach dem Stande vom 1. Februrar 1926*, F. Vahlen, Berlin, 1926, 102–113.

5 German literature about the Constitution of Hamburg includes Michael DUNKELBERG: *Bürgerausschuss in der Verfassung der Freien und Hansestadt Hamburg*, Diss. Hamburg, Hamburg, 1980; Max MITTELSTEIN: *Die Verfassung der Freien und Hansestadt Hamburg vom 7. Januar 1921*, Hartung, Hamburg, 1924. In Poland, these issues were the subject of interest of: Tadeusz MACIEJEWSKI: *Konstytucje wolnych miast Europy w okresie międzywojennym = Społeczeństwo a władza. Ustrój, prawo, idee*, Jacek PRZYGODZKI, Marian PTAK (eds.), Kolonia Limited, Wrocław, 2010, 624–630; Tadeusz MACIEJEWSKI: *Konstytucja Wolnego i Hanzeatyckiego Miasta Hamburga z 7 stycznia 1921 r. = Świat, Europa, Mała Ojczyzna. Studia ofiarowane Profesorowi Stanisławowi Grodzickiemu w 80-lecie urodzin*, Marian MAŁECKI (ed.), Wyższa Szkoła Administracji, Bielsko-Biała, 2009, 801–812; WĄSICKI: *op. cit.*, 142, 144.

days and convene the Assembly for the first session taking place within eight days of the date of the elections. Until then, the previous Assembly enjoyed its full powers.

Organisationally, the main agency of the Assembly was its Presidium consisting of seven members: the president, two vice-presidents and four secretaries. The president headed its operations and enjoyed powers related to supervising the chancellery, budget management, external representation, the police force and representation in disputes with administrative authorities (Article 17). The Assembly was convened for a session by its chancellery on the president's order, decision of the Presidium, the Assembly's own resolution, the decision of the Citizens' Commission, by motion of the Senate or twenty deputies but only when the next session was scheduled to take place in more than two months (Article 22).

The Assembly's primary area of competence was legislation. The right to propose initiatives extended to the Assembly itself and to the Senate, although only the former could pass acts (Article 51), needing only a simple majority of votes except where the constitution provided otherwise (Article 18). The quorum was more than eighty deputies, the number having to be verified before voting (Articles 20, 19). The method of voting was laid down in the regulations. The sessions of the Assembly were open but could be made secret by a motion of thirty deputies or of the Senate (Article 21).

In order to counterbalance the Senate's executive power, the Constitution of Hamburg, in addition to the Assembly itself and potential investigative committees, provided for the appointment of a special body known as the Citizens' Commission (*Bürgerausschluss*), consisting of the Assembly's president as chairman and twenty deputies as members. These were selected in proportion with the number of deputy mandates obtained by each party. However, only those parties were considered which had obtained at least ten votes in the Assembly. The parties were prevented from combining their tickets, making it more difficult for parties wishing to form a coalition to integrate votes. Each Commission member had one vote. Deputies could withdraw from the Commission on election or while it was active. In the latter case, they were replaced by successive deputies. The seat remained vacant if it proved impossible to fill for lack of candidates (Article 27).

The republican Reich constitution clearly stipulated that the executive power in the state rested with the president (Article 41) appointed by the chancellor (Article 53) and nominated ministers (Article 53). It prevented each state from electing its own president. The executive in federal states rested with state governments. These were known as senates in Hamburg, Bremen and Lübeck in line with Hanseatic traditions; in Prussia, Baden, Württemberg and

Thüringen, as state ministries and, in Bavaria and Saxony, general ministries. The other states used the term "state presidium".

The constitution of Hamburg stated only that the Senate is the state government without specifying the number of its members (Article 32). Any German citizen could be elected to it as long as he or she had attained thrity years of age, had been a citizen of the Reich for at least a year, was domiciled in the state of Hamburg and done nothing to become ineligible. At the same time, the acceptance of a seat in the Senate was not obligatory (Article 33). The senators were elected by the Citizens' Assembly by majority vote. Vacated seats were to be filled within a month. Candidates were always presented by the Citizens' Commission, which could demand that a representative of the Senate attend its sessions (Article 35).

The Senate as a whole, as well as its respective members, had to enjoy the Assembly's trust or else were liable to be recalled by it. A motion of no confidence could be proposed by at least forty deputies. Notice of this had to be provided to all other deputies and the Senate or its individual members a week before it was debated and voted on. A resolution to recall had to be passed by an absolute majority vote. Failing that, a vote could be re-taken a week later, but then the motion required a qualified majority (2/3). A recalled Senate could, as a last resort, move for a popular referendum to decide if the Senate itself or the Citizens' Assembly should be dissolved (Article 36). However, the old Senate would remain in office until a new one was ready to take over (Article 37).

The Senate selected from among its own members in a secret vote a president (first mayor) and his deputy (second mayor) for a one-year term of office. Re-election was allowed. The president's task was to direct the Senate's work, represent it abroad, ensure the proper conduct of internal and foreign policy and be personally involved in the exercise of legislative and executive powers (Articles 7, 41).

The Senate passed all resolutions by a majority vote. Ties were decided by the president's casting vote, as it was counted double, while the individual senators had the right to record separately a dissenting opinion in the minutes (Article 38).

The Senate's broad executive but also partially legislative, judicial and representative powers were treated only generally by the constitution, leaving them to be regulated precisely in specific acts. The Senate's main powers included directing the administration and resolving issues falling within its subject-matter competence (Article 38), legislative initiative (Article 38), overall supervision of the administration (Article 43), representation of Hamburg before the Reich, other German states and abroad, including the ratification of agreements made by the city (Article 45), acting as the highest supervisory authority for municipalities (Article 46), appointing officials (Article 48), administering oaths of office (Article 42), maintaining public order and ensuring state security (Article 44) as well as exercising the right of pardon, with the reservation that amnesty or annulment of a proceeding could only be granted under an act and, in the case of a conviction by the State Tribunal, only by a motion of or in consultation with the Assembly (Article 47).

The city was administratively divided into municipalities with the city itself being a separate municipality governed by the Citizens' Assembly and Senate (Article 67). The remaining urban and rural municipalities within its territory were self-governing organisations under the direction of the competent local authorities. These institutions enjoyed freedom in the exercise of their state duties, to the extent that these related to administrative tasks, including ensuring compliance with applicable laws, financial discipline and honest conduct, although they were supervised by governmental authorities (Article 68). Municipality and state officials alike were obliged to take an oath of allegiance to the Constitution (Article 69).

In 1933, Hamburg and its adjacent areas covered 769 sq. km and was home to approximately 1,220,000 people. That year also marked the beginning of the unification of the Reich initiated by Hitler. In Hamburg, this was finished with the Great Hamburg Act of 26 January 1937, enlarging the city's territories to include the districts of Altona, Wandsbeck and Hamburg-Wilhelmsburg along with twenty-seven municipalities formerly belonging to Prussia. The administration of the state was supervised by the Minister of Internal Affairs in consultation with the Minister of Finance. Eventually, an act was passed on 9 December 1937 to place the Reich governor at the head of state and local administration, with the president (governmental administration) and mayor (municipal administration) acting as his deputies. As a result, Hamburg lost its status as a state.

1.b Lübeck

On 7 April 1875, a new constitution was passed, with later amendments of 2 October 1907. It was amended by the State Constitution of Lübeck promulgated on 23 May 1920.[6] It consisted of a preamble and seventy-one articles gathered into seven chapters (General Provisions, Senate, Citizens' Assembly, The Powers of the Senate and the Citizens' Assembly, Standing Commissions,

---

6 Text of the constitution: *Lübeckische Landverfassung. Veröffentlich am 23. Mai 1920 = Sammlung der Lübeckischen Gesetze und Verordnungen*, 78(1920), 114; RUTHENBERG: *op. cit.*, 131–143.

Proceedings in the Case of Persistent Discrepancies between the Two Bodies, Referendum). It concluded with interim provisions regarding five articles of the constitution (5, 21, 44, 53). The preamble made a reference to the previous joint constitutional efforts of the Council Commission and the Citizens' Commission at the end of and following the First World War. These took place on 28 March 1917, 11 December 1918, 26 February and 26 March 1919, the last of them taking into account the principles contained in the Weimar Constitution of 11 August 1919, concerning the substance of future state constitutions.[7]

The general provisions defined Lübeck's state system as a "Free State under the name of Free and Hanseatic City of Lübeck, an independent state of the Reich" (Article 1). This was an expression of the existing independence, also reflected in the constitutions of other states of the republic, especially Hamburg and Bremen, which considered themselves to be free and Hanseatic cities. Other states did not use such formulations, regarding themselves, above all, as separate republics within the German Reich.

According to the constitution, the power in Lübeck came from the people and was exercised by the Senate and the Citizens' Assembly (Article 2). Any German could be a citizen as long as he or she enjoyed suffrage but only for the local Assembly (Article 3). The constitution was to apply not only in Lübeck, but also to those municipalities within its borders which remained under the authority of the Senate and the Citizens' Assembly (Article 4). The constitution did not contain any mention of the municipalities or their system.

The Citizens' Assembly consisted of eighty deputies. Active voting rights extended to all citizens of the Reich, regardless of their gender, who had been living in Lübeck state for at least three months (Article 17). The rights were not granted to interdicts, persons under temporary custody as a result of mental illness and those sentenced to the loss of public rights (Article 18). Passive voting rights extended to Reich citizens who enjoyed full public rights and had been living in Lübeck for at least six months, as well as non-members of the Senate (Article 19). It was not compulsory to accept election to office (Article 20). Elections by universal, equal, direct, secret and proportional suffrage took place every three years, on the second or third Sunday of November. A newly elected Citizens' Assembly entered into office on 1 December (Article 21) The deputies represented the nation (Article 19). They could lose

---

7 Günter KRABBENHÖFT: *Verfassungsgeschichte der Hansestadt Lübeck. Eine Übersicht*, Schmidt-Römhild, Lübeck 1969; MACIEJEWSKI: *Konstytucje wolnych ..., op. cit.*, 630–635; Tadeusz MACIEJEWSKI: *Krajowa Konstytucja miasta Lubeki z 23 maja 1920 r.* = *Vetera Novis Augere. Studia i prace dedykowane Profesorowi Wacławowi Uruszczakowi*, Dorota MALEC et al. (eds.), vol. 2, Wydawnictwo Uniwersytetu Jagiellońskiego, Krakow, 2010, 635–644; WĄSICKI: *op. cit.*

their position at their own request or for failure to comply with the conditions necessary for passive voting rights (Article 24). The Assembly selected its chairman and two vice-chairmen at the first session for a one-year term, with no right decline the election. Re-election was allowed (Article 25). The chairman was usually elected by a majority vote. If the vote proved inconclusive in the first round, those three candidates who had received the most votes advanced to the second round. If this also proved inconclusive, the third round began with two of the second-round contenders. In the case of the last round still being indecisive, the offices were distributed by lot (Article 26). Besides these officers, the Assembly also selected its secretary.

The Assembly was convened by the chairman by a motion of twenty deputies or the Senate (Article 28). This was done through a public announcement seven days in advance and, in the case of the Senate advancing the motion, each deputy was to receive a proposed agenda five days prior to the session (Article 29). The quorum required more than half the members (Article 30). Senate representatives could also attend the proceedings of the Citizens' Assembly, although their presence was not required if the subject-matter related to elections or matters which could be decided without senators (Article 31). Resolutions were passed by a majority vote (Article 33).

State powers in Lübeck were exercised jointly by the Senate and Citizens' Assembly unless otherwise provided for by the constitution (Article 41). Their powers covered matters relating to:
– amendments to the constitution, with two readings required for proposed revisions, a resolution by a 2/3 qualified majority vote and a two-week interval between the readings (Article 37);
– the acquisition and disposal of sovereign rights;
– the issuance, repeal and interpretation of acts and orders;
– the levy, change and abolition of taxes and other monetary performances;
– amnesty;
– passing resolutions on compulsory purchases for charitable purposes and social welfare;
– passing the state budget and the public budgets of charitable institutions;
– decisions on major changes in the structure of administrative authorities (Article 42).

The Citizens' Assembly had auxiliary bodies in the form of four standing commissions. The most important of these was the Citizens' Commission. There were also the Budget, Petition, and Election Commissions (Article 49). The Citizens' Commission consisted of twenty-four members selected from among the deputies of the Assembly for a one-year term. Re-election was allowed, but an outgoing member could decline it. Candidates for the commissions were reported to the Assembly chairman at the latest three days before the elections (Article 53). The commissions were headed by chairmen and their deputies. All of them were obliged to accept the offices, for which they had been selected (Article 54). A commission was convened by its chairman (Article 55). Its sessions were public but could be made secret by a motion of the Senate or the Citizens' Assembly (Article 56). The quorum required for passing a resolution was 2/3 of all members (Article 57).

The Citizens' Commission was competent with regard to:
- granting funds of up to 10,000 marks in total but not exceeding 500 marks annually in individual cases, where applications for such funds to be allocated for the same purpose were made repeatedly in the same accounting year;
- utilizing budget items not allotted to any individual office
- acquiring and disposing of real estate for the benefit of the "Lübeck state" as well as real estate belonging to Old Lutheran municipalities, public charities and private foundations with a value of up to 20,000 marks if this did not involve the exercise of the sovereign rights of these institutions;
- making offers for the sale of real estate belonging to the "state" regardless of their value;
- changing the principles of the administration and use of state-owned property and public charities with a value of up to 20,000 marks.

In accordance with Hanseatic traditions, the executive in Lübeck was known as the Senate, consisting of twelve members. Seven of them were principal ones, as they were banned from employment in institutions, in which they could earn a steady income, though they were allowed, subject to the Senate's consent, to sit on supervisory boards of various enterprises. This did not apply to the remaining five senators, although the Citizens' Assembly could, in individual cases, impose such a ban on them as well (Article 5). Senators were elected by the Citizens' Assembly for a ten-year term. Re-election was allowed. The elections were organised by the Assembly's Elections Commission.

The Senate held independent powers with regard to:
- foreign policy;
- "state" representation abroad and performance of international agreements;
- the right of pardon;
- the issuance of administrative decisions;
- the direction and supervision of governmental and municipal administration as well as control of the property of recognized religious associations;
- passing resolutions, ordinances and orders in matters falling within the Senate's exclusive competence and ensuring their proper execution;

- the appointment and recall of governmental and municipal officials;
- granting titles (Article 45).

"The Lübeck State" survived as a constituent member of the Weimar Republic until 1933. In that year, pursuant to the temporary unification of the Reich act, it was incorporated into Prussia as a separate urban district with the exception of two municipalities. At its abolition, the "state" covered an area of 298 sq. km. and was inhabited by a population of 136,000.

1.c   Bremen

In the early 20th century, the political system of Bremen was regulated by the Constitution of 1 January 1894. In the aftermath of the revolutionary events in the city, which took place in November 1918, the National Assembly was appointed the following year to act jointly with the former Senate, resulting in the issue on 9 April 1919 of a temporary law regulating the system of city government and establishing a special constitutional deputation which was to draft a new constitution. Two sessions were held to discuss it at the end of 1918 and early 1919. The draft was passed by the National Assembly of Bremen as the new constitution on 18 May 1920, effective from 6 June of that year, after three readings held on 16 January, 7–8 and 11 May 1920.[8]

The constitution consisted of five chapters concerning: "the State of Bremen" in General (I); Referendum, State Assembly and State Government (II); Legislature, Administration and Judiciary (III), Public Law Corporations (IV) and Interim Provisions (V), all of which contained eighty-nine paragraphs, some of which were subdivided internally into parts.[9]

The city, known officially as the Free Hanseatic City of Bremen, covered an area of 258 sq. km. and had a population of approximately 370,000. It consisted of the cities of Bremen, Bremenhafen and Vegesack and rural territories. Its status within the Reich was that of a federal state (*Land*) entitled to all rights and obligations resulting from the Federal Constitution (Article 1). In honour of long-standing tradition, the text of the constitution used that term interchangeably with "the State of Bremen" understood as forming a democratic

---

[8]   Text of the constitution: *Die Verfassung der Freien Hansestadt Bremen. Vom 18. Mai 1920*, Gesetzblatt der Freien Hansestadt Bremen, 46(1920), 183; RUTHENBERG: *op. cit.*, 90–102.

[9]   Overview of the constitution: Herbert SCHWARZWÄLDER: *Geschichte der Freien Hansestadt Bremen*, vol. 3, Röver, Hamburg, 1983; Georg BESSEL: *Bremen – Die Geschichte einer deutschen Stadt*, Insel, Leipzig, 1935; MACIEJEWSKI: *Konstytucje wolnych miast...*, *op. cit.*, 630–635; Tadeusz MACIEJEWSKI: *Konstytucja Wolnego Hanzeatyckiego Miasta Brema z 18 maja 1920 r. = O prawie i jego dziejach, księgi dwie. Studia ofiarowane Profesorowi Adamowi Lityńskiemu*, Marian MIKOŁAJCZYK (ed.), vol. 2, Wydawnictwo Uniwersytetu w Białymstoku, Białystok-Katowice, 2010, 245–254.

parliamentary republic. The state power came from the people and was exercised directly by the nation as a whole in popular referenda and through elected representatives as well as indirectly by the State Assembly (*Landtag*), also known as the Citizens' Assembly (*Bürgerschaft*) and State Government (*Landregierung*), also known under its traditional designation of Senate (§2).

The State (Citizens') Assembly consisted of 120 deputies. Elections were held by universal, equal, direct, secret and proportional suffrage (§10). All citizens of the Reich (regardless of gender) were entitled to passive and active voting rights as long as they had reached twenty years of age and had been living the "Bremen State" (§11).

The State Assembly members elected a president from among their number as head of the body, who together with his deputy and secretary (clerk) formed its Presidium, under whose direction the Assembly operated. The Presidium could be enlarged to include a honorary registrar (§ 23). The term "parliamentary session" was nowhere to be found in either the rules of the Assembly or the constitution. As a result, the term was divided into sittings held when necessary. The Assembly was convened by the President at its own discretion, when required by the Senate or when requested in writing by at least twenty-four deputies. Each deputy had to be invited to a sitting in writing with at least two days' notice. This rule could be ignored in urgent need or when notifying all deputies was impossible (§ 25). The Assembly's proceedings were open but could be held *in camera* if at least fifteen deputies or the Senate proposed an appropriate motion and obtained a simple majority vote in support (§17, 27). The agenda and the text of resolutions were null and void unless the Senate was consulted (§24).

Legislative initiative was given to the State Assembly, the Senate (§56) and citizens themselves acting through a referendum (§55).

The executive in the "Bremen State" was exercised by the State Government, also known as the Senate in line with Hanseatic traditions. It consisted of fourteen members (§ 35). These were elected by the State Assembly by a simple majority vote. The elections were conducted by a fifteen-member commission of the Assembly. The line-up of the parliament had to match the current partisan composition (§2). Entitlement to passive voting rights was conditional upon the attainment of thirty years of age, eligibility for the Assembly and, subject to exemption in special cases, living the state for a minimum period of one year (§38, 42).

After elections to the Assembly, the Senate selected from time to time by secret ballot two mayors from among its own members. In another round, one of the mayors was, also by secret ballot, made president. The constitution allowed reshuffles in these positions on occasions other than parliamentary elections, provided that these affected the Senate's make-up. Re-election was allowed but refusal of or resignation from office required the consent of the entire State Government (§45). The president was in charge of: heading the Senate, ensuring the proper conduct of work related to the powers entrusted to him and supervising the tasks entrusted to individual senators (§47). For these purposes, he could be replaced by the mayor or other specially designated Senate members (§46).

Besides legislative powers, the Senate was fully in charge of the executive. Within its scope, the State Government represented the state externally, exercised general administration, supervised governmental matters, appointed and recalled officials, granted the right of pardon on prior consultation with the courts, as well as amnesties (§60). Its activity in that respect was subject to supervision by the Citizens' Assembly as set forth in the constitution and specific acts (§61). The financial interests of the "Bremen State" were the responsibility of a specially appointed Finance Commission. In particular, its powers included drafting and presenting the budget for the State Assembly's approval, supervising governmental property and other economic undertakings of a public nature, the control of revenues and expenses, governmental debt repayments, ensuring proper accounting practices in administrative bodies as well as regular collection of state-owed court fees.

The parliamentary democracy of the "Bremen State" collapsed after the issue on 31 March 1933 of the temporary unification act dissolving the *Landtag* and ordering new elections, with the Nazis emerging as winners. A governor of the Reich was also appointed. Successive changes within the system were introduced pursuant to ministerial ordinances, especially those of the minister of the interior. The borders of the state were re-drawn in 1939 when Bremerhafen broke away to join with Hanover, for which Bremen was compensated with the addition of eight rural municipalities.

1.d   *The Free City of Danzig (Gdansk)*

The Supreme Council of the Paris Peace Conference, the so-called Council of Ten, known from March 1919 as the Council of Four, appointed a Commission for Polish Affairs on 12 February under the direction of Jules Cambon. Initially, the Commission's reports recommended that Danzig be annexed by Poland, but in the end it was the idea of making it a free city, proposed by David Lloyd George and supported by Woodrow Wilson, which prevailed. The relevant provisions on the matter were included in Chapter XI and Articles 100–108 of the Treaty of Versailles of 28 June 1919. Germany waived all rights and titles to Danzig and the neighbouring areas to the Allied and Associated Powers (Article 100). The borders of the Free City were to be drawn by a special commission (Article 101). Eventually, its area covered 1952 sq. km. with a population of 330,000 including 40,000 Poles. Protection of Danzig was made the responsibility of the League of Nations (Article 102) represented by the High Commissioner. The constitution of the Free City was to be drafted by the local population in consultation with the High Commissioner and submitted to the League of Nations, which was to guarantee it. The founding of the Free City was announced on 15 November 1920.[10]

Work on the constitution began in July 1919, when a special delegation was sent to the Hanseatic cities in the Weimar Republic, i.e. Hamburg, Lübeck and Bremen, with the aim of collecting information on their state system. At the same time, a constitutional commission of fifty-three members was appointed under the leadership of senior mayor Heinrich Sahm to represent all the political parties. The commission held plenary sessions only twice (29 September and 6 October 1919). The second session saw the election of a fifteen-member subcommittee to discuss two proposed drafts of the constitution. The first, consisting of sixty-four articles, was penned by Sahm and dealt only with the political system with the exclusion of citizens' rights, thereby adopting the concepts embodied in the constitution of German Hanseatic cities. It envisioned Danzig becoming a "Free and Hanseatic City" with a republican form of government, with a twenty-six-member Senate as its supreme authority. The Senate was to consist of primary senators elected by the Citizens' Assembly for a twelve-year term and auxiliary senators elected for six years. It was to have legislative (jointly with the Citizens' Assembly), executive and self-governmental powers as well as to act as head of state. The second most important authority was the Citizens' Assembly elected democratically by the population for a four-year term and consisting of seventy-two members. It had legislative powers only in deciding matters unreserved for the Senate but even then required the Senate's consent.[11] During the second session of the subcommittee, Social Democrats, who were in the majority, presented a counter-draft

---

10 About the creation of the Free City of Danzig in Polish literature e.g.: Antoni ROMAN: *Ustrój polityczny Wolnego Miasta Gdańska*, Warsaw, 1926; Marceli PODLASZEWSKI: *Ustrój polityczny Wolnego Miasta Gdańska w latach 1920–1933*, Wydawnictwo Morskie, Gdynia, 1966. In German literature recently: Hans Viktor BÖTTCHER: *Die Freie Stadt Danzig. Wege und Umwege in die europäische Zukunft*, Kulturstiftung der deutschen Vertriebenen, Bonn, 1997.

11 *Entwurf einer Verfassung für die Freie und Hansestadt Danzig*, Boenig, Danzig, 1920; Tadeusz MACIEJEWSKI: *Projekty konstytucji wersalskiego Wolnego Miasta Gdańska = Księga dedykowana Profesorowi Marianowi Kallasowi*, Sławomir GODEK, Dariusz MAKIŁŁA, Magdalena WILCZEK-KARCZEWSKA (eds.), InterLeones Halina Dyczkowska, Warsaw, 537–552.

consisting of seventy articles but also dealing only with the city's political system. It called for a parliamentary republic. Authority was to be exercised only by the Citizens' Assembly consisting of 120 deputies elected by five-point suffrage for a two-year term. The Senate's role as a government elected by the Assembly was limited to executive powers.[12]

Both drafts were debated by the subcommittee from 17 October 1919 to 29 March 1920, with twenty-one sessions in total and culminating in the publication of the final version in April 1920. It was based on solutions adopted in the Weimar Republic's constitution and the constitution drafts of Hanseatic cities. A democratically elected People's Assembly serving a four-year term was to exercise supreme authority. The Senate was in charge of the executive, with primary senators elected for six-year terms and auxiliary ones – four. Following the debate, it was decided that legislation should be the joint responsibility of the People's Assembly and the Senate.[13]

The elections to the Constitutional Assembly were on 16 May 1920, with its first session taking place on 14 June. Preliminary debate, which began in that same month, resulted in the appointment of a seventeen-member subcommittee. It held eighteen meetings before presenting the final draft of the constitution in a plenary session of the Assembly of 27 July 1920. It was accepted after two readings on 11 August. The text was published on 9 December.[14]

Eventually, after many months' discussion, the High Commissioner accepted the text on 11 May 1922, which had also been approved by the Council of the League. This enabled the Senate to publish it on 30 June 1922 in the Journal of Laws. At last then, the day came, nearly three years after the Treaty of Versailles, for Danzig to have its constitution.[15]

The constitution consisted of 117 articles divided into two parts. The first (Articles 1–70) regulated the political system and contained general provisions and regulations on the People's Assembly, the Senate, legislation, administration, judicature and self-government. The second (Articles 71–115) regulated citizens' rights and freedoms, also including those related to natural persons, officials, religion, education, the school system and the economy. The text ended with final and interim provisions (Articles 116–117).[16]

---

12   *Ibid.*
13   *Ibid.*
14   PODLASZEWSKI: *op. cit.*, 46–50.
15   *Verfassung der Freien Stadt Danzig in der Fassung der Bekantmachung vom 14. Juni 1922*, A.W.Kafemann, Danzig, 1922.
16   PODLASZEWSKI, *op. cit.*, 46–50.

The Free City of Danzig's constitution deemed it to be a free republican state (Article 1). Its emblem depicted two silver crosses in a red field with a crown above them (Article 2). The authority came from the people (Article 3). The official language was German, but the Polish minority was guaranteed the right to use its mother tongue and cultivate its national identity (Article 4). Danzig was subject to considerable military restrictions at the wish of the League of Nations (Article 5).

Due to its republican form of government with a democratic regime, the principal state authority in the Free City of Danzig was constituted by the People's Assembly (*Volkstag*) which consisted of 120 elective (Article 6) deputies serving a four-year term (Article 9) and acting as people's representatives (Article 7). They were elected democratically by universal, equal, secret, direct and proportional suffrage. In that respect, the constitutional provisions were supplemented by the electoral law of 20 April 1923.

The People's Assembly was chaired by a president who together with his deputy and secretaries formed the Presidium (Article 11). In constitutional practice, there were two deputies and eight secretaries. The Assembly convened at the request of the president, the Senate or by a motion of 1/6 of all members (Article 12).

The sessions of the Assembly were open to the general public but could be held *in camera* by a motion of 1/6 members with the required quorum of 2/3 of all members (Article 14). The presence of at least half the deputies was required for the passage of resolutions to be validly (Article 16). These were usually adopted by a simple majority vote unless the constitution required absolute qualified majority (Article 17). The representatives of the Senate or persons acting on their behalf were allowed to attend and take the floor at the Assembly's sessions. On some occasions, their attendance was compulsory (Article 18).

The Senate was, alongside the People's Assembly, one of the principal state authorities in the Free City of Danzig, vested with supreme executive powers and consisting of twenty-two members, i.e. the president (chairman), his deputies and twenty senators, all of them elective. The senators formed two groups: seven principal senators (*im Hauptamte*) and thirteen auxiliary senators (*im Nebenamte*). The president and principal senators served a four-year term and were elected by the People's Assembly no earlier than six months but no later than a year into its term of office. When a principal senator died or resigned from office, his successor served only the remainder of the term. The deputy president and auxiliary senators were elected by the Assembly for an indefinite term by secret ballot, with the candidate who received the majority of votes winning the election. The principal seats were filled by professional civil servants, while the auxiliary ones with representatives of political parties. Eligibility to serve as either was limited to persons who had reached twenty-five years of age.

As the supreme executive authority, the Senate was empowered to:
- promulgate laws and executive orders necessary to enforce them,
- administer the state and supervise all state authorities,
- prepare budget estimates,
- manage state property and public revenues as well as decide on the state's revenues and expenditures,
- protect the rights of the Free City and its citizens,
- appoint officials (Article 39),
- set guidelines for the internal and foreign policies of the state (Article 38),
- grant pardons (Article 40).

Additionally, the Senate represented the Free City abroad except where this was in breach of the Treaty of Versailles. The Free City's foreign affairs were the responsibility of the Polish government (Article 41). The Senate was required to account for any public matters as requested by the League of Nations (Article 42).

The Senate's operations were directed and supervised by its president who could, in special cases and in consultation with his deputy and the longest-serving senators, decide on matters falling within the powers of the Senate as a whole. However, such decisions required subsequent approval from the plenum (Article 36). The president signed all documents on behalf of the Free City but was allowed to delegate this duty to his deputy (Article 41). The president was also tasked with presiding at the Senate's sessions and casting the deciding vote in the event of a tie (Article 37).

Both of the above-mentioned authorities of the Free City of Danzig collaborated on legislative matters. Consequently, legislative initiative was vested in the People's Assembly, the Senate, the Labour Representation and, last but not least, citizens themselves through popular initiatives (Article 46). The Assembly and the Senate, however, played a superior role in the legislative process.

The form of an act of law was required for budget estimates, loans contracted by the state, the establishment of monopolies and privileges, the re-drawing of municipality borders, general amnesty and international agreements (Article 45). A separate procedure was prescribed for amendments to the constitution. The Assembly was obliged in such cases to adopt the proposed amendments in two readings by a 2/3 majority vote with 2/3 of all members present. Amendments could be petitioned for by the majority of the electorate through a referendum. However, an constitutional amendment in the end took effect only when approved by the League of Nations (Article 49).

The Free City of Danzig was administratively divided into urban and rural districts (Article 67), each with its own self-government supervised by the Senate (Article 68). Within that structure, the city of Danzig itself formed a separate municipality with its own property ruled by the Citizens' City Council elected by the People's Assembly (Article 69).

The second part of the Free City's constitution dealt with citizens' rights and duties. Personal rights and freedoms were partially regulated.

The political freedoms and rights set forth in the constitution may be divided into universal and purely civic ones. The first group included active and passive voting rights (Article 8, 26), the right to form unions and associations (Article 85) and the freedom of peaceful (unarmed) assembly (Article 84). The second, on the other hand, included equal access to public offices according to aptitude and usefulness (Article 91), with officials serving the general good rather than a particular political party (Article 93), the right to vote in referendua (Articles 47–49) and the right to information on the activities of public authorities, for example, through attending the open sessions of the Citizens' Assembly and the Senate (Article 37).

The cultural rights and freedoms included the freedom of art and education protected by the state (Article 101), state supervision of the school system staffed by professional and competent teachers (Article 102), maintenance of schools at various levels in cooperation with the municipalities (Article 103), free-of-charge primary education (Article 103) as well as state protection and custody of artistic, cultural and natural heritage (Article 109).

Civic duties were relatively few and limited to compliance with the law and protection of the constitution from unlawful infringement (Article 87), assuming an equal share of public obligations (Article 88), rendering personal performances for the state and municipality (Article 89), holding honorary offices (Article 90) and completing primary education (Article 103).

On 1 September 1939 at 4:45 AM, the battleship *Schleswig-Holstein* fired at the Polish outpost on the Westerplatte, starting the Second World War. The Free City of Danzig was incorporated into the German Reich to later become the capital of the Danzig – West Prussia district divided into three regencies: Danzig, Bromberg and Marienwerder.[17]

---

17   BÖTTCHER: *op. cit.*, 129–147.

2 The Memel (Klaipeda) Territory

As early as 1919, German doctrine pointed out the need for the Memel Territory to be converted into a Free State (*Freistaat*) rather than a Free City (*Freistadt*), as was the case with Danzig, for Memel's urban area was not as important as that of Danzig. At any rate, both territories were to connect East Prussia from the West and the East.

In the end, the Conference of Ambassadors assigned the territory to Lithuania on 16 February 1923. This was conditional, however, upon Lithuania's compliance with the following demands: accept the territory's autonomy, safeguard free trade taking into account Polish interests, reimburse financial outlays hitherto incurred by the Allies, enforce the compensation obligations imposed on Germany after the war and ratify the statute defining Memel's political system. The document consisted of an extensive protocol justifying the decision as well as six points. Lithuania accepted most of the conditions but rejected Poland's entitlements, including its right to nominate members of the Supervisory Committee of the Harbour and the Free Zone as well as demands for the reimbursement of administrative costs incurred from 1919 to 1923. Lithuania's memorandum of 23 November emphasized not only that country's compliance with the resolution of 16 February but also its intent to allow no concessions to Poland regarding its rights to the use of the harbour and free transit of goods in foreign trade.

Following international discussions, it was finally decided that Lithuania would be granted sovereignty over Memel under a separate resolution, while the territory's political and legal status, harbour and transit of goods would be regulated in three annexes forming an integral whole with the resolution. As a result, the Council of the League of Nations at its 28th session made an appropriate resolution signed by its signatories, i.e. Great Britain, France, Italy and Japan, on one hand, and Lithuania on the other. On 14 October, the resolution was recorded in the League of Nations' register.[18]

The convention itself consisted of fourteen articles. The introduction defined the Memel Territory in line with Article 99 of the Treaty of Versailles as an area located between the Baltic Sea, the north-eastern border of East Prussia and the former German-Russian border (Article 1). It was to exist under

---

18 Tadeusz MACIEJEWSKI: *Status prawny Kłajpedy w okresie międzywojennym* = Państwo, prawo, społeczeństwo w dziejach Europy Środkowej. Księga Jubileuszowa dedykowana Profesorowi Józefowi Ciągwie w 70–lecie urodzin, Adam LITYŃSKI (ed.), Wydawnictwo Towarzystwa Słowaków w Polsce, Katowice-Kraków, 2009, 433–440; Albrecht ROGGE: *Die Verfassung des Memelgebiete*, Deutsche Rundschau, Berlin, 1928.

Lithuanian sovereignty as an entity with autonomy as regards judicial legislation, administration and finance (Article 2). At the same time, Lithuania undertook to implement the provisions on the harbour and transit of goods (Article 3). Lithuania was to reimburse the Allies for the costs of occupation and administration of the area in the years 1919–1923, together with half of all expenses related to the demarcation of the Region, with the mode and time-limits for repayment to be set by a special committee of two representatives (Article 4). German property remaining in the Region, excluding railways, post, telegraphs, customs and harbour facilities, was to be transferred by Lithuania to the autonomous authorities (Article 5). Lithuania also agreed to be charged with all other financial obligations resulting from its withdrawal from the Region and ensure that they be fulfilled in accordance with the conditions set down by the League of Nations Compensation Commission (Article 6) and have such obligations recorded in a special mortgage register (Article 7).

An integral part of the convention were three annexes. The first, doubtless the most important one, was entitled "The Statute of the Memel Territory". It consisted of thirty-eight articles, dealing with the Region's autonomy and issues of citizenship. The second annex covered the legal status of the harbour in Memel, while the third one concerned transit.[19]

The Statute, which was formally enacted by the Lithuanian government, made the Memel Territory an autonomous entity founded on democratic principles under Lithuanian sovereignty (Article 1). Their interests were protected by a governor nominated by the president (Article 2). He was entitled to veto the acts of the House of Representatives insofar as such acts exceeded the House's powers or infringed upon the constitution of Lithuania or international obligations of that state (Article 10). The governor was also tasked with making acts public within one month of the date, on which they were submitted to him. Also, the Territory selected six deputies to the Lithuanian parliament but in doing so was bound by the Lithuanian electoral law (Article 3). The Lithuanian parliament was entitled to give orders to the Region regarding the enforcement of international treaties and conventions (Article 4). The Statute also laid down the scope of autonomy of the local authorities in 15 points (Article 5), including the issues of local administration, religion, education, health care, social welfare, roads and railways, police, civil legislation, judiciary, citizenship, immigration, taxes, management of public property as well as commerce and, with the exclusion of the Neman river, sailing. Other matters fell within the authority of the competent Lithuanian institutions (Article 8).

---

19 Texts in Thorsten V. KALIJARVI: *The Memel Statue*, Hale, London 1937; Sergiusz MIKU-LICZ: *Kłajpeda w polityce europejskiej*, Książka i Wiedza, Warsaw, 1976, 289–331.

At the same time, the inhabitants of the Region were granted all civil rights enjoyed by Lithuanians (Article 9).

The legislative in the Region was the responsibility of the House of Representatives, with members elected by four-point (universal, equal, direct and secret) suffrage (Article 10). Passive voting rights extended to those inhabitants of the Region who had reached the age of 21 (Article 37). The House's term of office spanned 3 years. There was a 1:50,000 ratio between deputies and citizens (Article 11). The first meeting of the House took place within 15 days of the elections. Debates were held in ordinary or extraordinary sessions. The House was headed by the Chairman with the Presidium acting to assist him (Article 13). Each bill on financial and economic matters, prior to its submission for final voting in the House, had to be opined by the Economic Council which was a continuation of the Clearing House established in 1919 (Article 14). The right of legislative initiative extended both to the House and the Directorate (Article 18).

The executive was the responsibility of the Directorate headed by a president and consisting of no more than five members, all of whom had to be citizens of the Territory. The president was appointed by the governor from among people trusted by the House. The president appointed the other members. All of them were entitled to take the floor at the sessions of the House and the Economic Council. As the Directorate was dependent on the House, it could be forced to resign when it received a vote of no confidence (Article 17).

At the local level, the Territory was divided into districts and these into municipalities. Self-government was represented by democratically elected assemblies (Article 19). Officials remaining in service until 1 January 1923 were allowed to retain all their acquired rights. In the future, however, they were to be appointed from among the citizens of the Territory (Article 29). This, however, did not apply to persons opting for German citizenship (Article 30), the purpose of which was to eliminate them from public administration.

The relations between the Third Reich and Lithuania regarding the state affiliation of the Memel Territory deteriorated in 1938 and reached a critical point in the following year. On 7 January 1939, the pro-Nazi Wilhelm Bertuleit was elected president of the Directorate. Finally, on 21 March 1939, Hitler gave orders for the Wehrmacht to occupy Memel. On the evening of the same day, the Lithuanian government accepted and ratified the German ultimatum. The following day, around midnight, an official pact was signed between the Third Reich and Lithuania to incorporate the Memel Territory into Germany. The pact, which consisted of five articles, re-affirmed the annexation of the Memel Territory by Germany, separated from it under the Treaty of Versailles (Article 1).

The German army seized Memel on 23 March 1939. The city was also visited by Hitler, who was greeted enthusiastically by the local populace. The autonomous Memel Territory had ceased to exist.

3   Fiume (Rijeka)

On 26 April 1915, the Allies signed a secret pact with Italy in London, preparatory to Italy's entry into the First World War. In exchange, Italy was offered territorial gains such as Dalmatia, initially without the city of Fiume, though Italy came to occupy it late in the war. At the Paris Peace Conference in 1919, the Italian delegation did not manage to push through the annexation, but a plebiscite was held in that area, in which most of the population supported the idea. The solution was opposed by the American president, Woodrow Wilson. As a result, the Italian delegates (Vittorio Emanuele Orlando, Sidney Sonnino) left Paris, giving rise to the so-called mutilated victory myth.

In the meantime, nationalist sympathies had emerged in Italy. The reason was the city of Fiume, inhabited in 1918 by 29,000 Italians and 31,000 Slavs, the latter being dominant only around the city. In an effort to foil Italy's incorporation of Fiume, the Allies sent French and Greek forces to the city and established a special military commission. In response, the Sardinian garrison stationed there invited a nationalist politician and writer Gabriele D'Annunzio, who arrived in Fiume on 12 September 1919 to take control as a dictator and to proclaim the city's annexation to Italy. The Italian government, however, refused to accept this state of affairs, proceeding to blockade the city and continuing border negotiations with the Kingdom of Slovenes, Croats and Serbs (Yugoslavia), culminating in the Treaty of Rapallo of 12 November 1920. In it, the Italians forwent their claim to the city, but forced D'Annunzio to leave. This meant Italy's official acceptance of the existence of the Free City of Fiume.[20]

The question of Fiume re-emerged in Italy's foreign policy with Mussolini's rise to power. The Italian parliament ratified the earlier border treaties with the Kingdom of Slovenes, Croats and Serbs and decided to partition the Free City of Fiume, with the city itself falling to Italy on 3 September and the rural areas (Sisak) to Yugoslavia.

The city's political system was regulated by the constitution of 27 August 1920, also known as the Charter of Carnaro (Carta del Carnaro), consisting of

---

20   Ferdinando GERRA : *L'impresa di Fiume*. Longanesi et Co., Milano, 1978.

sixty-five articles and penned by D'Annunzio. The constitution was proclaimed on 8 September 1920.[21]

The constitution of the Free City of Fiume consisted of an extensive preamble and sixty-five articles grouped into no less than twenty chapters. These were entitled as follows: Fundamentals (Principles) – fourteen articles, Citizens – three articles, Corporations – four articles, Municipalities – five articles, Legislation – eight articles, Executive – two articles, Judiciary – six articles, Commandant – four articles, National Defence – three articles, Public Education – five articles, Amendments to the Constitution – one article, Legislative Initiative – one article, Referendum – one article, Right to Petition – one article, Ban on Concurrent Holding of Multiple Offices – one article, Recalling Officials – one article, Liability of Officials – one article, Salaries of Officials – one article, College of Aediles – one article, Music – two articles. The text ended with a Latin maxim: *Statutum et ordinatum est. Juro ego.*

It is noteworthy that the constitutional provisions were arranged rather haphazardly, especially the last ten articles, distributed across no less than nine chapters, which could be easily included, with the possible exception of "Music", in the provisions on the legislative and executive. The arrangement was due to a number of factors, not the least of which was the author himself, D'Annunzio, a poet and politician rather than a lawyer, his views on the nature of the state and the origin of power, attitude to the rights of the individual as well as the political situation. As a result, the constitution was a conglomerate of syndicalist, pro-Fascist, democratic and even anarchist concepts, making it a singular phenomenon among 19th and early-20th-century constitutions. This is underlined by all those who have research its contents. But after all, perhaps this is what makes it special.

The sovereignty of the nation was considered to be the most essential foundation of a state; of a nation which held power that extended not only to the city itself, but also along the coast and railways which must naturally have stretched beyond the Free City. Additionally, it was stipulated regarding the sovereignty that in the West, it would be based on close relations with Italy, but in the East, Fiume would never waive its territorial claims, striving to mark out a fair and secure border (Article 1). This article was testimony to the bloodshed between Italians and Yugoslavs, in which the city played a central role. Despite

---

[21] Tadeusz MACIEJEWSKI: *Konstytucja Wolnego Miasta Fiume (Rijeka) z 27 sierpnia 1920 r.* = *Regnare – Administrare – Gubernare: prawo i władza na przestrzeni dziejów. Prace dedykowane Profesorowi Jerzemu Malcowi z okazji 40-lecia pracy naukowej*, Stanisław GRODZISKI, Andrzej DZIADZIO (eds.), Oficyna Wydawnicza AFM, Krakow, 2012, vol. 1, 175–184.

some hopes for stabilisation, the issue of national minorities living not only in the Kingdom of the Slovenes, Croats and Serbs, but also in Austria (Upper Tyrol) and Albania, was hotly debated in Rome. The situation was fuelled by the fact that Fiume's constitution claimed that the province of Carnaro had always belonged to Italy, as did the Venetian islands which had declared themselves as such (Article 2).

Furthermore, the constitution followed basic principles created by its author, D'Annunzio. The most important of them were national sovereignty, syndicalism, and the age-old Italian autonomy (Article 3). All of this was contained in a single article, a mixture of slogans fashionable at the time, harking back to the Roman Empire as well as to the nascent Fascist doctrine. Next in importance was the equality of all citizens regardless of gender, race, language, origin or religion. All of this, however, was subject to a syndicalist model of a state-controlled society subject to excessive state centralism, on one hand, but on the other expected to appoint officials and reduce its own social rights for a better community harmony (Article 4).

The second chapter of the constitution dealt with citizenship in the province of Carnaro, which extended to all persons recorded in the register of the Free City of Fiume and associated municipalities as well as those who had received it under a separate decree (Article 15). Full civil and political rights were enjoyed by them, however, upon reaching twenty years of age, especially with regard to active voting rights and employment (Article 16). On the other hand, the same rights were lost through a court judgment, failure to comply with the duty of defence and military service, non-payment of taxes or a parasitic lifestyle (Article 17).

Following the so-called mutilated victory in the First World War, Italy underwent a severe economic crisis, causing a wave of strikes and peasant revolts. As a result, the Italian Socialist Party became the dominant force on the political scene. It competed for support with the Italian People's Party and the Communist Party. At the opposite end stood Benito Mussolini's Italian Fasci of Combat propagating populist and later Fascist slogans. The movement soon gained widespread social support. Generally, it advocated syndicalism.

Legislation in Carnaro was bicameral, with the Commission of Senators as the upper and the Commission of Provisors the lower house. The Senate was elected for a 10-year term by direct, secret, proportional and equal suffrage. Active and passive voting rights extended to all citizens who had reached the age of twenty and enjoyed full political rights (Article 28). This was in a majority system where the senator-citizen ratio was 1:1,000, but the Senate could never consist of more than thirty members (Article 29). It performed legislative functions with regard to legal acts on substantive and procedural judicial law (civil and criminal), the arts and relations between the municipality and the province (Article 30). The Commission of Provisors consisted of sixty members elected by a majority vote in universal, equal, secret and proportional elections. The elections were based exclusively on a syndicalist system.

The term of office of the Commission of Provisors was two years (Article 32). It held sessions usually twice a year, in May and November. Its deliberations were "laconic". The Provisors had the privilege of issuing legal acts on commercial and maritime law, labour inspection, transport, public works, duties and tariffs, industry, banking, arts and crafts (Article 33). Also, it was decided that the Senate and the Commission of Provisors would hold a joint session (Arengo del Carnaro) annually to discuss issues related to foreign affairs, finance, colleges, extension of citizens' rights and amendments to the constitution (Article 34). It should be added that all normative acts passed by the parliament of Fiume could be rejected in a referendum requested by ¼ of all eligible voters (Article 57). The voters also had legislative initiative, as they could propose law bills to either house (Article 56).

The executive was exercised by seven ministers: of Foreign Affairs, Finance and Treasury and Public Instruction. They were elected by the National Assembly; the Ministers of Internal Affairs and Justice were elected by the Senate, while the Ministers of Public Economy and Labour were elected by the Commission of Provisors. The position of prime minister went to the Minister of Foreign Affairs but only on the *primus inter pares* principle, which meant heading the cabinet, but not directing it (Article 35). All of them were chosen for a one-year term, with re-election allowed (Article 36). The constitution prevented ministers and other officials from concurrently holding multiple positions (Article 59) and provided for removal from office in the event of a court sentence to the loss of political rights or a vote of no confidence being passed by the absolute majority of both houses (Article 60). They were also constitutionally liable for damage to the state, the corporations, society and individual citizens if they were guilty of "a crime, negligence, cowardice or carelessness" (Article 61).

An extraordinary position provided for by the constitution was that of commandant, appointed by the National Council at *Arengo del Carnaro* in the event of extreme danger facing the island. The voting was oral. The Council also decided on the time-limit of this office (Article 43). At such times, the commandant held supreme powers, with executive authority in the hands of commissioners and secretaries under the commandant's control (Article 44). Depending on the commandant's performance, the National Council could extend his term of office, replace, dismiss or even banish him (Article 45).

4 Conclusion

1. The origins of free cities in Europe date back to the Middle Ages when, starting in the 12th century, a great number of cities became directly subject to the Emperor. The trend was started by Lübeck which set a blueprint for their political system. This category also includes urban republics in Italy such as Milan, Florence or, in what would become Russia, i.e. Novgorod the Great or Pskov. The political changes that occurred within them led them to transform with time into separate territorial states.
2. A large majority of free cities and republics collapsed at the turn of the 19th century as a result of the Napoleonic Wars.
3. The 19th century saw the rebirth of just a few free cities. These included, in the Reich, Hamburg, Lübeck, Bremen, and Frankfurt am Main; in the former Polish-Lithuanian Commonwealth, these were Gdansk (Danzig) (1807–1815) and Krakow (1815–1846).
4. Following the First World War, Europe saw six free cities created, pursuant to the Treaty of Versailles and the Constitution of the German Reich of 11 August 1919, such as Hamburg, Lübeck and Bremen in Germany, more as a throwback to historical Hanseatic tradition rather than existing socio-cultural realities; Danzig, Fiume and Memel, the last of which was considered to be not a free city, but a free territory.
5. The free cities in the Reich were created due to its internal situation, resulting from the belief that establishing a uniform German state was impossible. The ones created outside the Reich were more due to political and democratic factors considering there were sizeable German (Danzig, Memel) and Italian (Fiume) national minorities, but to a lesser extent, to historical considerations.
6. The political systems of the free cities around the Baltic Sea were largely similar due to direct contacts between the commissions working on these cities' constitutions. For example, Danzig sent its representatives to Hamburg, Lübeck and Bremen, and Memel to Danzig.
7. All the constitutions were based on democratic principles and a republican system, with the addition of federalism in Germany. It was normal to hand over legislative power to a democratically elected majority, which selected the executive supported by the legislative with a vote of confidence.
8. Constitutions regulated only basic matters related to the political system, such as the central government, leaving the details to be dealt with in future legislative action (acts, regulations, etc.).

9. Citizens' rights and freedoms were regulated extensively only in the constitution of Danzig; in others, they were treated cursorily (Hamburg, Memel) or omitted altogether (Bremen, Lübeck).
10. Free cities declined under the influence of interwar totalitarianism, especially Nazism, which led to the unification of Hamburg and Bremen with the Reich, the dissolution of the free city of Lübeck and annexation in 1939 of Memel and Danzig.

Bibliography

Gerhard ANSCHÜTZ: *Die Verfassung des Deutschen Reichs vom 11. August 1919. Ein Kommentar für Wissenschaft und Praxis*, Stilke, Berlin, 1933.

Willibalt APELT: *Geschichte der Weimarer Verfassung*, Biederstein Velt, München, 1946.

Johann Viktor BREDT: *Der Geist der deutschen Reichsverfassung*, Stilke, Berlin, 1924

Georg BESSEL: *Bremen – Die Geschichte einer deutschen Stadt*, Insel, Leipzig, 1935.

Hans Viktor BÖTTCHER: *Die Freie Stadt Danzig. Wege und Umwege in die europäische Zukunft*, Kulturstiftung der deutschen Vertriebenen, Bonn, 1997.

Dokumente zur Deutschen Verfassungsgeschichte, Ernst Rudolf HUBER (ed.), vol. 3, Kohlhammer, Stuttgart, 1966.

Michael DUNKELBERG: *Bürgerausschuss in der Verfassung der Freien und Hansestadt Hamburg*, Diss. Hamburg, Hamburg, 1980.

Entwurf einer Verfassung für die Freie und Hansestadt Danzig, Boenig, Danzig, 1920.

Hans FENSKE: *Deutsche Verfassungsgeschichte. Vom Norddeutschenbund bis heute*, Copress, Berlin, 1981.

August FINGER: *Das Staatsrecht des Deutschen Reichs. Der Verfassung vom 11. August 1919*, Enke, Stuttgart, 1923.

Ernst FORSTHOFF: *Deutsche Verfassungsgeschichte der Neuzeit*, Stuttgart, Kohlhammer, 1972.

Werner FROTSCHER, Bodo PIEROTH: *Verfassungsgeschichte*, C.H. Beck, München, 2003.

Fritz VON HARTUNG: *Deutsche Verfassungsgeschichte vom 15. Jahrhundert bis zur Gegenwart*, Koehler, Stuttgart, 1954.

Thorsten V. KALIJARVI: *The Memel Statue*, Hale, London 1937.

Otto KIMMINICH: *Deutsche Verfassungsgeschichte*, Nomos, Frankfurt a.M., 1970.

Lübeckische Landverfassung. Veröffentlich am 23 Mai 1920 = *Sammlung der Lübeckischen Gesetze und Verordnungen*, 78(1920).

Günter KRABBENHÖFT: *Verfassungsgeschichte der Hansestadt Lübeck. Eine Übersicht*, Schmidt-Römhild, Lübeck, 1969.

Tadeusz MACIEJEWSKI: *Konstytucja Wolnego Hanzeatyckiego Miasta Brema z 18 maja 1920 r.* = *O prawie i jego dziejach, księgi dwie. Studia ofiarowane Profesorowi Adamowi Lityńskiemu*, Marian MIKOŁAJCZYK (ed.), vol. 2, Wydawnictwo Uniwersytetu w Białymstoku, Białystok-Katowice, 2010, 245–254.

Tadeusz MACIEJEWSKI: *Konstytucja Wolnego i Hanzeatyckiego Miasta Hamburga z 7 stycznia 1921 r.* = *Świat, Europa, Mała Ojczyzna. Studia ofiarowane Profesorowi Stanisławowi Grodzickiemu w 80-lecie urodzin*, Marian MAŁECKI (ed.), Wyższa Szkoła Administracji, Bielsko-Biała, 2009, 801–812.

Tadeusz MACIEJEWSKI: *Konstytucja Wolnego Miasta Fiume (Rijeka) z 27 sierpnia 1920 r.* = *Regnare – Administrare – Gubernare: prawo i władza na przestrzeni dziejów. Prace dedykowane Profesorowi Jerzemu Malcowi z okazji 40-lecia pracy naukowej*, Stanisław GRODZISKI, Andrzej DZIADZIO (eds.), Krakow, Oficyna Wydawnicza AFM, 2012, vol. 1, 175–184.

Tadeusz MACIEJEWSKI: *Krajowa Konstytucja miasta Lubeki z 23 maja 1920 r.* = *Vetera Novis Augere. Studia i prace dedykowane Profesorowi Wacławowi Uruszczakowi*, Dorota MALEC et al. (eds.), vol. 2, Wydawnictwo Uniwersytetu Jagiellońskiego, Krakow, 2010, 635–644.

Tadeusz MACIEJEWSKI: *Konstytucje wolnych miast Europy w okresie międzywojennym*, in: *Społeczeństwo a władza. Ustrój, prawo, idee*, Jacek PRZYGODZKI, Marian PTAK (eds.), Kolonia Limited, Wrocław, 2010, 624–630.

Tadeusz MACIEJEWSKI: *Projekty konstytucji wersalskiego Wolnego Miasta Gdańska*, in: *Księga dedykowana Profesorowi Marianowi Kallasowi*, Sławomir GODEK, Dariusz MAKIŁŁA, Magdalena WILCZEK-KARCZEWSKA (eds.), InterLeones Halina Dyczkowska, Warsaw, 537–552.

Tadeusz MACIEJEWSKI: *Status prawny Kłajpedy w okresie międzywojennym*, in: *Państwo, prawo, społeczeństwo w dziejach Europy Środkowej. Księga Jubileuszowa dedykowana Profesorowi Józefowi Ciągwie w 70-lecie urodzin*, Adam LITYŃSKI (ed.), Wydawnictwo Towarzystwa Słowaków w Polsce, Katowice-Krakow, 2009.

Christian-Friedrich MENGER: *Deutsche Verfassungsgeschichte der Neuzeit*, Müller Juristicher Verlag, Heidelberg, 1980.

Sergiusz MIKULICZ: *Kłajpeda w polityce europejskiej*, Książka i Wiedza, Warsaw, 1976.

Max MITTELSTEIN: *Die Verfassung der Freien und Hansestadt Hamburg vom 7. Januar 1921*, Hartung, Hamburg, 1924.

Nowe konstytucje, Julian MAKOWSKI (ed.), Warsaw, Hoesisck, 1925.

Marceli PODLASZEWSKI: *Ustrój polityczny Wolnego Miasta Gdańska w latach 1920–1933*, Wydawnictwo Morskie, Gdynia, 1966.

Quellensammlung zum deutschen Reichsstaatsrecht, Heinrich TRIEPEL (ed.), 4th ed., Siebeck, Tübingen, 1926.

Reichgesetzblatt 152(1919), 1383.

Albrecht ROGGE: *Die Verfassung des Memelgebiete*, Deutsche Rundschau, Berlin, 1928.
Antoni ROMAN: *Ustrój polityczny Wolnego Miasta Gdańska*, Warsaw, 1926.
Otto RUTHENBERG: *Verfassungsgesetze des deutschen Reichs und der deutschen Länder nach dem Stande vom 1. Februrar 1926*, Berlin, 1926.
Herbert SCHWARZWÄLDER: *Geschichte der Freien Hansestadt Bremen*, vol 3, Röver, Hamburg, 1983.
Die Verfassung der Freien Hansestadt Bremen. Vom 18 Mai 1920, Gesetzblatt der Freien Hansestadt Bremen, 46(1920).
Die Verfassung der Freien und Hansestadt Hamburg. Vom 7 Januar 1921, Hamburgisches Gesetz und Verordnungsblatt 5(1921).
Verfassung der Freien Stadt Danzig in der Fassung der Bekantmachung vom 14 Juni 1922, A.W.Kafemann, Danzig, 1922.
Jan WĄSICKI: *Rzesza a kraje niemieckie 1914–1949*, Wydawnictwo Poznańskie, Poznań, 1977.

CHAPTER 9

Local Citizenship in the Croatian-Slavonian Legal Area in the First Yugoslavia (1918–1941): Breakdown of a Concept?

Ivan Kosnica

1   Introduction

The concept of local citizenship can be defined as a form of a person[1] belonging to a municipality that gives to a person certain rights and obligations in that municipality.[2] The concept was especially relevant in many legal systems before formation of modern national states.[3] However, with the rise of modern national states and the rise of concept of national citizenship, importance of local citizenship diminished.

Looking through the lens of modernity and modernisation one can say that local citizenship represented concept characteristic for *ancien regimée* while the concept of national citizenship was characteristic for modern national states. However, although one concept represented tradition and the other modernity, transition in dominant importance from one concept to another was often not easy. On the contrary, reduction of importance of local citizenship in legal systems was often *longue durée* process. Therefore in many European states during the long nineteenth century and in the first half of twentieth century both concepts coexisted and were both very relevant for public law status of a person. Interconnections between the concepts were many, and as tipical one could mention that formation of the concept of national citizenship was often supported with local citizenship. We will menton the case of

---

1   The research is part of a Scientific Research Project of the Faculty of Law, University of Zagreb.
2   For different understandings of local citizenship, cf. Peter J. SPIRO: *Formalizing Local Citizenship,* Fordham Urban Law Journal, 37(2009)/2, 559–572; Marc HELBLING: *Switzerland: Contentious Citizenship Attribution in a Federal State,* Journal of Ethnic and Migration Studies, 36(2010)/5, 793–798; Sophia WOODMAN: *Local Politics, Local Citizenship? Socialized Governance in Contemporary China,* China Quarterly, 226(2016), 342–362; Rainer BAUBÖCK: *Reinventing Urban Citizenship,* Citizenship Studies, 7(2003)/2, 149–156.
3   Peter N. RIESENBERG: *Citizenship in the Western Tradition: Plato to Rousseau,* University of North Carolina Press, Chapel Hill, 1992, 142.

registers of local citizens which were gradually transformed into registers of national citizens.[4]

Meaning and significance of concept of local citizenship in each legal system was different as well as was relation of this concept towards the concept of national citizenship. Our study aims to grasp in significance and transfomations of local citizenship on Croatian-Slavonian legal area in the First Yugoslav state in the period from formation of the state in 1918 until its occupation in April war in 1941.[5] The starting point of the research is argumentation about local citizenship as a specific element of Croatian legal identity established in the period before 1918 when Croatia-Slavonia was part of the Austro-Hungarian Monarchy. Having this in mind, in the chapter we analyze development of this form of legal identity in the Kingdom of Serbs, Croats and Slovenes/Yugoslavia. The issue is very interesting mostly because the first Yugoslav state represented quite differrent context for Croatia-Slavonia than was the Austro-Hungarian Monarchy. This mostly because until 1939 and formation of the Banovina of Croatia, the state was highly centralized and the ruling elite promoted uniform national identity and one national citizenship while at the same time took measures to abolish previously formed legal identities.

In the chapter we research therefore tensions between Croatian-Slavonian local citizenship as an element of Croatian legal identity and the concept of Yugoslav national citizenship as an element of Yugoslav legal identity. In doing so, we analyze efforts of central authorities in Belgrade in promotion of common national identity thorugh the lens of legal instrumentalism. The chapter therefore aims to provide deeper understanding of limits of enactment of new regulations as an instrument of legal and social change.

The chapter starts with argumentation about Croatian-Slavonian local citizenship as an important element of Croatian legal identity established before 1918. Here we discuss what made local citizenship to be an important element of Croatian legal identity and what were key elements of the concept before 1918. In addition, we discuss positon of national and local citizenships in the Kingdom of Serbs, Croats and Slovenes/Yugoslavia. After this, we analyze more in detail changes in the concept of local citizenship on Croatian-Slavonian legal area in the period from 1918 until 1941. In conclusion, we discuss limits of legal instrumentalism in creation of new legal and social order.

---

4 Cf. this argument in Leo LUCASSEN: *Between Hobbes and Locke. Gypsies and the limits of the modernization paradigm*, Social History, 33(2008)/4, 425–426.

5 The state was officialy called the Kingdom of Serbs, Croats and Slovenes and from 1929 on the Kingdom of Yugoslavia.

2 Local Citizenship in the Croatian-Slavonian Legal System Before 1918

The origins of local citizenship in Croatia-Slavonia date back to the feudal period before 1848 when belonging to a city or some other corporation was an important element of a person's public identity.[6] The first modern regulations about local citizenship were enacted under King Franz Joseph I as part of broader modernisation and centralisation in the Habsburg Monarchy in the period of neoabsolutism (1849–1860).[7] However, vital development and positioning of local citizenship as central in Croatian-Slavonian legal system happened after reaching the Austrian-Hungarian Compromise in 1867 and Croatian-Hungarian Compromise in 1868. The reason for this should have been searched in the division of competences in the matters of citizenship according to Compromises. Crucial was that according to the Austro-Hungarian Compromise there were two states within the Monarchy, Austria and Hungary and consequently two national citizenships in the Monarchy, Austrian and Hungarian, while special Croatian-Slavonian national citizenship did not exist. However, the Croatian-Hungarian Compromise recognized to Croatia-Slavonia autonomy in internal administraton including regulation of local citizenship.[8]

Importance of local citizenship in Croatia-Slavonia therefore steemed from special regulations about local citizenship, namely the Law on regulation of local citizenship (*Zakon o uređenju zavičajnih odnosa*) of 1880 which was different law than Austrian or Hungarian regulation and thus represented third model of regulation of local citzenship in the Austro-Hungarian Monarchy.[9] Besides this, other laws enacted by the Croatian-Slavonian Diet and decrees enacted by the Provincial Croatian-Slavonian Government gave specific meaning to the concept of local citizenship in Croatia-Slavonia which was not just legal connection of a person with a municipality but also a key link of a person

---

6 Ivan KOSNICA: *Utvrđivanje državljanstva u Hrvatskoj i Slavoniji 1849–1880*, Zbornik radova Pravnog fakulteta u Splitu, 51(2014)/3, 702.

7 KOSNICA: *Utvrđivanje...*, *op. cit.*, 702–704; Cf. the regulations in Koloman MUTAVDJIĆ: *Zavičajno pravo: Zakon od 30. travnja 1880. ob uredjenju zavičajnih odnošaja u kraljevinah Hrvatskoj i Slavoniji i prijašnji propisi o stečenju i gubitku zavičajnoga prava*, Naklada knjižare Lav. Hartmana (Kugli i Deutsch), Zagreb, 1894, 218–270.

8 Ivan KOSNICA: *Hungarians and Citizenship in Croatia-Slavonia 1868–1918* = David A. FRENKEL, Norbert VARGA: *Law and History*, Athens Institute for Education and Research, Athens, 2015, 61–62.

9 *Zakon od 30. travnja 1880. o uređenju zavičajnih odnosa u kraljevinama Hrvatskoj i Slavoniji*, Sbornik zakonah i naredabah valjanih za kraljevinu Hrvatsku i Slavoniju, vol. 9, 1880 (alex.onb.ac.at/cgi-content/alex?aid=lks&datum=18800304&seite=00000179, accessed 22.02.2019).

with Croatia-Slavonia thus representing an important element of Croatian-Slavonian legal system. Such position of the concept of local citizenship argued prominent Croatian pubilic law scholars of that time, namely Josip Pliverić, Vinko Krišković and Ladislav Polić who all worked as professors at the Faculty of Law in Zagreb, the only Faculty of Law in Croatia-Slavonia thus having prominent role in formation of Croatian inteligentsia. In doing so, main thesis these scholars advocated was about Croatian-Slavonian local citizenship as a key insitute that served for defining Croatian-Slavonian citizens.[10] Finally, some politicians used the concept of Croatian-Slavonian local citizenship in debates about the issue who is and who is not a member of „Croatian political nation" arguing that members of Croatian political nation are only those who have local citizenship in Croatia-Slavonia.[11]

Key features of the concept of local citizenship in Croatia-Slavonia were that it was defined by the autonomous Croatian-Slavonian regulation and that Croatian-Slavonian Provincial Government was the highest authority in the matters of local citizenship in Croatia-Slavonia. Another very important aspect of Croatian-Slavonian local citizenship was that a person regularly proved Hungarian national citizenship (in Croatia-Slavonia this citizenship was officially called Hungarian-Croatian) with local citizenship certificate.[12] This mostly because the municipalities took care about registers of local citizens while centralized registers of national citizens did not exist. Important characteristic of the concept was that it based on *ius sanguinis* and was therefore very closed. This because all other possibilities of local naturalisations, except marriage, included an administrative act or in case of a settlement an explicit and

---

10 Mentioned scholars did not accept ideas about only one national citizenship in the lands of the Hungarian Crown but claimed that besides the common national citizenship there were special different citizenships for Croatia-Slavonia and Hungary. Dalibor ČEPULO: *Pravo hrvatske zavičajnosti i pitanje hrvatskog i ugarskog državljanstva 1868–1918 – pravni i politički vidovi i poredbena motrišta*, Zbornik Pravnog fakulteta u Zagrebu, 49(1999)/6, 802–803, 813; Ivan KOSNICA: *Das Problem der Staatsbürgerschaft in Kroatien und Slawonien im Ausgleichszeitraum (1868–1918)* = *Kroatisch-ungarische öfentlich-rechtliche Verhältnisse zur Zeit der Doppelmonarchie*, Gábor MÁTHÉ, Barna MEZEY (eds.), Eötvös University Press, Budapest, 2015, 203–207.

11 Some representatives in the Croatian *Diet (Sabor)* defined *Croatian political nation* on the basis of local citizenship in Croatia-Slavonia. Cf. some such debates in ČEPULO: *Pravo hrvatske...*, op. cit., 816–817; Ivan KOSNICA: *Hrvatsko-slavonska pripadnost u Hrvatskoj i Slavoniji u nagodbenom razdoblju*, Hrvatska i komparativna javna uprava/Croatian and Comparative Public Administration, 14(2014)/2, 481–482.

12 This was reflection of the rule that every Hungarian-Croatian citizen had to have local citizenship in one municipality (§ 2 the Law on regulation of local citizenship of 1880).

very formal notification of a settler to a municipality (§ 9, 10) while automatic naturalisation after certain period of time did not exist.

Finally, the concept of Croatian-Slavonian local citizenship was important for not just enjoyment of rights on local level, such as a right on poor relief in a municipality and voting rights on municipal elections,[13] but also in defining active and passive voting rights in elections for the Croatian-Slavonian Diet and also for enyojment of some privileges concerning social rights.[14] All said made the concept to be an important element of Croatian legal culture and identity in the Austro-Hungarian Monarchy.[15]

3 Regulation of National and Local Citizenships in the Kingdom of Serbs, Croats and Slovenes/Yugoslavia – General Remarks

With the formation of the Kingdom of Serbs, Croats and Slovenes in 1918, the context significantly changed. The central authorities in Belgrade promoted strong centralisation and abolishment of previously established legal identities. The aim was unification of laws and formation of one common national legal system with unitarian national citizenship as as basis of legal rights and oligations. Such development reflected visions of mostly Serbian political elite.

However, implementation of unitarian model of national citizenship did not go smooth. In fact, previous regulations about national citizenship status

---

13 Comp. § 6, *Zakonski članak XVI: 1870., sabora kraljevina Hrvatske, Slavonije i Dalmacije o uređenju općina i trgovišta,* Sbornik zakonah i naredabah valjanih za kraljevinu Hrvatsku i Slavoniju, III, 1871 (alex.onb.ac.at/cgi-content/alex?aid=lks&datum=18710304&seite=00000037, accessed 22.02.2019); Comp. § 19 and 20, *Zakon o ustroju gradskih općina u kraljevinama Hrvatskoj i Slavoniji,* Sbornik zakonah i naredabah valjanih za kraljevine Hrvatsku i Slavoniju, vol. 9, 1895 (alex.onb.ac.at/cgi-content/alex?aid=lks&datum=18950304&seite=00000219, accessed 22.02.2019).

14 KOSNICA: *Hrvatsko-slavonska pripadnost...*, op. cit., 480–485.

15 Despite evident problems in clear definition of the concept of legal culture here, for purposes of the paper, we will understand the concept in Friedman's' descriptive way that it consists of "attitudes, values, and opinions held in society, with regard to law, the legal system, and its various parts". Lawrence M. FRIEDMAN: *Law and Society: An Introduction,* Prentice-Hall, Englewood Cliffs NJ, 1977, 76 cited according to Roger COTTERRELL: *Law, Culture and Society: Legal Ideas in the Mirror of Social Theory,* Ashgate, Hampshire, 2006, 83; About law and legal culture cf. also Maciej KOSZOWSKI: *Medieval Iceland: The Influence of Culture and Tradition on Law,* Scandinavian Studies, 86(2014)/3, 333–334; About concepts as fundamental elements of legal system cf.: Imre ZAJTAY: *Immutability of Rules and Principles of Legal Development: The Permanence of Roman Law Concepts = European Legal Cultures,* Volkmar GESSNER, Armin HOELAND, Csaba VARGA (eds.), Dartmouth, Aldershot, 1996, 67.

initialy remained in force on each of legal areas and were only progresivelly replaced with new decrees, with some norms of the first Constitution of 1921 and with international treaties, namely peace treaties.[16] Full unification of citizenship law happened only in 1928 when the National Assembly accepted and the king Aleksandar Karađorđević sanctioned the first and the only Citizenship Code of the Kingdom of Serbs, Croats, and Slovenes/Yugoslavia.[17]

Despite obvious difficulties in the sphere of unification of laws, inlcuding the field of citizenship law, the central authorities of the Kingdom of Serbs, Croats and Slovenes during first years of the state succeded in promotion of national citizenship of the Kingdom of Serbs, Croats, and Slovenes as a key prerequisite for enyojment of numerous rights and obligations.[18]

While the authorities of the first Yugoslav state saw the concept of national citizenship as central for the new Yugoslav legal system, old concepts that reflected belonging to specific regions and lands should have been abolished and their importance in the legal system should have been annuled. According to this, the authorities very early, during 1919, enacted decrees which annuled importance of the concept of Croatian-Slavonian belonging (*hrvatsko-slavonska pripadnost*) as a basis of special rights on Croatian-Slavonian territory reserved for local citizens of Croatia-Slavonia.[19] Instead, all Yugoslav national citizens were declared as equal. Understanding of the concept of local citizenship as a concept exclusviely relevant in local, municipal affairs, reflected also the first Constitution of the Kingdom of Serbs, Croats and Slovenes of 1921 which contained only one clause about local citzenship stating that local citizen have the right to reside in the municipality he belongs and that he can not be expeled from the municipality without a court judgement.[20]

However, despite evident destruction of wider potential of Croatian-Slavonian local citizenship, which went hand in hand with strong administrative centralisation of the state and formation of the new regions (*oblasti*) instead of old lands, the old concept of local citizenship was not destroyed in full. This because the old Croatian-Slavonian regulations, namely the Law on

---

16   Igor ŠTIKS: *Nations and Citizens in Yugoslavia and the Post-Yugoslav States: One Hundred Years of Citizenship*, Bloomsbury Academic, London-New York, 2015, 32.

17   The Citizenship Code of the Kingdom of Serbs, Croats, and Slovenes of 1928 with commentary cf in Celso CAVALIERI: *Propisi o državljanstvu Kraljevine Srba, Hrvata i Slovenaca*, Vlastita naklada, Zagreb, 1929.

18   Ivan KOSNICA: *Definiranje državljanskog korpusa na hrvatsko-slavonskom području u Kraljevini SHS / Jugoslaviji*, Zbornik Pravnog fakulteta Sveučilišta u Rijeci, 39(2018)/2, 813–814.

19   *Ibid.*, 813.

20   Cf. art. 10. of the Constitution of the Kingdom of Serbs, Croats, and Slovenes of 1921. *Ustav Kraljevine Srba, Hrvata i Slovenaca*, Državna štamparija Kraljevine Srba, Hrvata i Slovenaca, Beograd, 1926.

regulation of local citizenship of 1880 remained in force until 1933 in municipalities and until 1934 in city municipalities. Similar was on Slovenian-Dalmatian and on former Hungarian legal area where also old pre-1918 regulations remained in force until 1933 and 1934.[21]

The unificaiton of regulations about local citizenship happened only in 1933 in municipalities or in 1934 in city municipalities. Then the National Assembly and the king enacted the law on municipalities (*Zakon o općinama*) of 1933 and the law on city municipalities (*Zakon o gradskim općinama*) of 1934.[22] The laws regulated local citizenship, mostly containing regulations about acquisition and loss of it. Significantly, the laws did not use Croatian terminology for local citizenship (*zavičajnost*) but instead Serbian terminology for membership in a municipality (*članstvo u općini*). This could mean that these new regulations were a kind of mixture of "western" and "eastern" traditions in regulation of local forms of belonging.

Finally, important changes in local citizenship on Croatian-Slavonian soil happened in the last stage of development of the Kingdom of Yugoslavia in 1939 with the formation of the Banovina of Croatia. The Banovina included almost whole Croatian-Slavonian legal area[23] and besides this, it also included Dalmatia as "Croatian" part of Slovenian-Dalmatian legal area, parts of Bosnian and Herzegovinian legal area populated mostly by Croats and part of Hungarian legal area (*Međimurje*), also populated dominantly by Croats. The Banovina got its autonomous organs; the Ban, the Ban's Government, the Croatian Diet (*Hrvatski sabor*).[24] Although the *Decree on the Banovina of Croatia* recognized separate Croatian entity, it did not establish separate national citizenship for the Banovina. However, it has brought some changes in competences in the matters of Yugoslav national citizenship. The most significant change was division of competences in a way that the government of Banovina became competent in regular naturalisations on the territory of the Banovina while extraordinary naturalisations and revocation of citizenship were still in competence of the central government and the king (§ 2 par. 3 point 2).[25]

---

21   CAVALIERI: *Propisi...*, op. cit., 34.
22   Ignjat M. TOLIĆ: *Zakon o opštinama*, Jugoslavenska štampa, Zagreb, 1933, 71; V.J. STEFANOVIĆ: *Zakon o opštinama (tekst sa komentarom, Zakonom o biračkim spiskovima, uredbama o izboru opštinskih odbora, uputstvima za sastav opštinskog budžeta i dr.)*, Themis, Zagreb, 1934, 11–308; *Zakon o gradskim opštinama*, Zakoni i naredbe, 2(1934), Izdavačko Preduzeće „M. Novine", Sarajevo, 1934.
23   Eastern Syrmia although part of the Croatian-Slavonian legal area was not included in the Banovina of Croatia. It administratively remained part of the Danube Banovina.
24   Ljubo BOBAN: *Sporazum Cvetković-Maček*, Institut društvenih nauka, Odeljenje za istorijske nauke, Beograd, 1965, 209–212.
25   For the text of The *Decree on the Banovina of Croatia (Uredba o Banovini Hrvatskoj) of* August 26 of 1939 see: http://www.pfsa.unsa.ba/pf/wp-content/uploads/2018/01/Uredba-o-Banovini-1939.pdf.

These new rules were in accordance with Croatian-Slavonian tradition of regulation of national citizenship, namely with the Hungarian-Croatian law about national citizenship of 1879 which recognized autonomy to Croatia-Slavonia in the executive matters of national citizenship, including regular naturalisations. Moreover, with the formation of the Banovina of Croatia established was belonging of persons to the Banovina of Croatia (*pripadnost Banovini Hrvatskoj*) based on the local citizenship in the Banovina.[26]

4 Local Citizenship and Determination of National Citizenship in the Croatian-Slavonian Legal Area

One of basic characteristics of the concept of local citizenship in Croatia-Slavonia before 1918 was the possibility to prove national citizenship with local citizenship. This characteristic of the concept could have been useful in the new Yugoslav state for determination of national citizenship of the Kingdom of Serbs, Croats and Slovenes in the Croatian-Slavonian legal area. This is especially so if we bear in mind the fact that the new state did not immediately enact citizenship law. The practice however indicates that the problem of the determination of citizenship in the Kingdom of Serbs, Croats and Slovenes, namely in the Croatian-Slavonian legal area, existed and was not easily resolved by mere use of local citizenship. With this in mind, Ladislav Polić, a professor of constitutional law at the Faculty of Law at the University of Zagreb, claimed in 1926 that during the first years of the new state it was disputable whom the Provisional Government and Provisional National Assembly considered a citizen of the state.[27] Polić's statement reflected the unstable situation in the legal practice concerning the definition of national citizenry.

The first draft of citizenship law of 1919 contained the rule that national citizens of the Kingdom of Serbs, Croats and Slovenes were all those who on 1 December 1918 had national citizenship in the Kingdoms of Serbia and Montenegro, local citizenship in Croatia, Slavonia and Dalmatia, belonged to Bosnia and Herzegovina or had local citizenship on other territories of the Kingdom.[28] As we can see, the draft contained a rule about local citizenship as a basis for determination of national citizenship in the "western" part of the Kingdom,

---

26 Juraj ANDRASSY: *Novo ustavno uređenje Hrvatske*, Mjesečnik: glasilo pravničkoga društva, Zagreb, 1939, 230.
27 Ladislav POLIĆ: *Pitanje državljanstva – referat = Spomenica na drugi kongres pravnika Kraljevine Srba, Hrvata i Slovenaca u Ljubljani od 9. do 11. rujna 1926*, Metod DOLENC, Rudolf SAJOVIC (eds.), Društvo "Pravnik" u Ljubljani, Ljubljana, 1927, 210–211.
28 *Ibid.*, 211.

including the Croatian-Slavonian legal area, and that was in accordance with the legal practice in this area in the period before 1918. However, the draft never became law, so this rule never entered into legal force.

A step forward was the Law about elections to the Constituent Assembly of 1920. The law contained rules for the determination of political citizenship, but only for the purposes of these elections. The law defined as national citizens all persons who before 1 December 1918 had national citizenship in Serbia and Montenegro, national citizenship in Croatia, Slavonia and Dalmatia, "Bosnian-Herzegovinian belonging", or had local citizenship in one of municipalities that became part of the Kingdom of Serbs, Croats and Slovenes.[29] The law for Croatia and Slavonia used the term national citizenship (*državljanstvo*), while it did not mention local citizenship. Additionally, the Law contained a rule that recognized national citizenship to all Slavs if they were permanently settled in the country in the period prior to the formation of voters' lists, regardless of their formal citizenship. The law also excluded from national citizenship and voting rights all those who had the right of option according to the peace treaties.[30] The electoral law thus broadened political citizenship to include persons who did not have formal citizenship but were ethnically connected,[31] while it excluded from citizenship all those who had the right of option.[32] Vague criteria (n.b. *all Slavs*) and exclusion of part of population with the right of option, eroded the principle of proving of national citizenship with local citizenship.

Key rules relevant for the determination of national citizenship were contained in the peace treaties concluded after the First World War between the Kingdom of Serbs, Croats and Slovenes and the Republic of Austria and Hungary. According to these treaties national citizenship of the Kingdom of Serbs, Croats, and Slovenes was acquired by all persons who had local citizenship (*Heimatrecht*) on ceded territories before 1 January 1910 and retained it until these agreements entered into force.[33] Persons who acquired local citizenship

---

29 Ladislav POLIĆ: *O pravnim osnovima budućega izbornoga reda*, Mjesečnik: glasilo pravničkoga društva, Zagreb, 2(1922), 49–51.
30 *Ibid.*
31 For more about concepts of formal and political citizenship, cf. Andreas FAHRMEIR: *Citizenship: The Rise and Fall of a Modern Concept*, Yale University Press, New Haven (CT)-London, 2007, 2–3.
32 The right of option was defined by international treaties between the Kingdom of Serbs, Croats and Slovenes and Austria and Hungary reached after the First World War. Celzije CAVALIERI: *Komentar Zakona o državljanstvu Kraljevine Jugoslavije*, Vlastita naklada, Zagreb, 1935, 131.
33 CAVALIERI: *Komentar...*, op. cit., 131; ČEPULO: *Pravo hrvatske...*, op. cit., 801.

on ceded territories after 1 January 1910 and wished to acquire national citizenship in the Kingdom of Serbs, Croats and Slovenes needed the approval of the state authorities.[34] The treaties therefore contained local citizenship as the fundamental criteria for the determination of national citizenship, if acquired before 1 January 1910. In cases when a person acquired local citizenship after 1 January 1910, local citizenship was not enough and it could be a starting point in the procedure of acquisition of national citizenship.[35]

Finally, the citizenship law of 1928 contained important norms for the determination of citizenship. The law defined as national citizens all those who had acquired local citizenship in Croatia-Slavonia before 1 January 1910 and retained it until peace treaties had entered into force. The law also recognized the national citizenship of persons who had acquired it according to peace treaties (§ 53 point 2). It recognized as citizens all those naturalized in the period before the citizenship law entered into force (§ 53 point 3). The law also recognized citizenship of Serbs, Croats and Slovenes who submitted a request for naturalisation if they were 21 years old, behaved well and had adequate income or wealth (§ 53 point 4) and provided a similar solution for certain other groups of Slavs (§ 53 point 5 and 6). Also recognized as citizens were persons whose initial ctizenship was unknown, if they were born in the territory of the Kingdom (*ius soli*) (§ 53 point 10) etc.[36]

All of these rules indicate that authorities used various criteria for the determination of who were national citizens. Although in 1919 the draft of the citizenship law contained the criterion of local citizenship as the only one for the determination of national citizenship in the Croatian-Slavonian legal area, later positive regulations partly abandoned this principle and introduced various criteria for determination of national citizenship, and local citizenship was only one of criteria. Distrust towards the concept of local citizenship reflected also the new sistem of proving national citizenship exclusively with national citizenship certificate. In the new state it was therefore not anymore possible

---

34   CAVALIERI: *Komentar...*, op. cit., 131; ČEPULO: *Pravo hrvatske...*, op. cit., 801; Dalibor ČEPULO: *Prava građana i moderne institucije: europska i hrvatska pravna tradicija*, Pravni fakultet Sveučilišta u Zagrebu, Zagreb, 2003, 86.

35   Giuseppe Motta states that in cases when local citizenship was acquired after 1 January 1910 it was „totally useless". Giuseppe MOTTA: *Less than Nations, Central-Eastern European Minorities after WWI, Volume 1*, Cambridge Scholars Publishing, Newcastle u. T., 2013, 372.

36   For more about provisions relevant for determination of national citizenship according to the citizenship law of 1928, cf. CAVALIERI: *Propisi...*, op. cit., 101–111; Otomar PIRKMAJER: *Zakon o državljanstvu sa tumačenjem*, Izdavačka knjižara Gece Kona, Beograd, 1929, 113–126.

to prove national citizenship simply with local citizensip certificate. Instead, national citizenship certificate was necessary. In line with this, Citizenship law of 1928 stated that a person could prove his national citizenship only with certificate of national citizenship issued by an administrative authority.[37] However, this rule did not reduced importance of local citizenship completely because in absence of registers of national citizens, the administrative authorities used local citizenship registers as a starting point for determination of national citizenship (§ 4 of the Citizenship Code of 1928).

5 Access to Local Citizenship in the Croatian-Slavonian Legal Area

After the establishment of the Kingdom of Serbs, Croats and Slovenes, the Provincial Government in Zagreb formally retained competence in the matters of local citizenship in the former territory of the Kingdom of Croatia-Slavonia.[38] However, despite this formally retained competence, real political circumstances had changed significantly. Aleksandar Karađorđević and the central government made frequent personnel changes in the Provincial Government and mostly appointed adherents of centralism in it.[39] In this way, they *de facto* abolished its autonomous position in the system of government. In the four years following enactment of the Constitution of 1921, the central authorities, centralized administration and the Provincial Government ceased to exist.[40]

Despite administrative centralisation, the legal distinctiveness of the Croatian-Slavonian legal area in the matters of acquisition and loss of local citizenship still existed. As noted earlier, particularly important was the Croatian system of acquisition of local citizenship based on *ius sanguinis*. A basic feature of the system was its closure. Especially problematic was a rule about the acquisition of local citizenship in a municipality after four years of residence but only after very formal notification of the intent to settle in a

---

37 CAVALIERI: *Propisi...*, op. cit., 10–12; PIRKMAJER: *op. cit.*, 45.
38 See a decision of the Provincial Government of 6 December 1919. In the decision, the Government explicitly declared its competence to determine local citizenship based on the Law on Regulation of Local Citizenship of 1880 in the former territory of Croatia-Slavonia while it refused to take action in cases of persons who wished to acquire local citizenship outside of its territory. Hrvatski državni arhiv, fond 79-Unutrašnji odjel Zemaljske vlade za Hrvatsku i Slavoniju, the box 4567, IV-2 4421/1919 (60791/1919); Ivan BEUC: *Povijest institucija državne vlasti u Hrvatskoj (1527–1945)*, Arhiv Hrvatske, Zagreb, 1969, 331–332.
39 Bosiljka JANJATOVIĆ: *Karađorđevićevska centralizacija i položaj Hrvatske u Kraljevstvu (Kraljevini) SHS*, Časopis za suvremenu povijest, 27(1995)/1, 59–60.
40 *Ibid.*, 63–67.

given municipality. In practice, it was true that many settlers neglected to provide such a notification. Because of this, many did not acquire new local citizenship.[41]

The Croatian model differed from the other two models of local citizenship in the Kingdom, namely the Austrian and Hungarian. The Austrian model was valid in the Slovenian-Dalmatian legal area and had been established by the laws of 1863 and 1896.[42] Although it prescribed the principle of *ius sanguinis*, this model from 1896 onwards also contained a right to local citizenship (*Heimatrecht*) after ten years of residence in a municipality.[43] The Hungarian model, valid in the former Hungarian legal area, contained *ius sanguinis* as a principle for the acquisition of local citizenship but it also contained various possibilities for local naturalisations by settlement. The most important of these was automatic naturalisation *ex lege* after four years of residence in a municipality, regulated by the Hungarian law of 1886.[44] All this made the Hungarian model of acquisition of local citizenship the most liberal.

A typical situation of the incompatibility of systems of local citizenship would be the case of national citizens who had local citizenship in the Hungarian legal area and had settled in the Croatian-Slavonian legal area. The local citizenship of these persons was regulated by the Hungarian law of 1886. According to this law, a citizen lost their local citizenship if he or she was absent four years from a municipality. The same law prescribed a rule about acquisition of new local citizenship in the municipality of settlement after four years. This system functioned when a person migrated within the former Hungarian legal area but did not if a person settled in the Croatian-Slavonian legal area. This mainly was because in the Croatian-Slavonian legal area, four years of residence was insufficient, but a person was also obliged to explicitly provide notice of their intention to settle in a municipality. Because of this, in many cases such settlers lost their previous local citizenship but did not acquire a new one. Therefore, they became persons without local citizenship.

---

41 Božidar MIRKOVIĆ: *Zavičajno pravo*, Općinski upravnik, 16(1924)/41, Zagreb, 161–162; BOGDANOVIĆ: *Automatsko stjecanje zavičajnosti po novom zakonu o općinama*, Općinski upravnik, 25(1933)/51, 223.

42 *Zakon o uređenju zavičajnih odnosa od 3. XII 1863*, Reichsgesetzblatt, 105(1863); *Zakon od 5. prosinca 1896. kojim se mijenjaju neke odredbe zakona 3. prosinca 1863 o uređenju zavičajnih odnosa*, Reichsgesetzblatt, 86(1896).

43 Ivan KOSNICA: *Croatian Law on Regulation of Local Citizenship (1880) – Context and Change*, 83–95, 93–94 = *Codification Achievements and Failures in the 19th-20th Century*, Mária HOMOKI-NAGY, Norbert VARGA (eds.), University of Szeged, Szeged, 2018.

44 Vinko ŽGANEC: *Zavičajno pravo u Vojvodini, Međimurju i Prekmurju*, Vladimir Takšić, Čakovec, 1924, 1–13; KOSNICA: *Croatian Law...*, op. cit., 94.

Different regulations and their incompatibility had disintegrative impacts on the legal situation of citizens. However, the problem of the multitude of regulations regarding municipalities and consequently regarding local citizenship had not been solved by 1933 and 1934. The first enacted was the Law on Municipalities (*Zakon o općinama*) of 1933. The Law regulated in articles 15–24 the issue of residents of a municipality and the issue of local citizens of a municipality (*članovi općine*). It stated that every national citizen should have one local citizenship in one municipality (§ 15). The Law prescribed *ius sanguinis* as the basic principle for the acquisition of local citizenship (§ 16).[45] Additionally, a person could acquire local citizenship by legitimation, by marriage (in the case of a woman), by public service and by local naturalisation. Naturalized should be moral national citizens, able to support themselves and not under criminal investigation or indictment for crimes for which the loss of civil rights was prescribed (§17). A municipality could not reject an applicant if they fulfilled these requirements and if they had lived five years in a municipality (§ 17).[46] The Law also regulated automatic local naturalisation for national citizens who lived in a municipality at least ten years, and during that time enjoyed civil rights and were not under criminal investigation or accusation for crimes for which loss of civil rights was prescribed (§ 17).[47] The law also prescribed the obligation of municipalities to maintain records of inhabitants and registers of local citizens (§ 24).[48] The Law on Municipalities of 1933 did not apply to cities, so local citizenship in cities was still regulated by previous legislation (§ 136). The Law on City Municipalities of 1934 regulated local citizenship in articles 11–20 on the same principles as the Law on Municipalities. These new laws replaced previous regulations about local citizenship, including the Croatian Law on Regulation of Local Citizenship of 1880, although according to some authors, like Stefanović, certain norms of the Croatian law were still valid.[49]

Comparison of the new regulations with the previous one valid in the Croatian-Slavonian legal area indicates two very important differences. The first is the introduction of five years' residence as an obligatory condition for regular naturalisation. The previous regulation did not contain such a provision or a similar one and that is why in this aspect the new regulation was more restrictive. However, more important was the second change. It was the

---

45 Tolić: *op. cit.*, 12.
46 *Ibid.*, 13; Stefanović: *op. cit.*, 86.
47 Bogdanović: *op. cit.*, 223; Stefanović: *op. cit.*, 86–87.
48 Stefanović: *op. cit.*, 91–92.
49 *Ibid.*, 83–85.

introduction of a system of automatic naturalisation after ten years' residence.[50] This was a quite new possibility for the acquisition of local citizenship that had been previously non-existent in the Croatian-Slavonian legal area, while a similar model existed in the former Hungarian and in the Slovenian-Dalmatian legal area.[51] This rule eased acquisition of local citizenship and consequently reduced the importance of *ius sanguinis*.

However, it is necessary to point out that the rule did not immediately have its full effect in the legal practice on Croatian-Slavonian legal area. Sources indicate incorrect interpretations of this rule. For example, in the professional journal *Općinski upravnik*, published in Zagreb on 9 December 9 1933, Spasoje Šarkić in his interpretation of the new regulation wrongly concluded that automatic naturalisation *ex lege* is not possible.[52] In addition, authorities of many municipalities also incorrectly interpreted the rule about automatic naturalisation.[53] Obviously, such incorrect interpretations were the result of traditional understanding of local citizenship as a closed concept.

6 Local Citizenship and Political and Social Rights in the Croatian-Slavonian Legal Area

An important feature of the concept of local citizenship in Croatia-Slavonia before 1918 was that it gave a citizen certain political and social rights in a municipality as well as in Croatia-Slavonia.

However, the authorities of the new state, immediately after its formation abolished wider potential of local citizenship as a prerequisite for enjoyment of rights in Croatia-Slavonia and limited its significance on local level. Moreover, even on the local level, the authorities weakened significance of local citizenship as the basis for political and social rights in a municipality. Such

---

50 BOGDANOVIĆ: *op. cit.*, 223.

51 The Hungarian Law of 1886 provided *ex lege* naturalisation after four years of residence without request, if a citizen fulfilled all legal requirements. In the Slovenian-Dalmatian legal area there was naturalisation on request after ten years residence according to the Law of 1896. The difference between this regulation and the new Yugoslav regulation was in the necessity of a request. While in the Slovenian-Dalmatian legal area request was necessary the new Yugoslav regime predicted automatic naturalisation after ten years *ex lege* and in this way was more similar to the Hungarian model. Therefore, one can view the formation of the new Yugoslav rule as "borrowing" and "adaptation" of already existing models.

52 Spasoje ŠARKIĆ: *Zavičajnost po novom zakonu o opštinama*, Općinski upravnik, 25(1933)/49, 217–218.

53 BOGDANOVIĆ: *op. cit.*, 223.

erosion of importance of local citizenship ilustrates the order of the central government that regulated local elections on Croatian-Slavonian legal area and was enacted on 1 November 1919. The order reserved active and passive voting rights in local elections to national citizens who had lived at least one year in a municipality, regardless of local citizenship.[54] In this way, the authorities abandoned local citizenship as the basis for voting rights in a municipality. Laws about local elections in Croatia-Slavonia enacted in the period 1921–1923 followed this regulation and therefore based political rights on local level, namely active and passive voting rights on local elections, on national citizenship and criteria of living in a municipality for a period longer than 6 months.[55]

Certain modification to the policy was made by the decree about local elections in municipalities in Croatia-Slavonia enacted by the central government on 31 May 1927. The decree followed the principle established earlier in the regulation of active voting rights and thus gave active voting rights to national citizens who had lived in a municipality longer than six months. On the other hand, the decree reserved passive voting rights for local citizens of a municipality who were at least thirty years of age.[56] In this way, the decree represented a step backward in the regulation of passive voting rights. The Law on Municipalities of 1933, as well as the Law on City Municipalities of 1934, followed the policy established by the decree of 1927. The law gave active voting rights to all inhabitants of a municipality (§ 26, 23). In this way, national citizens had active voting rights if they had lived at least six months in a municipality, regardless of local citizenship.[57] On the other hand, the Law on Municipalities of 1933 and the Law on City Municipalities of 1934 reserved passive voting rights for the local citizens of a municipality (§ 27, 24).[58]

As well as in the sphere of political rights, the central authorities negated local citizenship as a key prerequisite for enjoyment of social rights. In line with this, the Constitution of 1921 prescribed obligation of state to support poor citizens and vulnerable social groups (§ 22, 27, 31, 32). The Constitution of 1921 did not mention similar obligation of municipalities. Although Croatian law about local citizenship of 1880 contained a rule about obligation of

---

54 MIRKOVIĆ: *op. cit.,* 161; Ivo KRBEK: *Izborni red za odbore seoskih upravnih općina u Hrvatskoj i Slavoniji sa Sremom prema odredbi od 31.v.1927.,* Naklada Gospodarskih novena, Zagreb, 1927, 5.
55 KRBEK: *Izborni...*, op. cit., 7, 10.
56 *Ibid.,* 8–9, 15–16, 18–19.
57 STEFANOVIĆ: *op. cit.,* 93, 325–326.
58 Anto MILUŠIĆ: *Izborni sistem Banovine Hrvatske,* Zbornik Pravnog fakulteta u Zagrebu, 33(1983)/3–4, 360, 365; STEFANOVIĆ: *op. cit.,* 93–94.

municipalities to support poor citizens, the sources indicate that in the twenties municipalities did not provide poor relief.[59] The regulations about municipalities of 1933 and about city municipalities of 1934 did not bring change. Although these regulations contained norms about alternative duty of municipalities to support poor local citizens in cases when there are no other persons obliged by law or when there was no other support according to some other law (§ 22, § 18), other laws significantly reduced this obligation. For instance, in the case of covering hospital expenses for a poor patient, positive regulations abandoned local citizenship as a basis of supprot and instead of this contained five years residence in a municipality as crucial for determination of municipality obliged to cover the expenses.[60]

Specific revival of the concept of local citizenship as a basis of rights, both on local but also regional level happened at the end of the state, in the period of the Banovina of Croatia. On the regional level crucial was the decree about elections and about composition of the Parliament (*Sabor*) of the Banovina of Croatia of 14 January 1940.[61] The decree *inter alia* defined active and passive voting rights for the Croatian Diet stating that active voting right have male Yugoslav national citizens, at least 24 years old with local citizenship in some of municipalities in the Banovina of Croatia. Passive voting right belonged to citizens with active voting rights if they were at least thirty years old, literate and if they spoke the „national" language.[62] Thus in both cases, local citizenship in the Banovina of Croatia was the key dimension that connected a Yugoslav citizen with the Banovina of Croatia.

On local level crucial was the autonomous decree about municipalities of 1940.[63] The Decree defined active voting right for local elections in the Banovina of Croatia on similar basis as for elections for the Croatian Parliament and this meant that active voting right had a citizen listed in register of voters, at least 24 years old with local citizenship in one of municipalities in the Banovina of Croatia.[64] In this way local citizenship in Croatia-Slavonia

---

59 MIRKOVIĆ: *op. cit.*, 161.
60 Ivo KRBEK: *Upravno politički zakoni: (skripta): predavanja Ive Krbeka*, Klub slušača prava, Zagreb, 1940, 30.
61 *Uredba o izbornom redu i ustrojstvu Sabora Banovine Hrvatske*, January 14 of 1940, Narodne novine, 12(1940).
62 MILUŠIĆ: *op. cit.* 354–355; ANDRASSY: *op. cit.*, 230, 233.
63 *Uredba o izmjenama i dopunama Zakona o općinama*, April 9 of 1940, Narodne novine, 84(1940). On the other hand, regulation about city municipalities of 1934 has not been changed. MILUŠIĆ: *op. cit.*, 364–365.
64 *Ibid.* 359–360.

became fundamental prerequsite for enjoyment of active voting rights in local elections.

7 Conclusion

Analysis of transformations of the regulation of local citizenship in the Croatian-Slavonian legal area in the period of the First Yugoslav state indicates significant changes as a result of efforts taken by the central authorities in Belgrade in building of common and unified Yugoslav legal system. In line with this, the authorities reduced importantce of local citizenship. Therefore, the authorities conducted effective measures which abolished previous practice of proving of national citizenship with local citizenship certificate. Instead, the central authorities introduced new cerficates about national citizenship issued by the state administration. Another argument in favour of sucessfull abolishment of previously established legal models and identities by enactment of new regulations would be new regulation of acquistion of local citizenship in the Yugoslav municipal laws of 1933 and 1934 and the rule about automatic naturalisation *ex lege*. Such change annuled closure as an important characteristic of regulation of local citizenship on Croatian-Slavonian legal area. Finally, the central authorities in the period from formation of the state in 1918 until formation of the Banovina of Croatia in 1939 enacted new regulations which did not recognize local citizenship as a basis of political and social rights in Croatia-Slavonia and weakened importance of local citizenship as a basis of local political and social rights on local level.

However, in changing legal reality the central authorities faced some obvious limitations. First of all, the chapter indicates that reliance on the concept of local citizenship, namely on the records about local citizens, as a starting point in determination of Yugoslav national citizenship was necessary in the western part of the state, including Croatian-Slavonian legal area. Therefore, radical split with tradition was not possible. Another argument that clearly demonstrates limits of legal instrumentalism is the one about wrong interpretations and applicatons of new Yugoslav regulations about local citizenship of 1933 and 1934 in legal practice. This signales that closure was in some circles understood as an important characteristic of the concept of local citizenship, and was therefore resistant on immediate change of regulation. And finally, specific vitality of the concept and its long term resistance on normative changes, reflects new regulation enacted after 1939 in the Banovina of Croatia. This new regulation redefined institute of local citizenship in a way that was more in line with Croatian-Slavonian tradition relevant in pre-1918 times. Here especially relevant was that local citizenship was key prerequisite of active and passive voting rights in elections for the Croatian Diet. Previous remarks clearly indicate limits of legal instrumentalism. Moreover, they also show that we cannot speak about breakdown of a concept of local citizenship but rather about its redefinition.

Bibliography

Archival Sources

Hrvatski državni arhiv [Croatian State Archives], fond 79-Unutrašnji odjel Zemaljske vlade za Hrvatsku i Slavoniju, the box 4567, IV-2 4421/1919 (60791/1919).

Literature

Juraj ANDRASSY: *Novo ustavno uređenje Hrvatske*, Mjesečnik: glasilo pravničkoga društva, Zagreb, 1939, 226–240.

Rainer BAUBÖCK: *Reinventing Urban Citizenship*, Citizenship Studies, 7(2003)/2, 139–160.

Ivan BEUC: *Povijest institucija državne vlasti u Hrvatskoj (1527–1945)*, Arhiv Hrvatske, Zagreb, 1969.

Ljubo BOBAN: *Sporazum Cvetković-Maček*, Institut društvenih nauka, Odeljenje za istorijske nauke, Beograd, 1965.

BOGDANOVIĆ: *Automatsko stjecanje zavičajnosti po novom zakonu o općinama*, Općinski upravnik, 25(1933)/51, Zagreb, 223–224.

Celso CAVALIERI: *Propisi o državljanstvu Kraljevine Srba, Hrvata i Slovenaca*, Vlastita naklada, Zagreb, 1929.

Celzije CAVALIERI: *Komentar Zakona o državljanstvu Kraljevine Jugoslavije*, Vlastita naklada, Zagreb, 1935.

Dalibor ČEPULO: *Prava građana i moderne institucije: europska i hrvatska pravna tradicija*, Pravni fakultet Sveučilišta u Zagrebu, Zagreb, 2003.

Dalibor ČEPULO: *Pravo hrvatske zavičajnosti i pitanje hrvatskog i ugarskog državljanstva 1868–1918 – pravni i politički vidovi i poredbena motrišta*, Zbornik Pravnog fakulteta u Zagrebu, 49(1999)/6, 795–825.

Roger COTTERRELL: *Law, Culture and Society: Legal Ideas in the Mirror of Social Theory*, Ashgate, Hampshire, 2006.

Andreas FAHRMEIR: *Citizenship: The Rise and Fall of a Modern Concept*, Yale University Press, New Haven (CT)-London, 2007.

Marc HELBLING: *Switzerland: Contentious Citizenship Attribution in a Federal State*, Journal of Ethnic and Migration Studies, 36(2010)/5, 793–809.

Bosiljka JANJATOVIĆ: *Karađorđevićevska centralizacija i položaj Hrvatske u Kraljevstvu (Kraljevini) SHS*, Časopis za suvremenu povijest, 27(1995)/1, 55–76.

Ivan KOSNICA: *Croatian Law on Regulation of Local Citizenship (1880) – Context and Change = Codification Achievements and Failures in the 19th–20th Century*, Mária HOMOKI-NAGY, Norbert VARGA (eds.), University of Szeged, Szeged, 2018, 83–95.

Ivan KOSNICA: *Das Problem der Staatsbürgerschaft in Kroatien und Slawonien im Ausgleichszeitraum (1868–1918) = Kroatisch-ungarische öfentlich-rechtliche Verhältnisse zur Zeit der Doppelmonarchie*, Gábor MÁTHÉ, Barna MEZEY (eds.), Eötvös University Press, Budapest, 2015.

Ivan KOSNICA: *Definiranje državljanskog korpusa na hrvatsko-slavonskom području u Kraljevini SHS / Jugoslaviji*, Zbornik Pravnog fakulteta Sveučilišta u Rijeci, 39 (2018)/2, 809–832.

Ivan KOSNICA: *Hrvatsko-slavonska pripadnost u Hrvatskoj i Slavoniji u nagodbenom razdoblju*, Hrvatska i komparativna javna uprava/Croatian and Comparative Public Administration, 14(2014)/2, 465–492.

Ivan KOSNICA: *Hungarians and Citizenship in Croatia-Slavonia 1868–1918*, 59–72, in: David A. FRENKEL and Norbert VARGA: *Law and History*, Athens Institute for Education and Research, Athens, 2015.

Ivan KOSNICA: *Utvrđivanje državljanstva u Hrvatskoj i Slavoniji 1849–1880*, Zbornik radova Pravnog fakulteta u Splitu, 51(2014)/3, 697–713.

Maciej KOSZOWSKI: *Medieval Iceland: The Influence of Culture and Tradition on Law*, Scandinavian Studies, 86(2014)/3, 333–351.

Ivo KRBEK: *Izborni red za odbore seoskih upravnih općina u Hrvatskoj i Slavoniji sa Sremom prema odredbi od 31.v.1927*, Naklada Gospodarskih novina, Zagreb, 1927.

Ivo KRBEK: *Upravno politički zakoni: (skripta): predavanja Ive Krbeka*, Klub slušača prava, Zagreb, 1940.

Leo LUCASSEN: *Between Hobbes and Locke. Gypsies and the limits of the modernization paradigm*, Social History, 33(2008)/4, 423–441.

Anto MILUŠIĆ: *Izborni sistem Banovine Hrvatske*, Zbornik Pravnog fakulteta u Zagrebu, 33(1983)/3–4, 343–372.

Božidar MIRKOVIĆ: *Zavičajno pravo*, Općinski upravnik, 16(1924)/41, 161–162.

Giuseppe MOTTA: *Less than Nations, Central-Eastern European Minorities after WWI*, Volume I, Cambridge Scholars Publishing, Newcastle u. T., 2013.

Koloman MUTAVDJIĆ: *Zavičajno pravo: Zakon od 30. travnja 1880. ob uredjenju zavičajnih odnošaja u kraljevinah Hrvatskoj i Slavoniji i prijašnji propisi o stečenju i gubitku zavičajnoga prava*, Naklada knjižare Lav. Hartmana (Kugli i Deutsch), Zagreb, 1894.

Otomar PIRKMAJER: *Zakon o državljanstvu sa tumačenjem*, Izdavačka knjižara Gece Kona, Beograd, 1929.

Ladislav POLIĆ: *O pravnim osnovima budućega izbornoga reda*, Mjesečnik: glasilo pravničkoga društva, 2(1922), 49–63.

Ladislav POLIĆ: *Pitanje državljanstva – referat = Spomenica na drugi kongres pravnika Kraljevine Srba, Hrvata i Slovenaca u Ljubljani od 9. do 11. rujna 1926*, Metod DOLENC, Rudolf SAJOVIC (eds.), Društvo "Pravnik" u Ljubljani, Ljubljana, 1927.

Peter N. RIESENBERG: *Citizenship in the Western Tradition: Plato to Rousseau*, University of North Carolina Press, Chapel Hill, 1992.

Peter J. SPIRO: *Formalizing Local Citizenship*, Fordham Urban Law Journal, 37(2009)/2, 559–572.

V.J. STEFANOVIĆ: *Zakon o opštinama (tekst sa komentarom, Zakonom o biračkim spiskovima, uredbama o izboru opštinskih odbora, uputstvima za sastav opštinskog budžeta i dr.)*, Themis, Zagreb, 1934.

Spasoje ŠARKIĆ: *Zavičajnost po novom zakonu o opštinama*, Općinski upravnik, 25(1933)/49, Zagreb, 217–218.

Igor ŠTIKS: *Nations and Citizens in Yugoslavia and the Post-Yugoslav States: One Hundred Years of Citizenship*, Bloomsbury Academic, London-New York, 2015.

Ignjat M. TOLIĆ: *Zakon o opštinama*, Jugoslavenska štampa, Zagreb, 1933.

Uredba o Banovini Hrvatskoj, August 26 of 1939, http://www.pfsa.unsa.ba/pf/wp-content/uploads/2018/01/Uredba-o-Banovini-1939.pdf.

Uredba o izbornom redu i ustrojstvu Sabora Banovine Hrvatske, January 14 of 1940, Narodne novine, 12(1940).

Uredba o izmjenama i dopunama Zakona o općinama, April 9 of 1940, Narodne novine, 84(1940).

Ustav Kraljevine Srba, Hrvata i Slovenaca. Državna štamparija Kraljevine Srba, Hrvata i Slovenaca, Beograd, 1926.

Sophia WOODMAN: *Local Politics, Local Citizenship? Socialized Governance in Contemporary China*, China Quarterly, 226(2016), 342–362.

Imre ZAJTAY: *Immutability of Rules and Principles of Legal Development: The Permanence of Roman Law Concepts = European Legal Cultures*, Volkmar GESSNER, Armin HOELAND, Csaba VARGA (eds.), Dartmouth, Aldershot, 1996.

Zakon o uređenju zavičajnih odnosa od 3. XII 1863, Reichsgesetzblatt, 105(1863).

Zakonski članak XVI: 1870, sabora kraljevina Hrvatske, Slavonije i Dalmacije o uređenju općina i trgovišta, Sbornik zakonah i naredabah valjanih za kraljevinu Hrvatsku i Slavoniju, vol. 3, 1871.

Zakon od 30. travnja 1880. o uređenju zavičajnih odnosa u kraljevinama Hrvatskoj i Slavoniji, Sbornik zakonah i naredabah valjanih za kraljevinu Hrvatsku i Slavoniju, vol. 9, 1880.

Zakon o ustroju gradskih općina u kraljevinama Hrvatskoj i Slavoniji, Sbornik zakonah i naredabah valjanih za kraljevine Hrvatsku i Slavoniju, vol. 9, 1895.

Zakon od 5. prosinca 1896. kojim se mijenjaju neke odredbe zakona 3. prosinca 1863 o uređenju zavičajnih odnosa, Reichsgesetzblatt, 86(1896).

Zakon o gradskim opštinama, Zakoni i naredbe, 2(1934), Izdavačko Preduzeće „Movine", Sarajevo, 1934.

Vinko ŽGANEC: *Zavičajno pravo u Vojvodini, Medjimurju i Prekmurju*, Vladimir Takšić, Čakovec, 1924.

CHAPTER 10

Nazi Law as Pure Instrument: Natural Law, (Extra-)Legal Terror, and the Neglect of Ideology

Simon Lavis

1   Instrumentalism and Nazi Law

The impetus for the presentation of the paper that forms the basis of this chapter, at the 2016 European Society of Comparative Legal History conference at the University of Gdańsk, was the conference's focus on the question of the instrumentality of law. In particular, one of the strands of inquiry incorporated within the conference theme was law's use as an instrument to "transform reality", as a tool to "shape and strengthen national identity". The particular panel in which this paper was presented centred on the nexus of this point with law's role in political projects of total domination, specifically in 20th century authoritarian and totalitarian regimes. The subject of this contribution, the role of and relationship between law and ideology in the Third Reich, fits well within this given the transformative (and destructive) aims of the regime and its strong nationalistic (and racist) element.

There can be little doubt that the Nazi leadership wished to, and in many respects did, transform reality in the Third Reich, and that law was to some extent an instrument at the service of their ideological objectives to that end. However, as the theme of the conference attests, law is often instrumentalised, whether functionally or axiologically. Simply put, a ruling party or government has policy objectives and the law is one of the key normative and institutional operators through which it can implement them. This occurs in governments of all political stripes and is not limited to so-called totalitarian regimes. In this sense, the particular application of this question to Nazi law, and to the other 20th century authoritarian administrations considered by the panel's papers, is uncontroversial: a comparative examination of how law was used to further the national interest (as defined by the regime) and specifically the role of ideology in this.

However, it is arguably in the specific case of authoritarian and totalitarian regimes that our interpretation of this relationship between policy objective and legal implementation becomes obfuscated by an overriding ideological component. When it is an authoritarian ideology at the heart of government, such as that in Nazi Germany, we tend to interpret the relationship between policy and law, and in particular between governing ideology and legal ideology in a different way. The contention of this chapter, therefore, is that in the case of the Third Reich, given the discursive development of the academic understanding of the role of law in Nazi Germany, there is an *a priori* theoretical question about the nature of both the concept of instrumentalism and the concept of "law" at play when we confront the regime that brought about the Second World War and perpetrated the Holocaust. This is because the idea of law as a blunt instrument, a crude tool, at the service of state power, with little attention to the real nature and significance of ideological considerations for law, has dominated our legal theoretical understanding of the Nazi legal system. This pure instrumentalisation of law at the service of a repressive regime is particularly prevalent in natural law interpretations of wicked legal regimes, and especially Nazi law.

According to this view, it is a case of the Nazi leadership in the early 1930s initially presenting as a party of law and order, and feigning defence of the existing German *Rechtsstaat* in order to pacify the ruling and influential conservative elites. Over time this turned into the cynical manipulation of the residue of legal norms and processes, primarily to maintain the regime's hold on power and repress any resistance, and ended with the undermining of the legal system to leave a state of chaos, barbarity and terror, a state of non-law. The naturalistic belief in the necessary connection between law and morality limits the concept of law at play in this account to the rule of law, with the consequence that other Nazi measures intended to implement ideological objectives, which increasingly emerge as their hold on power strengthens, are not conducted through "law" at all and so do not merit historical or theoretical examination *as a matter of law*. This concept of instrumentalism – cynical manipulation of law for oppressive purposes – and of law – as the rule of law, the *Rechtsstaat* – is the predominant hermeneutic lens through which Nazi law is understood as a matter of legal theory. Nevertheless, positivism too is open to accept the "cynical manipulation" paradigm of instrumentalism in relation to Nazi law, just within a slightly broader definition of what constitutes the concept of law. In both cases the centrality of Nazi racial ideology to all aspects of the state, and the possibility of this ideology manifesting itself in an alternative, but recognisably legal, reality, is overlooked, as is an array of recent historiography about other aspects of the Third Reich that attests to its importance.

This chapter is not concerned with broader debates about or between positivism and natural law within the legal academy, or with critiquing the complex theories that underlie each position generally. Its focus is in part much narrower than that, and in part moves in another direction entirely. Its thesis is twofold. The first part is that this particular version of instrumentalism and concept of law has often been applied to Nazi Germany and is the paradigm that most determines our understanding of Nazi law. The second part is that this interpretation is problematic in light of the historical evidence, both because it oversimplifies the nature of the Nazi legal state and because it completely overlooks the role of ideology in Nazi law; the relationship "between law as a normative order and the overarching ideological framework" of the regime, as the conference panel abstract stated it. Ultimately, the biggest problem for legal theory presented by a simplified interpretation of law in the Third Reich, focused on crude instrumentalism and the separation between law and non-law, is that it renders unnecessary further investigation of the Nazi regime as a matter of law. It excludes from relevance for our dominant concept of law a significant and devastating period of European legal history and prevents us from trying to make sense of, and coming to terms with, what this means for law and legality today.

In order to demonstrate this thesis, this chapter will examine a number of influential analyses of Nazi law advanced since the 1940s to demonstrate their reliance on the approach set out above and highlight problems with this. These include Franz Neumann's *Behemoth*, Lon Fuller and HLA Hart's positions in the 1958 Hart-Fuller debate, and more recently the conclusions of Nigel Simmonds and Kristin Rundle. It will then conclude with some preliminary thoughts on applying a broader concept of instrumentalism, such as that implied by the conference theme, to Nazi law.

2   Instrumentalism in the Behemoth State

At the heart of an examination of the instrumentalism of Nazi law at the service of its ideology is the question of whether Nazi law was really "law" at all; whether the legal system in the third Reich was recognisable and valid as law. Some of the most enduring thinking on the nature and operation of the Nazi system of government with a bearing on this issue, which continues to be influential among historians and others today, comes from two studies by political scientists contemporary to the Third Reich: Ernst Fraenkel's "dual state" theory of Nazi legality, and Franz Neumann's "behemoth" account of the structure of the Nazi state.[1] These two conceptualisations of Nazi government are

---

1   Ernst FRAENKEL: *The Dual State: A Contribution to the Theory of Dictatorship*, Octagon Books, New York, 1969 [1942]; Franz NEUMANN: *Behemoth: The Structure and Practice of National Socialism 1933–1944*, 2nd ed., Frank Cass & Co, London, 1967.

significant because of the extent to which they have subsequently directed the focus of scholarly attention on the constitution of Nazi rule towards the "prerogative" aspect of the Nazi state or away from notions of law and legality altogether. In both cases, the "non-law" aspect is considered the area most interesting and worthy of study because that is taken to encapsulate the true nature of Nazi Germany; "a tyranny, characterized by arbitrary rule, enforced through intimidation and terror".[2]

This is most evident in Neumann's characterisation of the Third Reich as a behemoth in his book of the same name. This term "depicts a non-state, a chaos, a situation of lawlessness, disorder, and anarchy", and, according to Neumann, Nazi Germany fit this description as it had "'swallowed' the rights and dignity of man, and is out to transform the world into a chaos by the supremacy of gigantic land masses".[3] There is much that can be learned from Neumann's structural analysis of National Socialism and the text devotes a few pages to a discussion of the concept of law, positivism and natural law, and the particular manifestation of law in the Third Reich.[4] However, while he states that Nazi law could be considered law "if law is merely the will of the sovereign",[5] Neumann's evaluation and argument is that Nazi law is non-law, because it is not "rational either in form or content".[6] The implications of this for an examination of the instrumentalism of Nazi law are apparent, it is "nothing but a technique of mass manipulation by terror":[7]

> Since law is identical with the will of the Leader, since the Leader can send political opponents to their death without any judicial procedure, and since such an act is glorified as the highest realisation of justice, we can no longer speak of a specific character of law. Law is now a technical means for the achievement of specific political aims. It is merely the command of the sovereign ... Law is merely ... a means for the stabilisation of power.[8]

It is a combination of the loss of the specific character of law – a specific ideology of law – separate and distinct from the political will of the regime, with an

---

[2] *The Law in Nazi Germany: Ideology, Opportunism, and the Perversion of Justice*, Alan STEIN-WEIS, Robert RACHLIN (eds.), Berghahn Books, New York, 2013, 1.
[3] NEUMANN: *op. cit.*, vii, "Note on the name Behemoth".
[4] *Ibid.* 440–458.
[5] *Ibid.*, 458.
[6] *Ibid.*
[7] *Ibid.*
[8] *Ibid.*, 447–448.

analysis of Nazi law focused exclusively on violence and terror that denies it the quality of law and renders it a pure instrument in Neumann's analysis.

The former of these two points is dependent on an acceptance of Neumann's natural law application of the concept of law, and the latter on an ultimately concomitant denial of both a specific Nazi vision of legality and the use of law in the Third Reich for anything more than terror and repression. While Neumann acknowledges that, in a political sense, law may be "will and nothing else", the version of law he endorses is a rational concept "…determined by its form and content, not by its origin. Not every act of the sovereign is law. Law in this sense is a norm, comprehensible by reason, open to theoretical understanding, and containing an ethical postulate, primarily that of equality. Law is reason and will".[9] On this basis Nazi law cannot be considered law, because it undermines the "generality and the abstractness of law together with the independence of the judge":[10]

> …legal standards of conduct acquire greater significance than before because even the restrictions set up by parliamentary democracy … insufficient as they may have been, have been removed. By its very vagueness the legal standard of conduct serves to bring pre-National Socialist positive law into agreement with the demands of the new rules. National Socialism postulates the absolute subjugation of the judge to the law, but the standards of conduct make it possible for him to introduce political elements even when they conflict with positive law.[11]

This reveals the interdependence of Neumann's preferred concept of law with his description of Nazi law as an instrument. The particular ethical standard at the centre of this concept of law and the principles that are seen to emanate from that standard, are anathema to the Nazi version of law. As this forms the very definition of valid law, Nazi "law" cannot be valid law, it must be non-law. Absent of any recognisable normative content, Nazi (non-)law is reducible to the will of the sovereign, and this will is intent only on conserving power through terror; "true generality is not possible in a society that cannot dispense with power".[12] This appears to be the only possibility for a regime intent on being both authoritarian and totalitarian.

---

[9] Ibid., 440.
[10] Ibid., 444.
[11] Ibid., 447.
[12] Ibid., 451.

A critique of this is not based on its elucidation of some of the characteristics of Nazi legality – use of retroactivity, political influence on judiciary, vagueness of the legal standard of conduct – in Neumann's analysis, but rather lies elsewhere and is two-fold. First is not accounting fully for the centrality of Nazi racial ideology to the regime, and its potential for a Nazi vision of legality. It is argued that Nazi law was not *only* used for repression, terror and the maintenance of power but was also used for the substantive advancement of Nazi policy objectives beyond merely stabilising power. It did have its own normative and (un)ethical content. While Neumann hints at the centrality of Nazi ideology in acknowledging that "[t]he main function of National Socialist law is to preserve racial existence",[13] the implications of this for the nature of Nazi law and how law was instrumentalised by the regime are not fully realised in his evaluation. The function of Nazi law according to Neumann is to spread terror to maintain power.

Second is that the conclusions drawn about the nature of Nazi law emanate from the theory of law that is adopted to invalidate the Nazi legal regime, so that law apparently cannot have any normative content if it is not the rule of law and accordingly law as terror is the only possible alternative. The natural consequence of this, as noted in the introduction to this chapter, is that Nazi law is now readily excluded from serious conversations about the nature of law and what law may be used for. While it might be appropriate – indeed arguably imperative – to adopt a particular concept of law as a method of furthering resistance to a contemporary tyrannical regime,[14] the enduring influence of an analysis of Nazi law that emphasises its perceived lawlessness has acted as an obstacle to our better understanding of how the Nazi regime operated as a matter of law even as more and better historical evidence about the institutions and governance of the Third Reich has become available since the postwar period.

In his discussion of the Nazi legal system, while disagreeing with Fraenkel's views on the presence of law in the Third Reich, Neumann makes some reference to the divide between the "normative" and "prerogative" state that characterises Fraenkel's dual state analysis. He notes that "[t]he average lawyer will be repelled by the idea that there can be a legal system that is nothing more than a means of terrorizing people. He will point out that hundreds of thousands, perhaps millions, of transactions in Germany are handled according to

---

13   Ibid., 452.
14   Douglas G. MORRIS: *Write and Resist: Ernst Fraenkel and Franz Neumann on the Role of Natural Law in Fighting Nazi Tyranny*, New German Critique, 42(2015)/3, 197–230.

calculable and predictable rules. That is true".[15] These "'culturally indifferent rules' of a predominantly technical character", are a function of "the increasing complexity of modern society" according to Neumann.[16] He also concedes that "even in the so-called 'prerogative state'", we can witness the rational application of such technical rules,[17] but these are not the sort of laws that Neumann is primarily concerned with when drawing conclusions about Nazi legality.

The contrast between Neumann's behemoth and Fraenkel's dual state comes in the assertion by the latter that the normative state in particular operated in the Third Reich as part of the legal system, that there was to an extent law in the Third Reich. The normative state consisted of the vestiges of the pre-existing "normal" legal state of affairs and was "an administrative body endowed with elaborate powers for safeguarding the legal order as expressed in statutes, decisions of the courts, and activities of the administrative agencies".[18] The prerogative state, by contrast, was the arbitrary rule of the government, unrestrained by formal law: "that governmental system which exercises unlimited arbitrariness and violence unchecked by any legal guarantees".[19] The prerogative state was parasitic, over time, on the normative state, as radicalisation and chaos took hold, and more and more aspects of the state were pulled into the arbitrary realm, away from the safeguards of "normal" law.

It is possible to draw a rough parallel, even if not exact, between Fraenkel's normative state and Neumann's "culturally neutral" technical rules; and Fraenkel's prerogative state and Neumann's law as violence and terror. However, while the normative state may have tended towards a narrower realm of technical rules, an important feature of it is that it encompassed the residue of the pre-existing, *Rechtsstaat* and legal institutions, which continued to function to varying degrees and for differing periods into the Third Reich. Fraenkel argued that the state comprised a combination of arbitrariness (the prerogative state) and efficient order (the normative state),[20] rather than merely arbitrariness, but still made a distinction between the legal norms governing society and the exercise of political power in asserting the prerogative of the sovereign while emphasising the instrumentalism of the law at the hands of the regime:

---

15   NEUMANN: *op. cit.*, 440.
16   Ibid.
17   Ibid.
18   FRAENKEL: *Op. cit.*, xiii.
19   Ibid.
20   Ibid., xvi.

> The entire legal system has become an instrument of the political authorities. But insofar as the political authorities do not exercise their power, private and public life are regulated either by the traditionally prevailing or the newly enacted law ... Normal life is ruled by legal norms. But since martial law has become permanent in Germany, exceptions to the normal law are continually made. It must be presumed that all spheres of life are subjected to regulation by law. Whether the decision in an individual case is made in accordance with the law or with 'expediency' is entirely in the hands of those in whom sovereign power is vested.[21]

According to the dual state, the exercise of arbitrary rule, governed by the politics of the regime, comes within the prerogative sphere whereas the application of the ordinary law, less influenced by political concerns, falls within the normative state. The realm of terror and disorder, the lawless realm, is devoid of the sort of legal safeguards that Neumann associates with the rule of law. The "normal law", by contrast, is largely free from influence by the ideology of the state.

While the dual state provides a more differentiated vision of Nazi law than Neumann's lawless Behemoth state, therefore, we still find within it a concentration on the prerogative sphere as the political realm of the law, parasitic on the pre-existing legal system. To an extent, of course, this was what happened, the Nazi regime gradually changed the law and introduced new, Nazified principles and instruments, and the regime continued to operate within both systems for a long time. It is problematic, however, to characterise them in this way, as two parallel legal systems, because it excludes Nazi legality from consideration as "normal" law and, conversely, excludes ideology from the normative state. This tends to return to a position where the prerogative state is a lawless, arbitrary, barbarous, law as terror and the prerogative state is the rule of law, manipulated and undermined by the regime.

Fraenkel's analysis has remained popular among historians of the Third Reich as an explanation of how the legal system operated in tandem with the regime,[22] and Neumann's account become hugely influential in the framing of the Nazi legal system in the Nuremberg Military Tribunals,[23] and has continued to be the prevailing understanding of Nazi law, at least in the Anglo-American

---

21 Ibid., 57.
22 Cf., for example *The Law in Nazi Germany...*, op. cit., 2.
23 *Reassessing the Nuremberg Military Tribunals: Transitional Justice, Trial Narratives, and Historiography*, Kim C. PRIEMEL, Alexa STILLER (eds.), Berghahn Books, New York, 2012.

historical academy, in the period since. It is possible see some of the key characteristics of these analyses in a number of subsequent studies of Nazi law. In particular, the application of the natural law theoretical paradigm and the characterisation of Nazi "law" as exclusively terror, has resulted in the prevalence of a narrow conception of the regime's aims – as attaining and preserving power – and how law was used to achieve those aims – as a form of pure instrumentalism with no independent ideological content.

3 Instrumentalism in the Hart-Fuller Debate

The 1958 Hart-Fuller debate between Lon Fuller and HLA Hart provides an important forum in which Nazi law was discussed in terms of legal philosophy, and in which the trope of pure instrumentalism and associated characteristics evident in from the earlier scholarly interventions about Nazi law, were applied to the Nazi legal system.[24] The academic significance of the debate in framing the central issues for analysis of the concept of law and the terms of the ongoing debate, particularly for the Anglo-American jurisprudential community, should not be underestimated, and its merits and influence continue to be eagerly discussed.[25] The purpose of this section is not to rerun the debate or describe in detail the arguments of the two protagonists, but rather to highlight how both Fullerian natural law and Hartian positivism endorsed the application of a concept of pure instrumentalism to the Nazi legal system. Aside from providing further examples of the prevalence of this approach, this also reveals that this approach is not exclusively the domain of natural law, even though it has a specific correspondence to that theory. The positivist paradigm too is compatible with an historical interpretation of the Nazi regime that views it entirely as a terror state and overlooks the role of a constructive ideology in the framing of the legal system.

The Hart-Fuller debate famously took a post-war "grudge informer" case from the federal Republic of Germany as a starting point for a dispute about how best to understand the concept of law. The main questions engaged by the debate were the validity question – what are the conditions of validity for law – and the separability question – is law necessarily connected to morality.

---

24   The Hart-Fuller debate primarily consisted of H.L.A. HART: *Positivism and the Separation of Law and Morals*, Harvard Law Review, 71(1958)/4, 593–629 and Lon FULLER: *Positivism and Fidelity to Law – A Reply to Professor Hart*, Harvard Law Review, 71(1958)/4, 630–672.

25   Cf., for example *The Hart-Fuller Debate in the Twenty-First Century*, Peter CANE, (ed.), Hart Publishing, Oxford, 2010 and *New York University Law Review Symposium: Fifty Year Later*, New York University Law Review, 83(2008)/4, 993–1212.

Natural lawyer Fuller claimed that law had its own "inner morality" comprising eight fundamental principles, with much in common with the tenets of the rule of law, that meant it was necessarily connected to morality. As Nazi law did not conform to these principles, Fuller argued it was not a valid legal system:

> To me there is nothing shocking in saying that a dictatorship which clothes itself with a tinsel of legal form can so far depart from the morality of order, from the inner morality of law itself, that it ceases to be a legal system. When a system calling itself law is predicated upon a general disregard by judges of the terms of the laws they purport to enforce, when this system habitually cures its legal irregularities, even the grossest, by retroactive statutes, when it has only to resort to forays of terror in the streets, which no one dares challenge, in order to escape even those scant restraints imposed by the pretence of legality – when all these things have become true of a dictatorship, it is not hard for me, at least, to deny to it the name of law.[26]

Positivist Hart argued that the conditions of validity for law were much less substantial than this, with the requirement being that it was correctly enacted according to the internal, formal rules of the system, regardless of other characteristics and principles, supplemented by a very minimal natural law content. Law and morality could be connected in practice, but were conceptually separable, so Nazi law could be considered valid as law.

This chapter so far has highlighted the connection between natural law, law as terror, and pure instrumentalism, and in the above quotation from Fuller, it is possible to see some of the features of Neumann's analysis present. Fuller refers to the regime "cloth[ing] itself with a tinsel of legal form", "depart[ing]" from legal standards, "resort[ing] to forays of terror" and maintaining the "pretence of legality". Fuller predominantly examines Nazi law through a few examples and with reference to breaches of certain tenets of the rule of law (morality of law), such as stability, consistency of administration, and the prohibition on retroactivity.[27] Nazi Germany is a presented as a regime that attempted to maintain the façade of formal legality while manipulating and undermining the substance of law, not through ideological infusion of an alternative substance into the law, but through resort to terror at every turn.

---

26 FULLER: *Positivism...*, op. cit., 660.
27 Lon FULLER: *The Morality of Law*, Yale University Press, New Haven (CT), 1964.

For Fuller the question is "[h]ow much of a legal system survived the general debasement and perversion of all forms of social order that occurred under the Nazi rule".[28] Nazi "law" was a "debasement and perversion" of real law, against which the pre-existing legal system struggled to survive. As with Fraenkel this creates a false opposition between "normal" law and lawless, arbitrary terror and, as with Neumann, depicts the entire system that results as non-law, such was the undermining of what law actually is. Fuller's natural law paradigm brings with it a narrow definition of what constitutes law, which was anathema to the Nazi regime. Consequently the Nazi approach to law can only be treated as something else entirely, and any relationship to actual law could only be in the form of pure instrumentalism – the pretence of law used to terrorise, repress and preserve power. While these attributes of the Nazi regime should certainly not be discounted, Fuller's theory gives no consideration to the role of ideology in Nazi law. For Fuller, it was not a system "...where lawyers are still at least as interested in asking 'What is good law?' as they are in asking 'What is law?'".[29] In reality, however, the opposite was the case. The Nazis were not ultimately very interested in what constituted law in the formal sense, but only what constituted substantively "good" law; law that furthered the national community.

Hart says very little about the nature of Nazi law, partly because his theory applied much less onerous standards for achieving validity as a legal system, and partly because in his case "the appearance of law is all that matters",[30] so it was not considered necessary to dig too deep into the actual workings of the system. However, the embrace of positivism and with it a broader concept of law and legality based on formal and procedural criteria does not, in the case of the Third Reich, bring with it a rejection of pure instrumentalism as a lens through which to view Nazi law. While it entails a rejection of natural law and the tenets of the rule of law as conditions of validity for law, and consequently accepts Nazi law as law, at least in theory, it is still possible within the positivist paradigm to interpret that Nazi use of law as pure instrumentalism. It is, for Hart as much as Fuller, the manipulation of law for the exercise of tyranny with no attention to its underlying ideological substance. In this version too "...the Nazi regime in fact depended on a kind of blindness to anything but the formal semblance of legality in order to gain legitimacy for its actions".[31] Accordingly,

---

28   FULLER: *Positivism...*, *op. cit.*, 646.
29   *Ibid.*, 648.
30   Desmond MANDERSON: *Two Turns of the Screw: The Hart-Fuller Debate* = *The Hart-Fuller Debate in the Twenty-First Century*, Peter CANE (ed.), Hart Publishing, Oxford, 2010, 204–205.
31   *Ibid.*

while there is a necessary connection between natural law and pure instrumentalism as applied to the Third Reich, this does not preclude the possibility of positivism also being associated with this interpretation in discursive practice.

4 The Instrumentalism of Law in "Wicked Legal Regimes"

The connection between natural law theory and a particular interpretation of the instrumentalisation of law in Nazi Germany is clearly expressed in some of Nigel Simmonds' writings about so-called wicked legal regimes. In his discussion of "evil regimes" in *Law as a Moral Idea*, Simmonds in fact discounts real historical cases of wicked law (including Nazi law) from further consideration as serious subjects of study for those interested in the use of law for evil ends – and in the battle between positivism and natural law for hegemony over the concept of law – because, he argues, it is only hypothetically possible to imagine a regime able to "follow the rule of law closely, while making no pretence of governing justly".[32] It is the *pretence* of governing justly that is important for Simmonds, and most relevant to the connection between natural law and instrumentalism at issue here because, according to this theory, wicked rulers exclusively manipulate the law and know they are manipulating the law. Simmonds' aim is to demonstrate the divergence in principle between self-interest and the rule of law, and the convergence in principle of moral considerations with the rule of law, and for this actual wicked legal regimes are all too easily explained because they only ever pretend to follow the rule of law when it suits their ambitions for power.

While, for Simmonds, there might be examples of individual wicked laws within an established historical system, these say nothing about the serviceability of a legal system generally for evils ends. In historical instances of wicked regimes (although absent a detailed consideration of any particular case), the evil regime is aware that law is good, and knowingly manipulates the law for reasons of self-interest, primarily in order to maintain power. This, therefore, only serves to enhance the case for natural law against positivism because a wicked regime adopting the cloak of legality automatically "invokes an assumed connection between those institutions and moral motivation of precisely the kind that the mundane view [legal positivism] seeks to question".[33] Consequently, "[w]icked rulers motivated by pure self-interest are unlikely to

---

[32] N.E. SIMMONDS: *Law as a Moral Idea*, Oxford University Press, Oxford, 2007, 63.
[33] *Ibid.*, 60–62.

find that observance of the rule of law is in their interests, for a willingness to deploy violence outside the bounds of the published rules is a highly effective device for the securing and entrenching of a regime's grip on power".[34]

When addressing hypothetical wicked regimes, which are suggested to pose a stronger potential challenge to the natural law paradigm, a similar overarching point is made, that evil rulers are motivated by self-interest and are incentivised to manipulate the law (the rule of law) to these ends rather than to comply with it for genuine, if malevolent, reasons. For example, wicked regimes "typically allow some room for laws and policies aimed at improving the overall expectations of the populace, so as to stiffen incentives for compliance with the law".[35] And:

> ...while wicked rulers will have good reason to publish rules and enforce them, they will have no reasons of self-interest for respecting a most fundamental requirement of the rule of law: the requirement that official violence should be used only in response to the violation of the law by others. Wicked rulers ... will have powerful reasons for departing from this requirement, while the only good reasons for respecting the requirement are grounded in moral considerations.[36]

Again here, adherence to the principal tenets of natural law, including the necessary connection between law and morality – law as the rule of law – is strongly connected to a particular understanding of the nature of wicked regimes, including the Third Reich, according to which law can only be used as a crude instrument; a means of quelling resistance and strengthening power. Whether in a real, historical case of an evil regime, such as in Nazi Germany, or a hypothetical case, the regime, motivated by self-interest, uses the cloak of legality to "stiffen incentives for compliance" and buttress support among those who value the rule of law, They gradually move away from adherence to the rule of law in order to repress resistance and maintain power, still motivated by self-interest. Meanwhile, it is not possible to be evil and comply with the rule of law because the only "good" reasons for respecting the rule of law are moral reasons.

In this view, as with Fuller, the rule of law is law, and law that does not comply with the moral substance we attribute to the rule of law cannot be considered law at all. Logically, Nazi policies could not be carried out through legal

---

34   Ibid., 100.
35   Ibid., 95.
36   Ibid., 78.

means, and so Nazi law must be non-law. Law is only every instrumentalised by the Nazi regime to further self-interest, ensure the endorsement of society and incentivise compliance with the law. And whereas for natural law, law is not always an instrument, because it maintains its own separate, inherent morality, law in wicked regimes is a crude instrument cynically manipulated by leaders motivated entirely by self-interest and only concerned with ensuring control and oppression of the population.

This application of natural law to wicked legal regimes displays similar characteristics to the analyses of Neumann and Fuller, and brings with it similar problems. Chief among these is that it underplays the potential importance of ideology to the Nazi project, and the extent to which this had a bearing on the type of laws and legal system that were put in place. The attribution of pure self-interest as the dominant if not exclusive motivation of the Nazi regime enables a clear distinction to be drawn between the "good" of (the rule of) law and the (cynical, manipulative) wickedness of the regime. It also means that, according to this world view, law must only be an instrument in the hands of the regime. A more complex understanding of the motivations and policies of the Nazi regime and the possibility of alternative ethical criteria being used to judge what constitutes "good" law and justice undermines the evidential support for this sort of instrumentalism in the case of the Third Reich.

Again, that is not to say that the Nazi leadership, especially in the earliest years of power after 1933, did not claim to defend the *Rechtsstaat* in order to secure and maintain the support of the conservative elite and some sections of German society, nor that they did not have a different vision for the Nazi legal system, which was not dependent on the rule of law. It would be wrong to say the Nazis were wedded to the idea of the rule of law, and Hitler had no interest in maintaining the *Rechtsstaat* beyond that which was necessary. As German legal historian Michel Stolleis has stated;

> We know that the National Socialist regime took a strong interest in preserving the impression of normality. Its rule was based essentially on its ability to gain the cooperation of the bourgeois economic elites and, above all, the civil servants and judges who were discontent with the Weimar Republic. Those elites were largely nationalistic and antiparliamentarian in their thinking, but they also had a strong dislike of open terror. Before they could come to terms with the Nazi regime, they needed to be reassured that a national Rechtsstaat (state based on the rule of law) would be established, that everything would be done in accordance with the law, and that excesses would not be tolerated. ... As far as the legal system was concerned, the initial strategy of the National Socialists was

therefore to change only those elements that were indispensable to securing power and demarcating the main ideological positions.[37]

The Nazi vision of legality was starkly different to the liberal vision, which presented many obstacles to what the Nazis wanted to achieve with German society. But this is not the same as saying the Nazis only wanted power for power's sake, and only used law in order to spread terror and maintain power. This grossly underestimates the conviction of the Nazi leadership to a broader ideological vision, beyond an authoritarian struggle for power, involving the transformation of the German state, society and legal system, as unsupportable, objectionable and ultimately disastrous as their vision was.

The Stolleis quotation makes reference to the necessity, even at the start of the regime, to use law to stake out its fundamental ideological positions as well as to secure power. A complete focus on the latter to the exclusion of the former misrepresents the nature of both law and ideology in the Third Reich. As in earlier cases, this interpretation aligns the implementation of Nazi policy through "law" as terror, exclusively with the prerogative state and excludes it from the ambit of what is considered to be law. It allows us to make the clear distinction between what "law" is capable of – discrimination, emergency rule, perhaps some repressive measures – and what it is not capable of – mass deportation, large scale killing, the advancement of an ideological vision of law completely opposed to the principles of the rule of law.

5   Natural Law, Non-Law and Instrumentalism

When "(non-)law as terror" is the only or predominant paradigm used to interrogate and interpret the Nazi legal system, as well as often excluding from legal examination those elements considered to fall outside of the realm of law – the lawless barbarity, the criminal state, the acts of "murder"; the Holocaust[38] – the focus naturally shifts towards the undermining of the pre-existing safeguards within the legal state and specifically law's role in repression and persecution in the early years of the regime. The argument presented in this chapter does not wish to eradicate this focus as, to reiterate, terror, repression, the destruction of the *Rechtsstaat* and the maintenance of political control,

---

37   Michael STOLLEIS: *Law and Lawyers Preparing the Holocaust*, Annual Review of Law and Social Science, 3(2007), 215.
38   David FRASER: *Law After Auschwitz: Towards a Jurisprudence of the Holocaust*, Carolina Academic Press, Durham (NC), 2005.

were significant characteristics of the regime and, in the case of the first two of these elements in particular, not only in its earliest years. Rather it intends to advance the case that it was largely "law" that was used both for these purposes and the implementation of even more extreme measures, and that the consideration of Nazi law should extend to its normative role in constructing a Nazi identity and vision for society; its use as an instrument to transform reality, not exclusively to obliterate it.

However, the focus on law as terror and the themes of lawlessness and crude instrumentalism continue to permeate legal theoretical literature specifically focused on Nazi law. This is referred to in more recent legal historical engagements with Nazi law. For example, in the recognition that "[t]he agreed-on version in general historiography seems to be: the 12 years of National Socialist rule are 12 dark years that represent a rupture in German history",[39] the acknowledgement that "[i]t may seem paradoxical to speak of law and despotism in the same breath, for to do so raises the dilemma of the existence of law in a system that is on the whole unlawful and un-just",[40] or the assertion:

> A book about the law in Nazi Germany might strike some readers as an exercise in contradiction. They understand the Nazi regime as a tyranny, characterized by arbitrary rule, enforced through intimidation and terror. The hallmark of Nazi society, as they understand it, was not law, but lawlessness.[41]

An example of a legal theoretical analysis of Nazi law that illustrates a continued focus on lawlessness and makes the repressive aspects of Nazi law representative of the legal system as a whole, through the conceptual intermediary of natural law theory, is Kristin Rundle's advocacy of a deeper account of Fullerian natural law as it applies to the Nazi state.[42] Rundle's thesis centres on a defining legal moment around the time of *Kristallnacht* in November 1938 at which point, the claim is, legal discrimination and persecution became extralegal (non-law) oppression and extermination. Based primarily on an assessment of the 1935 Nuremberg Laws and some contemporary diary accounts of

---

39 Thomas VORMBAUM: *A Modern History of German Criminal Law*, Springer, Berlin, 2014, 172.
40 STOLLEIS: *op. cit.*, 214.
41 *The Law in Nazi Germany...*, *op. cit.*, 1.
42 Kristen RUNDLE: *The Impossibility of an Exterminatory Legality: Law and the Holocaust*, University of Toronto Law Journal, 59(2009)/1, 65–125 and Kristen RUNDLE: *Law and Daily Life – Questions for Legal Philosophy from November 1938*, Jurisprudence, 3(2012)/2 429–444.

Jews living in the Third Reich, Rundle argues that while in the early years of the regime repression was conducted through legal means, after 1938 the possibility of acting as a legal subject under the law ceased to exist and Nazi policy was implemented outside of the law.

Despite Rundle's assertion that "the Nazi legal campaign against the Jews is capable of carrying the label of law",[43] this only goes so far in time, and in fact her evaluation of Nazi law and application of natural law theory to it has much in common with other approaches discussed here that invalidate the Nazi legal system as a whole. Three points are particularly worthy of mention. The first is that the analysis is always drawn to the point of non-law, the significance of lawlessness to the regime's worst excesses, which, as in previous cases, denies the very possibility of law's complicity in the implementation of particularly evil objectives. Nazi policy after 1938 "...belonged to an extra-legal world of SS directives that remained, at all times, contingent on the whims of those who had the power to issue them",[44] which consequently renders those very acts of state that were most devastating uninteresting and irrelevant as a subject of legal study.

The second is the characterisation of the relationship between the regime and the legal system as one of the erosion and undermining of the latter by the former until it is no longer law. From November 1938, Rundle argues, the parasitic influence of Nazism on the legal system engendered "a degenerative process that involved successively greater departures from conventional standards of legality as time progressed".[45] While Rundle does not specifically resort to the language of instrumentality, cynical manipulation, the cloak of legality or the "tinsel of legal form", this is the implication of a focus on law being undermined, as opposed to it being reconstructed according to a different conception of legality. The narrative of descent into arbitrariness and lawlessness remains the same but is shifted in time to a later date. Consequently, Desmond Manderson's criticism of Fuller's 1958 analysis of Nazi law is equally apt here, as this "does not acknowledge Nazism did not merely corrupt a legal system. It realised a vision of it...".[46] This ignores the constructive objectives of Nazi ideology in favour of the destructive aspects, whereas both were important and both had an impact on the legal system.

The third point – related to the second – is the concentration on law as terror; the use of law (and non-law) to repress and persecute. This was undoubtedly

---

43   RUNDLE: *Impossibility...*, *op. cit.*, 102.
44   *Ibid.*, 76.
45   *Ibid.*, 87.
46   MANDERSON: *op. cit.*, 212.

a significant and substantial function of law in the Third Reich and a central aspect of the implementation of Nazi racial policy, and the argument here is not that attention should be drawn away from this entirely. However, Rundle's thesis assumes that criminal legislation directed at Jews is characteristic of the whole Nazi legal system, and that component should be exclusively rendered from the subjectivity of Jews suffering from persecution by the law. Again, this is undoubtedly important, but it does not capture either the whole system of law and especially, as noted in relation to the previous point, the relationship between law and the constructive aspects of Nazi ideology. It is problematic to invalidate (from November 1938) Nazi law as a system on this basis. The importance of natural law theory to the particular direction and scope of this argument is also noteworthy. As in other cases, its application goes hand in hand with these points, and its implication is that we need not be concerned with how the Nazi regime advanced its ideology and transformed the normative framework of society as a matter of law.

Some of the characteristics of the literature discussed in this chapter are also ostensible in other recent studies of Nazi law that do not necessarily or explicitly adopt a naturalist paradigm of the concept of law. In particular they tend to allude to the both law and non-law in the Third Reich without expressly addressing or resolving the tension between the two. Thomas Vormbaum writes about the "*manifest unlawfulness* of the National Socialist regime and its exorbitant crimes"[47] in a history of German criminal law in which it is also asserted, for example, that the Reichstag Fire Decree of February 1933 "*legitimised* the SA's system of terror".[48] Hans Petter Graver, in a book focused on the role of judges in anti-rule of law regimes, has also argued:

> From the point of view of legal theory, there must be something flawed with the legal system where judges can contribute to atrocities. *Either what seems to be a legal order is not a legal order at all* or there is something wrong with the approach and methods of judges in oppressive societies since they depart from their task as guardians of the rule of law. The answer may be a combination of both if one claims that it lies in the inability of such judges to distinguish between *law in the true sense and the oppressive non-law of authoritarian regimes.*[49]

---

47   VORMBAUM: *op. cit.,* 264. Italics are mine.
48   *Ibid.,* 181. Italics are mine.
49   Hans Petter GRAVER: *Judges Against Justice: On Judges When the Rule of Law is Under Attack,* Springer, Berlin, 2015, 207. Italics are mine.

Graver suggests that Nazi law constitutes a version of "oppressive non-law" as the potential "flaw" in the legal system that allows judges to be complicit in an atrocity like the Holocaust. The Nazi legal regime may have been flawed in many respects, including when measured against a particular standard of "good law", but it is not clear from evidence that this is because it "is not a legal order at all" or on what grounds this conditional claim is made. This view is advanced alongside indications that the Nazi legal system – at least by some measures – was law, although these appear somewhat confused in their mutual compatibility. There is some acknowledgement of the role of an alternative ideology in fashioning the legal system, as Nazi judges "...sought to construct a coherent and applicable normative body of principles from the programme and ideology of the Nazi party".[50] The focus, however, is clearly on the manipulation and re-purposing – not to say instrumentalisation – of the pre-existing legal state into an organ of terror. For Graver, "[t]he Nazi experience shows how a dictatorship can take over almost all of the legal norms of a preceding regime and transform them by legal reinterpretation to a system of oppression",[51] and "[t]he continuity of the legal order was ensured by maintaining legal language and concepts such as legislation, constitution, legal certainty, contract, property, public security, and the like, and by giving them a totally new content".[52]

In its incorporation of the idea of *legal* norms being infused with new ideological content, this interpretation entails a more subtle transformation of law than simply the gradual destruction of the pre-existing legal state into an extra-legal realm of barbarity and terror. It nevertheless continues the thrust of the academic narrative along the lines of pure instrumentalism and law exclusively used for terror, while making room for the idea of Nazi law as non-law. There are questions here both about the extent to which the Nazi regime did entirely co-opt existing legal norms as against the infusion of Nazi-specific concepts and principles into the legal system, and about the potential inconsistencies between the different interpretations presented. It may not be contradictory to say Nazi law did not measure up to a certain standard of "good law" and from that point of view, it can be criticised on grounds of morality, while also saying Nazi law was to all intents and purposes a functioning legal system and needs to be evaluated as such from an academic perspective. However, it is not always evident, as in the examples of Vormbaum and Graver, that this is the view being advanced. It is, often in legal historical accounts, the

---

50   Ibid., 229.
51   Ibid., 30.
52   Ibid.

omission to offer a clear legal theoretical interpretation of the nature of the Nazi legal system that enables the perpetuation of a narrative of pure instrumentalism. Indeed, it may be the prevalence of that narrative, and the other elements associated with it, that make a new systemic legal theoretical analysis of the Nazi regime appear unnecessary.

6 Ideology, Instrumentalism and the National Community

The various examples in this chapter of interpreting Nazi law primarily through a narrow concept of crude instrumentalism, founded on the twin and co-dependent pillars of natural law and law as terror have, as has been asserted, resulted in a neglect of the relationship between the overarching ideological framework of the regime and Nazi law as a normative order, as well as an undue concentration on the "non-law" interpretation of Nazi law. It has also had a further consequence, which has been to overlook, as a matter of legal theory, the important role of law in facilitating the realisation of the *Volksgemeinschaft* – the imagined Aryan "national community" – around which Nazi racial ideology and policy was constructed. This represents the essential "other side of the coin" to the use of law for discrimination, persecution and extermination without which these elements are unlikely to have been implemented to the same extent.

The overall impact of a dominant representation of Nazi (non-)law based on pure instrumentalism is that "...scholarship may have suffered from the erroneous perception that the law did not matter in Germany during the Nazi period".[53] This is not the case, and it is important to take steps to overcome this misperception, which involves first the acceptance that it is law that we are talking about that was complicit in some way in almost everything in Nazi regime up to and including the Holocaust: "Nazi law was law, in one form or another, and it is at the more nuanced levels of debate that we must address these questions".[54] Second is to recognise that this legal system was more than just a system of terror, as important as that aspect undoubtedly was, so the Nazi regime did not only instrumentalise the pre-existing *Rechtsstaat* to achieve and maintain power, before dismantling it to leave chaos and lawlessness. Third is to seriously examine the idea that the Nazis attempted to infuse law with a different normative basis and set of values based on its racial ideology, and to

---

53　*The Law in Nazi Germany*..., op. cit., 1.
54　David FRASER: *"This is Not like any other Legal Question": a Brief History of Nazi Law before UK and US Courts*, Connecticut Journal of International Law, 19(2003/04), 124.

consider the implications of this. Then it will be possible to properly consider the instrumentalism of Nazi law in the way intended in the conference proceedings that inspired this paper; its use to transform reality in the Third Reich.

When assessing how the Nazi regime instrumentalised the legal system in order to implement and achieve its ideological objectives, it is necessary to eschew a narrow concept of what constitutes "law" and consider more than what happened to the pre-existing legal regime, in the very early stages of the regime, and consequently look beyond crude and cynical instrumentalisation for purposes of terror and power preservation. Otherwise we do not see the full picture of how law was used to advance and realize National Socialist policy. Those limitations both preclude further research into, and understanding of, the part that law played in persecution, exclusion, and genocide across the whole period of Nazi rule, and prevent us from coming to terms with the complicity of law in authoritarian and totalitarian regimes; what law, as a concept, is capable of being used for, and how this happens in practice.

A concept of validity and legality based on the rule of law or other moral considerations may serve an important purpose as a standard of "good" law against which it is possible to measure the conduct of a regime in order to establish, for example, if it is indeed "wicked", and whether it might be necessary to consider resistance against it. In the historical case of Nazi Germany, however, the regime's iniquity is beyond reasonable doubt and the time for resistance has passed. More urgent now for lawyers and historians is to examine how the regime functioned as a matter of law and understand what implications this may have for the nature and operation of law generally. The primary aim of this chapter has been to elucidate and critique the prevailing interpretation of Nazi law as pure instrumentalism, and there is not space here to offer a full account of either the relationship between Nazi law and the overarching ideological framework of the regime or what an alternative version of instrumentalism based on this looks like. The remainder of this chapter, however, will consider some preliminary thoughts in this direction.

With reference to the idea of a lingering normative state and a racialized, parasitic, Nazified prerogative state, Stolleis argues that:

> it is a myth that some areas remained entirely untouched by the political claims of the system. Neither the frequently cited land register law, nor the social security or tax laws, nor the law concerning debts, property, family, and inheritance was in any way immune.[55]

---

55 STOLLEIS: *op. cit.,* 216.

This conclusion has two implications for the arguments in this chapter. The first is that law in Nazi Germany was not merely the leftover residue of the *Rechtsstaat*, largely untouched by ideology, until it was eroded by arbitrariness and terror so all that was left was pure, prerogative, non-law. Nazi ideology impinged upon and continued to impact all continuing aspects of the Nazi regime and changed the legal system as a whole so that it no longer looked like what had come before it, but nor did it resemble absolute terror. The second implication is that law continued to function in a recognisable – but different – form across the spectrum of the system, and this cannot just be seen as a set of technical rules engaged in the administration of society.

The difficulty that Nazi law presents for the concept of law and prevailing paradigms of interpretation is that, far from taking purely the form of law and manipulating it for personal (regime) gain absent any substantive ethical content, it was ultimately closer to pure substance, lacking the formal requirements of law but with a normative basis founded in Nazi ideology. According to this, "the primary Nazi standard of 'good law' was taken to be the advancement, purification and collective properties thought to be essential to the flourishing of the German 'Blood-community' (*Blutsgemeinschaft*)", rather than a formal rule of recognition or formalistic principles of morality.[56] Instead of the law being used in any way necessary to maintain power, the ultimate Nazi ideal was that "ethical principles should be embedded in law".[57] The national community was considered to have an ethical compass, a "healthy popular sentiment", embodied in the person of the Führer and embedded in the interpretation of the law. This was contrary to liberal principles of legality, and clearly "represented a gross departure from the rule of law"[58] and the obliteration of its key tenets, but it is not so simple as to say these were replaced with disorder, anarchy, lawlessness and barbarity.

An important consequence of the dissolution of law into ideology was the denial of a distinct and independent coherence to legality. This was in some ways the absolute instrumentalism of the law to the services of the ruling (totalitarian, authoritarian) ideology, but not merely the residue of the *Rechtsstaat*, and not just in the service of repression, terror and the pursuit of power. All law in all forms would have ultimately taken on the formless substance

---

56 Carolyn BENSON, Julian FINK: *Introduction: New Perspectives on Nazi Law*, Jurisprudence, 3(2012)/2, 342.
57 Herlinde PAUER-STUDER: *Law and Morality under Evil Conditions: The SS Judge Konrad Morgen*, (2012) 3(2) Jurisprudence, 3(2012)/2, 371.
58 BENSON, FINK: *op. cit.*, 341.

dictated by Nazi ideology, with the defective purpose of advancing the national community and supressing perceived racial and political enemies. Law in Nazi Germany was used, as an instrument of ideology, to construct and foster national and racial identity within the community, and at the same time to repress the population and ensure the maintenance of the stranglehold of Nazi rule. We can choose to call everything that departed from the pre-existing *Rechtsstaat* "non-law" if we so wish, but that misrepresents the history of Nazi rule and denies the complicity of law with Nazi ideology.

The essence of Franz Neumann's argument about law in the Nazi state, which constituted a lawless, anarchic chaos, is that "[i]f general law is the basic form of right, if law is not only *voluntas* but also *ratio*, then we must deny the existence of law in the fascist state".[59] More recently undertaken historical research, however, shows us that "the extent to which there was actually an internal logic to the legal system implemented by the Nazi regime is striking. There was an underlying ideology at the heart, driving the regime".[60] On the face of it these two statements about Nazi law may not appear incompossible, but the way the first analysis is argued and its strong connection to natural law theory and the claim that law was only crudely manipulated as an instrument of terror, means that it cannot really be reconciled with the second assertion. National Socialist ideology provided a rationale and reasoning for the legal system of the Third Reich. Therefore, while Nazi law did operate as a tool of repression and an instrument of terror, it also embodied a racial ideology that included a vision of legality that was often at odds with the *Rechtsstaat* that had come before it, but should not be denied interrogation as a matter of law on that basis. If we want to really understand the instrumentalism of law in the hands of the Nazi regime, we need to search beneath the "tinsel of legal form" and uncover the darker side of Nazi legal reality.

Acknowledgements

This article is partly based on the doctoral research titled "The Conundrum of Nazi Law: An Historiographical challenge to the Anglo-American Jurisprudential Representation of the Nazi Past" (2015), supported by the Arts and Humanities Research Council under studentship AH/I013404/1. The author

---

59   NEUMANN: *op. cit.*, 451. Italics in original.
60   Harry REICHER: *Evading Responsibility for Crimes Against Humanity: Murderous Lawyers at Nuremberg* = *The Law in Nazi Germany: Ideology, Opportunism, and the Perversion of Justice*, Alan STEINWEIS, Robert RACHLIN (eds.), Berghahn Books, New York, 2013, 143.

would like to thank Professor David Fraser, Dr Stephen Skinner and Dr Cosmin Cercel for their support on the conference panel in which this paper was presented.

Bibliography

Carolyn BENSON, Julian FINK: *Introduction: New Perspectives on Nazi Law*, Jurisprudence, 3(2012)/2, 341–346.

Ernst FRAENKEL: *The Dual State: A Contribution to the Theory of Dictatorship*, Octagon Books, New York, 1969 [1942].

David FRASER: *"This is Not like any other Legal Question": a Brief History of Nazi Law before UK and US Courts*, Connecticut Journal of International Law, 19(2003/04) 59–125.

David FRASER: *Law After Auschwitz: Towards a Jurisprudence of the Holocaust*, Carolina Academic Press, Durham (NC), 2005.

Lon FULLER: *Positivism and Fidelity to Law – A Reply to Professor Hart*, Harvard Law Review, 71(1958)/4, 630–672.

Lon FULLER: *The Morality of Law*, Yale University Press, New Haven (CT), 1964.

Hans Petter GRAVER: *Judges Against Justice: On Judges When the Rule of Law is Under Attack*, Springer, Berlin, 2015.

H.L.A. HART: *Positivism and the Separation of Law and Morals*, Harvard Law Review, 71(1958)/4, 593–629.

The Hart-Fuller Debate in the Twenty-First Century, Peter CANE (ed.), Hart Publishing, Oxford, 2010.

The Law in Nazi Germany: Ideology, Opportunism, and the Perversion of Justice, Alan STEINWEIS, Robert RACHLIN (eds.), Berghahn Books, New York, 2013.

Desmond MANDERSON: *Two Turns of the Screw*, ed. Peter CANE, Hart Publishing, Oxford, 2010.

Douglas G. MORRIS: *Write and Resist: Ernst Fraenkel and Franz Neumann on the Role of Natural Law in Fighting Nazi Tyranny*, New German Critique, 42(2015)/3, 197–230.

Franz NEUMANN: *Behemoth: The Structure and Practice of National Socialism 1933–1944*, 2nd edn, Frank Cass & Co, London, 1967.

New York University Law Review Symposium: Fifty Year Later, New York University Law Review, 83(2008)/4, 993–1212.

Herlinde PAUER-STUDER: *Law and Morality under Evil Conditions: The SS Judge Konrad Morgen*, Jurisprudence, 3(2012)/2, 367–390.

Reassessing the Nuremberg Military Tribunals: Transitional Justice, Trial Narratives, and Historiography, Kim C. PRIEMEL, Alexa STILLER (eds.), Berghahn Books, New York, 2012.

Harry REICHER: *Evading Responsibility for Crimes Against Humanity: Murderous Lawyers at Nuremberg* = *The Law in Nazi Germany: Ideology, Opportunism, and the Perversion of Justice*, Alan STEINWEIS, Robert RACHLIN (eds.), Berghahn Books, New York, 2013.

Kristen RUNDLE: *The Impossibility of an Exterminatory Legality: Law and the Holocaust*, University of Toronto Law Journal, 59(2009)/1, 65–125.

Kristen RUNDLE: *Law and Daily Life – Questions for Legal Philosophy from November 1938*, Jurisprudence, 3(2012)/2 429–444.

N.E. SIMMONDS: *Law as a Moral Idea*, Oxford University Press, Oxford, 2007.

Michael STOLLEIS: *Law and Lawyers Preparing the Holocaust*, Annual Review of Law and Social Science, 3(2007), 213–231.

Thomas VORMBAUM: *A Modern History of German Criminal Law*, Springer, Berlin, 2014.

Index of Names

A.B. Keith   87, 89, 91, 93, 96, 100, 108, 110
Abu Hamza al-Masri   108
Abu Qatada al-Filistini   108
Adam Lityński   160, 169
Adetokunbo Ademola   93
Adolph Hitler   148, 162, 163, 205
Ákos Mihályfi   79, 85
Alan C. Cairns   93, 110
Alan Forrest   114, 127
Alan L. Olmstead   115, 127
Alan Steinweis   195, 214–216
Alan Watson   137, 140–142
Albrecht Rogge   160, 170
Albrecht von Wallenstein   4
Aleksandar Karađorđević   176, 181
Aleksander Czaja   35, 49
Alexa Stiller   199, 215
Alexander Debner   6
Alexander I of Russia   45
Alexis Tocqueville   56
Alfred M. Boll   116, 126
Ambroise Jobert   37, 49
András Gergely   52, 53, 67
Andreas Fahrmeir   118, 127, 179, 188
Andrew III of Hungary   77
Andrew Lynch   103, 110
Andrzej Dziadzio   164, 169
Andrzej Zahorski   37, 50
Anna M. Drabek   17, 28
Antal Csengery   78
Antal Ocskay   63
Antal Szapáry   78
Antal Tasner   61
Anto Milušić   185, 186, 189
Antoni Roman   155, 170
Archduchess Mathilda of Austria   81
Archduke Albrecht (Albert), Duke of Teschen   81
Archduke Franz Karl (Francis Charles) of Austria   54, 74
Archduke Ludwig Viktor (Louis Victor) of Austria   54
Armin Hoeland   175, 190
Arnold Luschin von Ebengreuth   8, 15, 29
Árpád Károlyi   64, 67

Árpád Királyfi   115–117, 127
August Finger   144, 168

Balázs Pálvölgyi   113
Barna Buday   121, 126
Barna Mezey   51, 53, 54, 56–59, 64, 65, 67, 68, 71, 85, 174, 189
Bertalan Neményi   120, 128
Bertalan Szemere   64
Bodo Pieroth   144, 168
Bogdanović   182–184, 188
Bogusław Leśnodorski   36, 44, 50
Bonny Ibhawoh   88, 90, 92, 110
Bosiljka Janjatović   181, 189
Božidar Mirković   182, 185, 186, 189

Carolyn Benson   213, 215
Catherine Collomp   118, 126
Celso (Celzije) Cavalieri   176, 177, 179–181, 188
Charles I of Austria (IV of Hungary)   70
Charles Njonjo   104
Charles VI (Holy Roman Emperor – III of Hungary)   13, 70
Christian D'Elvert   17, 28
Christian-Friedrich Menger   144, 169
Christoph of Berbisdorf   22
Claud Schuster   92
Cosmin Cercel   215
Csaba Csapó   121, 130
Csaba Varga   175, 190
Cunow   15, 27

Dalibor Čepulo   174, 179, 180, 188
Dalibor Janiš   3, 8, 29
Dariusz Makiłła   37, 50, 155, 169
David A. Frenkel   173, 189
David Fraser   206, 211, 215
David Jayne Hill   115, 127
David Lloyd George   154
David Schneiderman   95, 111
David Swinfen   88, 93, 96, 104, 112
Dawid Michalski   143
Dénes Jánossy   113, 127
Dénes Kovács   78–81, 84, 85
Desmond Manderson   202, 208, 215

Dierk Walter 114, 129
Dieter Albrecht 1, 26
Dinshah Fardunji Mulla 92
Don H. Doyle 114, 128
Dorota Malec 149, 169
Douglas G. Morris 197, 215
Drew Keeling 122, 127

E.R. Cameron 91
Ede Zsedényi 78
Edoardo Vicario 136, 142
Edward McWhinney 91, 95, 111
Edward W.S. Tingle 115, 129
Elek Dósa 78
Elisabeth of Bavaria 79, 80
Emil Niederhauser 70, 84
Emil Trauschenfels 78
Emma Bartoniek 76, 81, 84
Ernst Birke 20, 27
Ernst Bruckmüller 17, 27
Ernst Forsthoff 144, 168
Ernst Fraenkel 194, 198, 202, 215
Ernst Mischler 8, 29
Ernst Rudolf Huber 143, 168
Errico Presutti 136, 137, 142
Eugene Tyler Chamberlain 122, 126

F.R. Scott 98, 111
Ferdinand I (Holy Roman Emperor) 53
Ferdinand I of Austria (V of Hungary) 54, 59, 70, 71, 73, 74
Ferdinand II (Holy Roman Emperor) 2, 16
Ferdinand von Seibt 17, 28
Ferenc Eckhart 51, 58, 59, 67, 73, 74, 84
Ferencz Deák 78
Ferencz Pulszky 78
Francesco Mastroberti 136, 142
Franz (Francis) Joseph I 51, 66, 70, 74, 75, 77–82, 173
Franz II (Holy Roman Emperor) (I of Austria) 55, 70, 71
Franz Neumann 194–199, 202, 205, 214, 215
Frederic Augustus I of Saxony 45
Friedrich Walter 15, 31
Frigyes Podmaniczky 78
Fritz von Hartung 144, 168

G.W. Bartholomew 90, 109
Gábor G. Kemény 120, 127

Gábor Máthé 174, 189
Gavin Wright 115, 127
Gejza Ferdinandy 116, 117, 127
Georg Bessel 152, 168
George Coldstream 92
George M. Stephenson 119, 129
Gerhard A. Ritter 122, 129
Gerhard Anschütz 144, 168
Giovanni Batista Ugo 139, 142
Giuseppe Motta 180, 189
Günter Krabbenhöft 149, 168
Günter Moltmann 114, 118, 128
Gusztáv Thirring 113, 129
György Apponyi 57, 62, 78
György Bartal 78
György Joannovics 78
György Károlyi 78
György Spira 52–55, 58, 61, 68
Gyula Andrássy 78
Gyula Rácz 120, 128
Gyula Szende 79, 85

H. Duncan Hall 90, 98, 106, 110
H.L.A. Hart 194, 200–202, 215
Hans Chmelar 123, 126
Hans Fenske 144, 168
Hans P. Vought 118, 129
Hans Petter Graver 209, 210, 215
Hans Viktor Böttcher 155, 159, 162
Hans-Wolfgang Bergerhausen 2, 26
Harry Reicher 214, 216
Hector Hughes 89–91, 97, 98, 102, 106, 110
Heikki Pihlajämaki 141, 142
Heinrich Triepel 143, 169
Helmut Rumpler 17, 31
Helmuth Feigl 17, 18, 28
Henri Bourassa 105
Henry Brougham 86
Henryk Suchojad 8, 31
Herbert Hassinger 8, 28
Herbert Schwarzwälder 152, 170
Herlinde Pauer-Studer 213, 215
Hermann Palm 14, 30
Hermengild Jireček 2, 3, 27, 30, 32
Hubert Izdebski 41, 49
Hugo Kołłątaj 44, 49

Ignjat M. Tolić 177, 183, 190
Igor Štiks 176, 190

INDEX OF NAMES

Imre Gonda 70, 84
Imre Képessy 51
Imre Szabó 78
Imre Zajtay 175, 190
Irene Bloemraad 119, 126
István Bittó 78
István Deák 53, 54, 57–59, 61, 63, 66, 67
István Kemény 78
István Rácz 120, 128
István Széchenyi 57, 58, 60, 63, 68
István Szigeti 61, 68
Ivan Beuc 181, 188
Ivan Kosnica 171, 173–176, 182, 189
Ivan Martinovský 3, 31
Ivo Cerman 17, 27
Ivo Krbek 185, 186, 189

J. Joachim Menzel 14, 28
J.A. Iliffe 90, 109
J.H. Thomas 101
J.N.D. Anderson 90, 109
J.S. Ewart 107, 110
J.W. Harris 89, 110
Jacek Przygodzki 145, 169
Jacqueline D. Krikorian 88, 111
Jan Kapras 9, 14, 29
Jan Wąsicki 144, 145, 149, 170
Jan Zdichynec 14, 31
Jan Županič 16, 32
Jana Janišová 3, 8, 29
János Király 76, 84
János Lutter 79, 80, 85
János Sára 70, 85
János Simor 78
János Sziklay 78–81, 84, 85
Jaroslav Pánek 1–3, 30, 31
Jeffrey G. Williamson 118, 127
Jeffrey Goldsworthy 105, 110
Jenő Barsi Rónay 70, 85
Jerzy Gordziejew 39, 40, 49
Jerzy Malec 42, 50
Jerzy Michta 8, 30
Jiří Brňovják 1, 12–16, 27
Jiří David 13, 27
Jiří Hrbek 14, 31
Jiří Šouša 11, 28
Joachim Bahlcke 1, 26
Johann Thomas Edler von Trattner 16, 31
Johann Viktor Bredt 144, 168

Johann von Jung 8, 29
Johann von Saalhausen 6
John Bowring 52, 67
John Higham 118, 127
John Kendle 95, 111
John M. Maguire 116, 128
John Moody 122, 128
John Palmer Gavit 116, 119, 127
John William Tate 105, 112
Jörg Nagler 114, 128
Josef Jireček 3, 32
Josef Kalousek 9, 11, 12, 14, 29
Josef Ulbrich 8, 29
Joseph Chamberlain 97
Joseph I (Holy Roman Emperor) 70
Joseph II (Holy Roman Emperor) 16, 55, 70
Josiah H. Symon 93, 112
Josip Pliverić 174
Józef Gierowski 40, 49
Józef Wojakowski 35, 50
József Eötvös 58, 63
József Hosszu 78
József Justh 78
József Parádi 121, 128
József Révai 52
József Ruszoly 58, 62, 63, 65, 68
Judit Beke-Martos 67, 69, 72, 74, 84
Jules Cambon 154
Julian Fink 213, 215
Julian Makowski 143, 169
Julius Count of Hardeff 22
Juraj Andrassy 175, 186, 188

Kálmán Ghyczy 61, 64, 78
Kálmán Tisza 78
Karel Malý 1–3, 11, 28, 30, 31
Karen Schniedewind 114, 129
Karl Lechner 8, 28
Karolina Adamová 1, 18, 26
Károly Szász 78
Katarzyna Bucholc-Srogosz 37, 49
Kenneth Roberts-Wray 90, 111
Kim C. Priemel 199, 215
Klára Kučerová 11, 28
Klaus Friedland 114, 128
Klemens von Metternich 54, 57
Koloman Mutavdjić 173, 189
Kristen Rundle 194, 207–209, 216
Kristofer Allerfeldt 114, 126

Ladislav Polić 174, 178, 179, 190
Ladislav Soukup 1, 11, 28, 30
Lajos (Louis) Kossuth 53, 57–62, 64, 74
Lajos Batthyány 57, 62, 63
Lajos Beck 120, 126
Lajos Vadnay 78
László Bezerédj 78
Lawrence M. Friedman 175
Leo Lucassen 172, 189
Leopold I (Holy Roman Emperor) 54, 70
Leopold II (Holy Roman Emperor) 16, 17, 55, 70, 71
Levente Völgyesi 56, 68
Ljubo Boban 177, 188
Lon Fuller 194, 200–202, 204, 205, 208, 215
Loren P. Beth 94, 109
Louis Riel 107
Louis-Philippe Brodeur 105
Luboš Velek 20, 31
Ludwig von Petry 14, 28
Ludwig von Wirkner 62
Ludwik Gutakowski 45
Lutz Rentzow 2, 4, 30

Maciej Koszowski 175, 189
Magdalena Wilczek-Karczewska 37, 50, 155, 169
Mahendra P. Singh 94, 112
Maja Maciejewska-Szałas 143
Manley O. Hudson 103, 110
Marc Helbling 171, 188
Marceli Handelsman 44, 49
Marceli Podlaszewski 155, 156, 169
Marcus Braun 122, 126
Marcus Gräser 114, 128
Marek Krzymkowski 35, 37, 43, 44, 50
Marek Starý 1, 7, 31
Mária Homoki-Nagy 56, 67, 182, 189
Maria Theresa 13, 70
Marian Kallas 44, 49
Marian Małecki 145, 169
Marian Mikołajczyk 152, 169
Marian Ptak 145, 169
Max Mittelstein 145, 169
Maximilian Leopold von Cantelmo 24
Megan Richardson 105, 111
Metod Dolenc 178

Michael Dunkelberg 145, 168
Michael R. Haines 115, 127
Michael Stolleis 205–207, 212, 216
Michael Walter 116, 129
Michał Gałędek 33
Mihály Latkóczy 78–81, 85
Mihály Singer 123, 129
Miklós Jósika 62
Miklós Vay 78
Miroslav Svoboda 8, 29
Montesquieu 40
Mór Jókai 79, 80, 84

N.E. Simmonds 194, 203, 216
Napoleon 41–43, 45, 46
Neil Larry Shumsky 118, 129
Nelson Moe 136, 142
Ninian Stephen 106
Norbert Varga 173, 182, 189
Norman Bentwich 89, 94, 99, 106, 108, 109

Oliver Faron 118, 127
Oliver Jones 103, 104, 106, 110
Olivier Chalin 4, 27
Oscar S. Straus 115, 129
Otomar Pirkmajer 180, 181, 189
Otto Kimminich 144, 168
Otto Ruthenberg 145, 148, 152, 170

P.A. Howell 86, 93, 96, 110
Pál Nyáry 52, 78
Pál Péter Tóth 121, 128
Pál Somssich 78
Pál Trifunácz 78
Partick Weil 118, 119, 127, 130
Pasquale Stanislao Mancini 139, 142
Patrick McGrath 96, 111
Paul Quigley 114, 128
Pavel Maršálek 20, 30
Paweł Cichoń 26, 49
Pedro I of Brazil 131
Pedro II of Brazil 132
Peter Cane 200, 202, 215
Peter F. Sugar 55, 57, 68
Peter H. Wilson 4, 27
Péter Hanák 55, 57, 68
Peter J. Spiro 114, 116, 129, 171, 190

INDEX OF NAMES

Peter Karl Jaksch   11, 15, 16, 29
Peter Mosný   18, 30
Peter N. Riesenberg   171, 190
Péter Simon   78, 80, 81, 85
Peter W. Hogg   105, 110
Petr Kreuz   3, 31
Petr Maťa   10, 14, 15, 29, 30
Petr Polehla   14, 31
Pierre Trudeau   104
Pietro Bastogi   135
Piotr Dymmel   42, 50
Piotr Kitowski   143
Prentis Webster   115, 129
Prescott F. Hall   118, 120, 127

R.J.W. Evans   2, 4, 27
Rafał Mańko   49
Rainer Bauböc   171, 188
Raymond L. Cohn   114, 126
Reinhard Binder-Krieglstein   18, 27
Richard B. Haldane   91, 92, 94, 109
Richard Sutch   115, 127
Robert Borden   92
Robert Rachlin   195, 214–216
Roger Cotterrell   175, 188
Rohit De   104, 110
Rudolf Sajovic   178, 190
Rudolf Stanka   1, 31
Rui Barbosa de Oliveira   131, 133–135, 137, 142

S.S. Shilwant   94, 111
Sámuel Bónis   78
Sándor Illés   121, 128
Sándor Petőfi   52, 60
Scott Sigmund Gartner   115, 127
Sebastian Macieja   143
Sergiusz Mikulicz   161, 169
Simon N.M. Young   104, 110
Sławomir Godek   37, 50, 155, 169
Sophia Woodman   171, 190
Spasoje Šarkić   184, 190
Stanisław August (Poniatowski)   34, 35, 37, 39, 40, 42–44
Stanisław Grodziski   164, 169
Stanisław Małachowski   45
Stanisław Potocki   45
Stefan Holcik   71, 84

Stephen I of Hungary   69
Stephen Skinner   215
Susan B. Carter   114, 127
Syed Ameer Ali   92

T.V. Thomas   2, 27
Tadeusz Maciejewski   143, 145, 149, 152, 155, 160, 164, 169
Thomas Mohr   86, 88, 90, 91, 96, 97, 100, 101, 103–105, 107, 111
Thomas Musgrave   87, 111
Thomas Vormbaum   207, 209, 210, 216
Thomas Winkelbauer   10, 29, 30
Thorsten V. Kalijarvi   161, 168
Tibor Frank   55, 57, 68
Timothy J. Hatton   118, 127
Tomáš Knoz   10, 29
Tomasz Knopp   43, 49
Torrie Hester   114, 117, 127
Torsten Feys   119, 122, 127

Ulf Brunnbauer   122, 126
Ulrike von Hirschhausen   116, 129
Urbano Rattazi   136

V.J. Stefanović   177, 183, 185, 190
Václav Elzner   15, 28
Vincent C. MacDonald   98, 111
Vinko Krišković   174
Vinko Žganec   182, 191
Vladimír Klecanda   7, 29
Volkmar Gessner   175, 190

W. Harrison Moore   96, 111
W.P.M. Kennedy   98, 105, 111
W.T. Cosgrave   100
Werner Frotscher   144, 168
Wilhelm Bertuleit   162
William Jowitt   98
William P. Dillingham   114, 118, 126, 129
William Watson   95
Willibald Rosner   18, 28
Willibalt Apelt   144, 168
Winfried Becker   1, 26
Witold Filipczak   35, 49
Władysław Konopczyński   35, 50
Władysław Rostocki   42, 50

Wojciech Organiściak 35, 50
Wojciech Witkowski 36, 50
Wolfgang Brinckmann 144
Woodrow Wilson 154, 163

Yash P. Ghai 104, 110

Zdeněk Veselý 1, 28
Zsolt László Kocsis 74, 84

Index of Subjects

Enlightened Absolutism   20
Absolutist
   Absolutist Monarch(s)   20
   Absolutist State   3
Administration   33, 34, 36, 38, 40, 41, 44–48, 55, 131, 134, 135, 137, 147, 151, 156, 161, 201, 213
   Bureaucratic Administration   40, 41, 47
   Central Administration   34, 45–47
   Centralized Administration   41, 181
   Consistency of Administration   201
   General Administration   154
   Governmental Administration   148, 151
   Local Administration   39, 40, 42, 43, 45–47, 148, 161
   Municipal Administration   148, 151
   Operations of Administration   39
   Organs of Administration   35, 39
   Public Administration   37, 40, 70, 162
   Self-Governmental Administration   45
   Stability of Administration   201
   State Administration   148, 187
Administrative
   Administrative Apparatus   39
   Administrative Authorities   40
   Administrative Organisation   41, 45
   Administrative Law   2, 136
   Administrative Power   42
   Administrative Structure(s)   36, 37, 39, 132
   Administrative System   40, 41, 47
   Collegial Administrative Bodies   38
   Administrative Offices   39
   Administrative Reforms   37, 38

Citizenship   125, 161, 165, 171–188
   Citizenship Code   176, 181
   German Citizenship   162
   Formal Citizenship   179
   Hungarian Citizenship   116, 117
   Local Citizenship   171–188
      Local Citizenship Access   181
      Local Citizenship Acquisition   180–184, 187
      Austrian Model of Local Citizenship   182
      Banovina's Local Citizenship   178
      Local Citizenship Certificate   174, 181, 187
      Concept of Local Citizenship   171–174, 178, 184, 186–188
      Croatian-Slavonian Local Citizenship   172, 174–178
      Determination of Local Citizenship   180
      Hungarian Model of Local Citizenship   182
      Importance of Local Citizenship   173, 185, 187
      Institute of Local Citizenship   187
      Loss of Local Citizenship   181
      Origins of Local Citizenship   173
      Regulation(s) of Local Citizenship   173, 176–178, 180, 181, 183, 187
      Right to Local Citizenship   182
      Significance of Local Citizenship   172, 184
      Transformations of Local Citizenship   172
   National Citizenship   171–181, 185, 187
      Banovina's National Citizenship   177
      National Citizenship Certificate   180, 181
      Concept of National Citizenship   171, 172, 175, 176
      Croatian-Slavonian National Citizenship   173, 179
      Determination of National Citizenship   178–181, 187
      Hungarian National Citizenship   174, 179
      National Citizenship of Serbs, Croats and Slovenes   179, 180
      National Citizenship in Serbia and Montenegro   178, 179
      Promotion of National Citizenship   176
      Unitarian National Citizenship   175
      Yugoslav National Citizenship   172, 177, 187
   Political Citizenship   179

INDEX OF SUBJECTS

Citizenship Registers 181
Revocation of Citizenship 177
Colony(ies) 87, 88, 90, 91, 93, 94, 97, 101, 106, 131, 138
Comparative
   Comparative Approach 104
   Comparative Examination 192
   Comparative Glasses 141
   Comparative Histories 141
   Comparative Law 137, 140
   Comparative Study(ies) 20, 89, 132, 137, 141
Constitution
   Australian Constitution 96
   Belgium Constitution of 1831 56
   Bohemian Renewed Land Constitution from 1619 1, 3, 4
   Bohemian Renewed Land Constitution from 1627/1628 9–13, 16
   Constitution of the Republic of Brazil 133, 134, 140
   Constitution of Free Hanseatic City of Bremen of 1 January 1894 152
   Constitution of Free Hanseatic City of Bremen of 18 May 1920 152–154
   Canadian Constitution 103
   Constitution of Free City of Danzig of 11 August 1920 155–157, 159, 168
   Constitution of the Duchy of Warsaw of 22 July 1807 41–43, 54
   Fiume's Free State Constitution of 27 August 1920 (Charter of Carnaro) 163–166
   German Reich (Weimar) Constitution of 11 August 1919 143–146, 149, 152, 156, 167
   Constitution of Free and Hanseatic City of Hamburg of 7 January 1921 144–148
   Hungarian April Laws of 1848 51, 53, 61, 64–67, 71
   Hungarian Constitution 54, 55, 58, 59, 62, 64, 65, 71
   The Fundamental Law of Hungary of 2011 52, 71
   Imperial Constitution of Olmütz of 4 March 1849 67, 74, 75, 82
   Irish Free State Constitution of 1922 91, 99, 103
   Lithuanian Constitution 161
   Constitution of Free Hanseatic City of Lübeck of 7 April 1875 148
   Constitution of Free Hanseatic City of Lübeck of 23 May 1920 148–150
   Moravian Renewed Land Constitution from 1628 2, 23
   Constitution of the Kingdom of Piedmont-Sardinia (*Statuto Albertino*) of 1848 139, 140
   Polish-Lithuanian Commonwealth Constitution (the Government Act) of 3 May 1791 34–37, 44, 45, 48
   Constitution of the Kingdom of Serbs, Croats, and Slovenes of 1921 176, 181, 185
   South Africa Constitution of 1909 103
   Vladislaus Land Constitution of 1500 5, 6
Constitutional
   Constitutional Amendment(s) 45, 159
   Constitutional Assembly 144, 156
   Constitutional Change(s) 58, 83
   Constitutional Commission (Deputation) 152, 155
   Constitutional Development 3, 51, 70, 71
   Constitutional Drafts 144
   Constitutional Efforts 149
   Constitutional Event 83
   Constitutional History 78
   Constitutional Issues (Questions) 3, 123
   Constitutional Law 95
   Constitutional Liability 36, 45, 166
   Constitutional Monarchy 17, 53, 61, 66, 71
   Constitutional Nature 51
   Constitutional Order 51, 69, 71, 72, 74–76, 80–83
   Constitutional Perspective 62
   Constitutional Position 116
   Constitutional Practice 157
   Constitutional Prevision 139
   Constitutional Provisions 42, 157, 164
   Constitutional Principles 144
   Constitutional Relevance 79
   Constitutional Reform 59
   Constitutional Relationship 116
   Constitutional Requirement 62
   Constitutional Revolution 51, 59
   Constitutional Significance 76
   Constitutional Situation 19
   Constitutional Status 53, 54
   Constitutional Structure 67
   Constitutional Struggle 69
   Constitutional System(s) 42, 43, 143

INDEX OF SUBJECTS

Constitutionalism 48, 65
Constitutionality 67
Coronation 63, 69, 70, 72, 73, 75–83
Court
   Bavarian Royal Court 81, 83
   Viennese Imperial (Royal) Court 4, 10, 53–55, 58, 62–65, 77
Court (Tribunal)
   Appellate Court of the Privy Council 86, 88, 89, 91, 97, 100, 104, 106–108
   Brazilians' Court of National Public Treasury 134, 138
   Brazilian's Federal Court of Auditors 131–135, 137–140
   Brazilian's Federal Supreme Court 138
   Canadian Supreme Court 99, 105
   Caribbean Court of Justice 104
   Commonwealth Tribunal 104
   Court of Counts 136
   Court of Justice at the Hague 133
   Court of Justice of the Economic Community of West African States 104
   East African Court of Justice 104
   European Court of Human Rights 108
   High Court of Australia 96
   Italian Court of Auditors 135–137
   Land Court 5
   Supreme Court of the United Kingdom 95
   Tribunal de Contas 131
   US Supreme Court 94
Criminal
   Criminal Appeals 107
   Criminal Cases 107
   Criminal Code 91, 107, 133
   Criminal Investigation 183
   Criminal Law 3, 166, 209
   Criminal Legislation 209
   Criminal State 206
   Criminal Trials 99
   Criminal Charges 106

Devolution 95
Devolved
   Devolved Government 87, 93
   Devolved Parliament 94
diploma inaugurale 70, 72, 73, 77, 78, 80
Dominion(s) 87–92, 94–98, 100, 102–107

Enlightenment 33, 38, 40, 48, 70
Estate(s) 2–5, 7, 11, 12, 14–18
   Estate(s) Admission 8–10, 14, 15, 17
   Estate Community(ies) 10–14, 16, 17
   Estate Constitutions 17
   Estate Corporations 9, 18, 20
   Estate(s) Domains 14
   Estates Engagement 7
   Estate Freedoms 17
   Estate Institutions 3, 5
   Knights Estate (*Ritter*) 2
   Land Estates 9, 11, 13, 15, 17
   Lords Estate (*Herren*) 2, 9
   Estates Membership 7
   Non-Catholic Estates 1
   Prelates Estate 2
   Estates Republic 3
   Estates Revolt (Uprising) 6, 9, 10
   Estate(s) Rights (Privileges) 9–12, 17
   Estate(s) Society 9, 12, 14, 16, 19
   Estate System 17, 18
   Estates State 2, 18
   Urban Estate 2, 9

Federal
   Federal Constitution (of Reich) 143, 145, 152
   Federal (Brazil) Court of Auditors 131, 133
   Federal Form 133
   Federal Government(s) 93, 94
   Federal Institutions 95
   Federal Law 144
   Federal Matter 96
   Federal Model 94
   Federal Republic of Germany 200
   Federal Republic of Brazil 133
   Federal Settlement(s) 95, 96, 104
   Federal State(s) 133, 138, 146, 152
   Federal Supreme Court 138
   Federal Systems 87
   Federal Unions 94
Federation(s) 87, 138
Federalism 102, 167

Instrumentalism 192, 194, 200, 203, 206, 211
   Absolute Instrumentalism 213
   Concept of Instrumentalism 193, 194, 200

Crude Instrumentalism   194, 207, 211
Examination of Instrumentalism   194, 195
Legal Instrumentalism (of the Law)   88, 102, 172, 187, 188, 198, 203, 212, 214
Paradigm of Instrumentalism   193
Pure Instrumentalism   200–203, 210–212
Sort of Instrumentalism   205
Version of Instrumentalism   194, 212

Judicial Committee of the Privy Council   86–97, 99, 100, 102–109

Human Rights   64, 65, 87, 88, 99, 102, 106–109

Legal
  Legal History   1
  Legal Instrumentalism   88, 102, 172, 187, 188, 198, 203, 212, 214
Legitimacy (Legitimisation, Legitimation)   75, 131, 183, 202
  Ceremonial Legitimisation   72, 73, 75, 77, 82
  External Legitimacy   131
  Formal Legitimisation   72, 73
  Political Legitimacy (Legitimation, Legitimization)   82, 131, 141
  Religious Legitimisation   73

Migration
  Migration Agents   119–121
  Migration Business   119, 120, 122
  Central and Europe Migration   118
  Circular Migration   118
  Migration Countries   114
  Migration Destination   117
  Migration Discussions   124
  Hungarian Migration   119, 124, 125
  Illegal Migration   120, 121, 123
  Migration Law (Legislation)   123, 125
  Migration Policy(ies)   118, 121–125
  Migration Problem(s)   120, 121, 124
  Migration Route(s)   120, 122
  Migration Rules   124
  Transatlantic Migration   114
  Unauthorized Migration   123
  Migration into the United States   118

Modernisation   33, 48, 51, 88, 102, 106, 113, 126, 131, 171, 173
Monarch   2–4, 9, 10, 12
  Absolutist Monarch(s)   20
Monarchical (Monarch's)
  Monarch's Consent (Permission)   6, 9, 11, 12
  Monarch's Intercession   6, 8
  Monarchical Offices   12
  Monarch's Power   3
  Monarch's Rule   16
  Monarch's Will   12
Monarchy
  Constitutional Monarchy   17
Municipal
  Municipal Administration   148, 151
  Municipal (Urban) Affairs   38, 176
  Municipal Elections   175
  Municipal Laws   187
  Municipal Officials   152
  Municipal Mayors   41, 42
Municipality(ies)   145, 148, 149, 151, 152, 154, 158, 159, 162, 164–166, 171, 173–177, 179, 181–186

Nation   62, 83, 131, 140, 149, 153, 164
  Nation-Building Policies   124
  Political Nation   66, 174
National
  National Character   94
  National Citizens(ship)   171–183, 185–187
  National Community   202, 211, 213, 214
  National Control   140
  National Identity   20, 51, 52, 57, 66, 69, 81–84, 88, 102–104, 106, 113, 124, 131, 140, 172, 192, 214
  National Independence   51, 52
  National Institution   136
  National Interest   192
  National Symbols   133
  National Legal System   175
  National Minorities   66, 165, 167
  National Modernisation   51
  National *Rechtsstaat*   205
  National Socialism   195, 196
  National Socialist Ideology   214
  National Socialist Law   197
  National Socialist Policy   212
  National Socialist Regime   205, 209

INDEX OF SUBJECTS

National (cont.)
    National Socialist Rule   207
    National Socialists   205
    National Solutions   33, 48
    National Sovereignty   164, 165
    National State(s)   113, 171
    National Struggles   52
    National Traditions   33
Nationalism   56
Nationalist
    Nationalist Interests   93
    Nationalist Sentiment   104
    Nationalist Symphaties   163
Nationalistic
    Nationalistic Element   192
    Nationalistic Elites   205
Nationalists   86, 97, 102
Natural Law   192, 193, 195, 196, 200, 201–209, 211
Nazi Law   192–197, 199–203, 205, 207–214

Positivism   193, 195, 200, 202, 203
Positivist Paradigm   200, 202
Public Law   171

Right(s)
    Active Voting Right(s)   145, 149, 153, 165, 185–187
    Burghers' Rights   12
    Citizens Rights   40, 61, 155, 156, 158, 159, 166, 168
    Civil Rights   162, 165, 183
    Cultural Rights   159
    Estate(s) Rights   9–12
    Human Rights   64, 65, 87, 88, 99, 102, 106–109
    Legal Rights   175
    Majorities Rights   100
    Minorities Rights   100
    Naturalisation Regulation Right   119
    Noble Rights   3, 40
    Passive Voting Right(s)   149, 150, 153, 159, 162, 165, 185, 186, 188
    Personal Rights   159
    Political Rights   56, 159, 165, 166, 185, 187
    Public Rights   149
    Right to Appoint Dignitaries   63
    Right to Cultivate National Identity   157
    Right of Dissolution   63
    Right to Elect the King   54
    Right to Emigration   115
    Right to Form Unions and Associations   159
    Right of Habeas Corpus   65
    Rights of Indigenous Peoples   101
    Right to Information on the Activities of Authorities   159
    Right of Legislative Initiative   146, 162
    Right to Local Citizenship   182
    Right to Nominate Committee Members   160
    Right of Option   179
    Right of Pardon   148, 151, 154
    Right of Patronage   62
    Right to Petition   164
    Right to Possess Real Estate   55, 57
    Right to Record Opinion in the Minutes   147
    Right to Reside in the Municipality   176
    Right of Residence (Residential Right, *ius incolatus*, Inkolat)   1, 4–10, 12–16, 18–21, 24
    Right of Self-Government   66
    Right to the Throne   72–74, 83
    Right to Use Mother Tongue   157
    Right to Vote in Referendum   159
    Social Rights   165, 175, 184, 185, 187
    Sovereign Rights   150, 151
    Subjective Rights   5
    Voting Right(s)   35, 64, 108, 175, 179, 185
Revolution   53, 58, 65
    Bourgeois Revolution   53
    Constitutional Revolution   51, 59
    French Revolution   60, 64
    Industrial Revolution   55
    Hungarian Revolution   52, 53, 55, 59–61, 66, 70, 74
    Legal Revolution   59
Legal Transplant(s) (Transfers, Reception)   33, 44, 131, 132, 137, 140, 141

Urban
    Urban Area   160
    Urban District(s)   152, 159
    Urban Estate   2, 9
    Urban Municipalities   148
    Urban Republics   167
    Urban Society   55

Index of Places

Africa   88
   East Africa   90
   Southern Africa   100
African Colonies   93
Albania   165
Alberta   103
Altona   148
America   118
   North America   94
   South America   141
Anhalt   144
Australia (Commonwealth of Australia)   87, 94–97, 102–104, 106
Austria (Austrian Hereditary Lands, Austrian Empire)   8, 9, 15, 18, 59, 62, 66, 67, 69, 82, 116, 123–125, 165, 173
Austria (Republic of Austria)   179
Austria-Hungary (Austro-Hungarian Monarchy)   83, 113, 115–117, 119, 123–125, 171, 175

Baden   144, 146
Baltic Sea   160, 167
Banovina
   Banovina of Croatia   172, 177, 178, 186, 187
   Danube Banovina   177
Bavaria   143, 144, 147
Belgium   56, 134, 136
Belgrade   172, 175
Bohemia (Kingdom of Bohemia)   1–16, 19, 20
Bohemian Crown Lands (Bohemian State)   1, 2, 4, 6, 8–20, 25
Bosnia and Herzegovina   178
Bratislava (Pressburg)   59–61, 66, 71
Brazil (Empire of Brazil, Federal Republic of Brazil)   131–134, 138–140
Bremen   146, 149, 152–155, 167, 168
Bremen State   152–154
Bremenhafen   152, 154
British Columbia   98, 103
British Dominions   87–92, 95, 97, 98, 102–107
British Empire   86–96, 99, 101, 102, 104–106, 108
Bromberg   159
Brunei   107
Buda   59, 70, 79, 81

Budapest   59, 113, 116, 117, 121–125
Burma   91

Calgary   99
Canada   87, 92, 94–96, 98–100, 103–105, 107
Caribbean   104, 107
Carnaro   163, 165, 166
Ceylon   92
Chile   134
Commonwealth of Nations   88
Croatia   66, 178, 179
Croatia-Slavonia   172–174, 176, 178, 180, 181, 184–187

Dalmatia   163, 177–179
Danube   81
Danzig Regency   159
Děčín   6
Dresden   14

Earth   44, 72
East Prussia District   160
England   59, 88, 90, 95, 106
Esztergom   77–79
Europe   35, 38, 41, 69, 70, 83, 115, 134, 167
   Central Eastern Europe (Central and East Europe)   33, 58, 118
   Western Europe   34, 48, 55, 69

Far West   91
Fiume   122, 123, 163, 167
Florence   135, 167
France   18, 41–43, 59, 134, 160
Frankfurt am Mein   167
   Kingdom of Galicia and Lodomeria   18

Gdansk (Danzig)   154–160, 167, 168, 192
Germany (German Reich, Weimar Republic of Germany, Third Reich, Nazi Germany)   66, 143, 145–150, 152–156, 159, 160, 162, 167, 192–195, 197–209, 211–214
Great Britain   95, 160
Greece   134

INDEX OF PLACES

Habsburg Monarchy (Habsburg Empire, Habsburg Hereditary Lands, Habsburg Territories, Danubian Monarchy)   4, 6, 15, 18, 20, 51, 53–55, 59, 62, 66, 74, 75, 173
Hague   133
Hamburg   144–149, 155, 167, 168
Hamburg-Wilhelmsburg   148
Hanover   154
Holy Roman Empire   4, 9, 18
Hong Kong   91
Hungary (Kingdom of Hungary)   8, 18, 51–55, 57, 59, 60, 62, 63, 65–67, 69–74, 77–83, 113, 116, 117, 120, 121, 123–125, 172–174, 179

India (West Indies Federation)   87, 92–94
Ireland (Irish Free State, Republic of Ireland)   91, 95, 97–100, 105, 106
Italy   132, 134–140, 160, 163–165, 167

Japan   134, 160

Kalocsa   79
Kenia   104
Krakow   167

Lithuania   37, 160–162
Lombardy   136
London   86, 97, 98, 168
Lübeck   146, 148–152, 155, 167, 168
Lusatia   8, 10
    Lower Lusatia   8, 14
    Upper Lusatia   8, 14

Malaya Federation   87
Manitoba   96, 103
Marienwerder   159
Memel (Klaipeda) Territory   160–163, 167, 168
Milan   167
Mohacs   70
Montenegro (Kingdom of Montenegro)   178, 179
Moravia (Margraviate of Moravia)   2, 3, 8, 10, 12–16, 19, 20

Naples   135
Neman   161
Netherlands   3, 18, 134

Newfoundland   96, 103
New Brunswick   103
New South Wales   96
New York   123
New Zealand   100, 102, 105
North Ireland   95, 96
Nova Scotia   103
Novgorod the Great   167
Nuremberg   199

Oldenburg   144
Olmütz   67, 74, 75, 82
Olympic Plaza   99
Ontario   96, 103
Ottawa   99
Ottoman Empire   16, 55, 70

Palermo   135
Paris   154, 163
Parliament Hill   99
Pest   52, 53, 59–61, 63, 80
Piedmont   136
Kingdom of Piedmont Sardinia   139
Poland (Crown, Polish State, Polish Territories, Kingdom of Poland)   8, 18, 33, 34, 37–41, 45–48, 145, 154, 160
Polish-Lithuanian Commonwealth   18, 34, 37, 38, 167
Portugal   132, 134, 138
Prague   2, 4, 6, 9
Prince Edward Island   103
Prussia   15, 114, 143, 144, 146, 148
Pskov   167

Quebec   87, 96, 103, 104

Rapallo   163
Rhine   143
Rhodesia (Southern Rhodesia)   101
Rhodesia and Nyasaland Federation   87
Roman Empire   165
Romania   134
Rome   165
Russia   45, 167

Sardinia   135
Saskatchewan   103, 107
Saxony   14, 147
Scotland   95

Serbia (Kingdom of Serbia)   134, 178, 179
Silesia (Silesian principalities)   8, 10, 14, 15, 19
Singapore   106, 107
Sisak   163
Slavonia   178, 179
South Africa   92, 98, 100, 101, 103
South Australia   96
Spain   18, 134
Sweden   134
Syrmia
   Eastern Syrmia   177
Székesfehérvár   77

Thüringen   147
Transylvania (Transylvanian Territories)   60, 66, 70
Turin   135
Turkey   134
Tyrol
   Upper Tyrol   165

United Kingdom   92, 94, 95, 97, 98, 108, 114
United States of America   94, 113–119, 124

Vegesack   152

Venetian Islands   165
Versailles   154, 156, 158, 160, 162, 167
Victoria   96
Vienna   10, 54, 57, 59, 60, 62–64, 113, 116, 123, 124
Vojvodina (Vajdaság)   66

Wales   95
Wandsbeck   148
   Duchy of Warsaw   39, 41–48
Warsaw   41
Washington   113, 115, 116, 118, 119, 122, 124, 125
Weimar   143, 144, 149, 155, 156
West Prussia District   159
Western Australia   87
Westerplatte   159
Westminster   97, 102, 103
White Mountain   6, 19
Württemberg   146

Yugoslavia (Kingdom of Serbs, Croats and Slovenes, Yugoslav State)   163, 165, 171, 172, 175–182, 187

Zagreb   171, 174, 178, 181

Printed in the United States
By Bookmasters